Sketches of Fiji

To all those wonderful men and women who worked with me to build a safe, strong, and profitable national airline for Fiji

---

Sketches of Fiji – Andrew Drysdale

Copyright © 2019 by Andrew Drysdale

Publisher – Mentor Aviation Services

mentoraviationservices701@gmail.com

All rights reserved. This book or any portion thereof may not be reproduced or used in any manner whatsoever without the express written permission of the publisher except for the use of brief quotations in a book review.

Printed in Australia

First Printing, 2019

ISBN 978-0-646-80026-4

Sketches of Fiji

Front Cover

The image on the front cover is of a Tabua. It is the tooth of a Sperm whale presented in Fijian tradition only on important ceremonial occasions.

The solemn atmosphere, the mutual respect and dignity amongst those gathered together for the presentation, and the deeply felt ancient words and form used in the ceremony say more to me about Fiji than anything else.

This particular Tabua is very old. It is in the collection of the Te Papa museum in Wellington New Zealand and I am indebted to them for permission to use the image here.

The name carved on the Tabua, 'Ratu Lejia' (biblical Elijah) may well refer to the Chief of Viwa Island in Bau Waters in the mid-1800s. Ratu Lejia, who was originally named Verani, converted to Christianity on Good Friday 1845. He took the name of Lejia on his conversion.

Bau Waters is where I spent many happy days spearfishing in my teenage and later years.

Sketches of Fiji

Appreciation

My thanks to lifetime friend Graham Southwick for our many shared experiences and for pointing out my mistakes, and to Tony Wong for all our aviation years together and his remarkable memory for detail. To Doug Nancarrow for his friendship and precise editing pen, and to Stephanie Blandin de Chalain for her artistry in cover design and layout, and for her patience. To Ron Rosalky and Garry Saunders for their advice and guidance. Together they have turned a collection of stories into a book.

And to all those whose life has touched mine in the past 73 years.

Contents

Tabua – front cover	i
Introduction	02
What Fiji means to me	04
A Local European in Colonial Fiji	11
Fiji Airways	113
Blue Lagoon Cruises	223
Air Pacific	300
So why these notes?	373

Introduction

Yonder the long horizon lies, and there by night and day
The old ships draw to home again, the young ships sail away

Gerald Gould

The quote is from a small book of poems my mother gave to my father called *The Open Road*. The inscription on the fly leaf in her hand is: *'To Tommy from Ellen wishing you a very happy birthday 1956'.* He would have been 46, that's the year they returned from Australia to live again in Fiji.

These notes are not intended as an historical record, nor even claim to be well written. It's just, as we would say in Fiji, 'telling story'. I hope that it helps to paint a picture of Fiji in the latter part of the 20th. Century from the perspective of a 'local European' as we were called. And if it helps the reader to understand some of the things that shaped me and the people around me, and tells of things achieved, then good.

I have deliberately called it a 'sketch' because that is all it can ever be. What I have covered is not a selection of stories drawn from a long list; it's just what came to mind as I typed. There are very many other stories that should be told, and probably some that should not. I ask your forbearance on that. They relate to my life, and those immediately around me. There are many other Drysdale stories that should be told; particularly that of my brother Peter, whose story eclipses any in these pages. If you find yourself saying "Why didn't he talk about…?" or perhaps feel I should have been more balanced in what I have said, then I ask your understanding.

Sketches of Fiji

It gets personal at times; I trust you will bear with me when that creeps in. I thought a lot about including those passages and finally decided it would be a hollow record if I didn't speak about the things that mattered to me.

What I've set down is the way I remember it, and if (more likely, when) there are errors then that is due to my memory, which I hope you will accept with a degree of humour. The reality of writing is that it can never replicate life. In life we constantly experience parallel stories, events, voices, people; indeed, all those things that we give the word 'life' to. The written word can only ever relate to one of these at a time and I tell you this now as an excuse as to why the pages ahead are at times inconsistent and jump all over the chronological place.

Assuming you are generous enough to accept that excuse, I'll get started.

What Fiji means to me

Back in March 2011 one of Fiji's leading businessmen asked me to write a chapter for a book he was intending to publish called "What Fiji means to me". For reasons I won't go into here, it didn't happen. But still, I thought you might find what I wrote of interest – it is a bit personal.

I have no idea how many times I've said, "I grew up in Fiji". I do know that I say it often, and with a sense of being a little unique, certainly with pride. Given my Scottish origins it usually brings a strange look; or from the bolder listener a comment 'you don't look Fijian'.

And so they fall into the trap and I can launch into my life's story.

Fiji is childhood memories: living in Samabula North next to the Hindu temple, my parent's tough life starting a business, and the freedom of those early years. Long school days at Saint Felix College in Toorak, looking out of the classroom door across the harbour to the reef and the island of Beqa beyond, wishing desperately to be there, not learning how many sheep they have in New Zealand. Memories of having to make sasa brooms as punishment for some misdemeanour and being given "six of the best" when the misdemeanour wasn't quite so small. Wonderful school holidays with friends in the village at Verata, having our bath in the stream and eating food collected that morning from the tei tei.

The 1959 industrial riots in Suva and my father going off with the other Defence Club members to keep the peace after martial law was declared

Sketches of Fiji

– how easily we forget those times. Making and paddling tin boats up the Tamavua river through the mangrove dogo and the hundreds and thousands of tiny crabs with bright yellow claws covering their faces; watching the amazing mud skippers, going past the 'night cart' *topasi* place and the abattoir. Fishing, swimming and getting sunburnt all the time.

Memories of being 'king of the skies' during kite season and of my secret 'maja' formula of Vics Vaporub glass pounded into a mush with dalo and hibiscus leaf that cut everyone else's string (now you know the secret). Of going to mass with the Sisters in the chapel at the Tamavua Home of Compassion every Sunday – well nearly every Sunday.

Then Marist Brothers High school and Brother Lambert's thin, lined face screwed up into strange contortions as he tried to show us how to pronounce "petit pommes" during French lessons – and us never quite getting it right. And those wonderful Marist Brothers who guided us towards a life in the real world of Fiji in the dying stages of the Colonial era. The teenage years with dramatically changed views on girls; parental grumbling about algebra marks and finger waving about the looming Senior Cambridge exams.

Getting into dad's gin when he was out, and never wanting to drink gin again – scotch of course is fine.

Then as the years went by, the long, happy, and admittedly sometimes best forgotten, hours at the Royal Suva Yacht Club. Water skiing at

What Fiji means to me

Mosquito Island, spear fishing at Toberua passage, and always desperate for petrol money.

We can talk of bushwalking most weekends through the jungles of South East Viti Levu, and the immense quiet of the Fiji bush that isn't really quiet at all. Of climbing Joske's thumb with no special gear, not even ropes; just Dunlop tennis shoes, strong young muscles and an empty head – at least that's what we were told afterwards. There's a small glass Ponds face cream jar on the summit containing the stub of a pencil and a scrap of paper so those who make it to the top can write their names. It was a very short list. Grahame Southwick and I slept on top one night just for fun, as you do at that age. It was a bit windy and very wet, and when we got home our parents weren't happy because a tropical depression had gone past that night.

Then there were the years as a volunteer fireman in the Suva Brigade under the strict discipline of Harry Le Vesconte. Oh dear, fire drill at 7.00am on a Sunday morning is not good when you are 20 years old and have just come from the Yacht Club bar. And the new world being opened up as an aircraft engineer with Fiji Airways. Five years of apprenticeship when my new wife was paid more than me in her job as a receptionist at the Club Hotel.

Memorable years being taught theory of flight by Forrester Lindsay who helped design the Spitfire. Of being part of that pioneering time when we flew 16- passenger de Havilland Heron aircraft thousands of

Sketches of Fiji

miles over the Pacific to tiny atolls like Tarawa. How proud we were when we got those Gypsy Queen 30 engines to 2000 hours between overhauls – something no-one else in the world came anywhere near. And later those exciting, high-risk, years working with wonderful people as we moved Air Pacific from Suva to Nadi and built a strong and profitable international airline for our country.

And so the memories roll on. But there's something more deeply ingrained, and more important, in what Fiji means to me – the characters that make Fiji what it is. It isn't until one leaves Fiji and the grey commuter world becomes real, that you begin to understand that at home we are fortunate to meet, and to work with, exceptional characters who touch our lives in so many ways. These are strong characters, leaders; both good people and the not so good. There are people we agree with, and those we don't. Yes, there are people like them in the countries beyond Fiji, but you don't get to meet them – they are names in a newspaper. Think of those leaders who took us into independence; Ratu Sir Kamasese Mara, Sir John Falvey, AD Patel. They were leaders, not only of their own people, but of all of us.

Or some others: Irene Jai Narayan, Ratu Sir George and Ratu Edward Cakobau, Ratu Sir Penia Ganilau, Sidiq Koya, Sir Ian Thompson, Don Aidney and yes, Major General Sitiveni Rabuka and Sakiasi Butadroka. And those who have stamped their mark more recently on Fiji's history, business and politics. All of them with their own vision for Fiji; all changing our lives in some way, and all people I have known personally.

What Fiji means to me

In Fiji we see the world on a much bigger canvas than those in the suburbia of the developed countries. That we have the opportunity to do so is both unique and incredibly important in framing our values and our perspectives on life.

But it's not only the political and business leaders who make Fiji what it is; it's also those we came to call the 'grassroots' and who, each in their own way, are characters as well. The peanut seller at Suva bus stand with his cry of "peanutbean"; the old Indian man who called me to stop work fencing our six-acre property at Saweni and to sit beside him on a plank under the Neam tree looking out over the Yasawa Islands. We sat, quiet, for a few minutes then he simply said "good", I said "yes" and returned to my work. My family still gets me to stop work by calling "it's old Indian man time"; and I stop. I don't know his name and I'm sorry for that.

Fiji's humour is unique and plays a large part in defining our people. Nowhere else in the world has that wonderful ability to poke fun at another without rancour, and to have it returned in like manner. Nor the ability to so happily laugh at oneself. It's not a loud-mouthed humour; it's quiet, almost reflective at times. The gentle joke in a quiet voice around the 'grog' bowl in the village, or in the cane field; or the quick response to a comment that turns a serious moment into a funny one in a way that cannot be described in Western terms. It's not the drawn-out structured joke of the West with a punchline at the end, but more a deep understanding of people conveyed in the form of a

Sketches of Fiji

joke. Sometimes it can be boisterous and give rise to an outburst 'Kaila', but even then, it's quick, and in a way intuitive of our inner person.

There's also a wisdom in Fiji. Like our humour it is different to the rest of the world. It comes from the heart, it cannot be learnt from books. One can't study to achieve Fiji wisdom, it is something instilled from childhood. It is a wisdom and a set of values that is sometimes shielded behind a busy world. At times it's difficult to find – but it is there. It is the wisdom and concern of the village or community leader for their people. It is in the caring of the nurse in the hospital, and the sharing of the little that we may have. It lies in the community, and the communal values from centuries past.

Those of us newer to Fiji can absorb some of these concepts over time provided we are open to seeing things in a different light, but we cannot truly understand it all. We will never know the true depth of the word 'Vanua'; perhaps we shouldn't try. It is enough that we know, and abide by, these values and respond in our lives to what they tell us. This wisdom, these values, cannot be overridden by the political adolescence that Fiji is dealing with today. They are a fundamental part of our people. When the day is done, and people are measured, it is the wisdom and these values that will matter.

This is what Fiji means to me.

Sketches of Fiji

A local European in Colonial Fiji

Living in Samabula

One day when I was young my father announced that we were going to live in Fiji and that the plan was for him to get back into the banana trade where he had worked in the 1930s, or to buy the Navua hotel. As it turned out they started Fiji's first ever dry-cleaning business. We were living in the Melbourne seaside suburb of Sandringham at the time, having moved there from a tiny hamlet in the Australian bush called Barmah.

I knew about Fiji because that was where my parents had lived, met, and married during World War II. They had moved to Australia at the end of the War and that's where I and my two brothers were born. Around the dinner table they would often speak with great fondness about their friends and life in the islands.

The next day I excitedly told my class the big news and the nun who was our teacher asked me to point out on a wall map where Fiji was. Mum and Dad had already shown me that on our home atlas, so I proudly fingered the two small, lonely dots in the South West Pacific Ocean. Along the bottom of the map were pictures of the people from the various countries, and there was this Fijian man with a huge smile and 'big hair'. That's the moment when it struck home that we were going to live in another country and to begin a new life.

Then it was off to Fiji. Dad went ahead of us. We sailed on the MV *Wanganella* to New Zealand in June of 1956 and stayed with Mum's family in Levin for a while. Then on MV *Oronsay* to Fiji. Our cabins were in the bowels of the ship with that peculiar smell that ships have. I don't know

Sketches of Fiji

what it is, or what causes it, but every ship I've ever been on has that same smell. There was a fair amount of seasickness and the stewards in their starched white P&O uniforms were always helpful and seemed not to mind. The cruise was just over three days and we woke very early on the morning of the fourth day to watch the sun rise behind us and light up a magnificent scene. We were cruising parallel to the reef past what I now know to be Naselai point, then Nukulau Island with Makaluva tucked in close by. Then we swung north around the corner of the reef and into the entrance to Suva harbour. I have a very clear recollection of that city lit up in the early morning light and looking magical. It still does today, at least from that vantage point it does. In later years I was to get to know Nukulau and those reefs like the back of my hand.

Clearing immigration was done on-board and clearance was relatively quick. I was fascinated with the colours and the smells, and the people, and the bustle of the wharf-side, and then the customs shed. People coming and going in every direction, passing each other on the narrow, canvas-sided gangway. People like us coming down, official-looking people in uniforms coming up, and Fijians and Indians going in both directions. Dad met us at the wharf, and I recall he had another man with him. This almost certainly would have been Noel McFarlane, a close family friend from the war years, one-time Mayor of Suva, lawyer and, I believe, the man who advised Dad on starting a dry-cleaning business in Fiji.

We went to the Garrick hotel, the same one where my parents had stayed so many times all those years ago. There are stories of these fine old hotels

Living in Samabula

with starched white tablecloths, polished silver cutlery, fine crockery and silent, attentive servants dressed in starched white uniforms. It really was like that. We used mosquito nets over the beds and went down the hall for the toilet and shower. There was a never-ending stream of old friends who came to see Mum and Dad. We were taken to dinners, lunches and high tea. In between all this Peter, John and I were taken to start school at Saint Felix College high on a ridge above the city. The school was run by Marist brothers who wore heavy long black tunics.

After a few weeks we moved to a small home. I think that this was the first time Mum and Dad began to realise that things were going to be different as they carved out their new life trying to build a business from scratch.

The house was a simple concrete block rectangle with two homes, apartments really, side by side in the same building, and two bedrooms in each home. They are called semi-detached or villas in Sydney, but this was a lot more basic than the Sydney houses. The address was Namuka Street Samabula North – no street numbers in those days. It was a suburb almost exclusively of Indian people and many of the homes around us were little more than shacks. Our landlord lived on the ridge above in a corrugated iron home, known euphemistically in Fiji as a 'wood and iron dwelling'. Around us were large blocks of land that were, at that time, undeveloped and completely covered in scrub, para grass and guava bush. The Lal family lived in a simple home over the road; they went on to become wealthy people in the bus business.

Sketches of Fiji

Except when at school we went bare feet all the time, and the soles of our feet became hard and leathery. We thought nothing of walking over prickly 'sensitive' grass, in mangrove mud up to our knees, along gravel roads, and even on the sharp coral of the reef. Our simple shorts and short sleeved shirts were made for us by our landlord in his tiny tailoring shop in Samabula, right next to the bus stop. He had a pedal operated Singer sewing machine and a small table for cutting out the cloth with very large scissors. The back wall of his shop was covered with large bolts of cotton fabric of all colours. There was no synthetic cloth in Fiji then.

It's difficult to describe our life in those days. Mum and Dad worked extremely long hours in a factory they leased at Walu bay. The factory was next to a stream that began at the top of the nearby ridge adjacent to the insane asylum, ran past the gaol next to a tall building housing the hangman's scaffold, through a wooden culvert under the main road heading towards Lami, and then past the factory. Across the creek was an area of soapstone fill that was later to become the Public Works Department (PWD) yard and where, many years later, I was to build ships for Blue Lagoon Cruises.

The factory was next door to the wooden hall of the Returned Serviceman's Club, old man Whippy's Boatyard, and Tom Pickering's United Engineers. At the back of Pickering's workshop was a fully equipped blacksmith's forge. I would stand for hours watching the big men heating the iron to the right colour in the forge, beating it out on the anvil, and 'quenching' it in oil or water depending on the temper they needed. Joy of joys when they invited me to operate the bellows.

Tom and Nell Drysdale

Let's step back for a moment to speak of my parents and their background. Theirs is an interesting story of Fiji in the years before and during World War II. It was that Fiji link that later framed my life.

My father, Thomas Andrew Drysdale, was born in Melbourne on 16th March 1910 and lived in Moonee Ponds. It's a family tradition going back many generations for the first-born son to be given those Christian names, and it is my name, although I go by Andrew. I don't know where Tom went to school, but given they were not wealthy I suggest a local public school. After high school he was indentured to a Melbourne law firm. At some point during this time he became interested in motorbikes and began racing Norton bikes. Norton was *the* English bike of the time and owning one of these would have been something the lads greatly desired.

The upshot though was that he lost his leg in an accident involving a Melbourne tram and a fellow driving his very pregnant wife to hospital to give birth. The resulting court case gave Dad some cash and the accident caused him to give up his law training. As a result of meeting a friend of a friend, he found his way to Fiji. To put that in perspective he was in his early 20s, had no formal qualifications, had a wooden leg, and the great depression of the 1930s was at its height, so there wouldn't have been too many jobs going for him in Melbourne.

So there we are, it's 1936, and with this good-looking young gentleman arriving in Fiji with some money in his pocket but needing an income. He found one trading bananas. How he got into this enterprise I don't

Sketches of Fiji

know, but what he did was to live in Suva, buy cases of bananas from the Fijian growers in Rewa and Tailevu, and ship them to Australia on the Matson boats *Monterey* and *Mariposa*. These would have been the originals – they built others of the same names later. The company installed chilled storage for him on the ships, very new technology for the day. He travelled with the bananas, sold them to the wholesalers in Sydney Markets (now in Chinatown) at a royalty of two and sixpence per case, and returned when the vessel sailed north.

However the war years were approaching and this enterprise was clearly not going to last, so he got into a business deal with a fellow called A J 'Percy' Turner, originally from Ellington on the Ra coast. Percy was a planter, entrepreneur and, by reputation, a drinker. He had a house at Nasese in Suva, near what is now called Turner's Bridge. I don't know what brought the two together, but Percy had lost his left arm in some accident – so fellow amputees perhaps? They eventually had a big blow up over money that Turner owed Dad. A lawyer friend, Noel Mc Farlane, ensured Dad got his money.

The business that Dad and Turner became involved in was timber milling on the Northern Fiji island of Vanua Levu. The sawmill was located at an absolutely beautiful place north east of Savusavu called *Buca* (Butha) bay. Dad moved to Buca bay and managed the mill; albeit he seems to have travelled regularly to Suva to stay at the famous (perhaps infamous) Garrick hotel in Suva. I gather he was also well known in the club circuit of Suva and was generally con-

Tom and Nell Drysdale

sidered a gentleman and a hardworking one at that. Travel between Vanua Levu and Suva was usually on the 150-foot MV *Yanawai*.

It was on the *Yanawai* that he first met my mother Ellen Teresa Gimblett. She was a New Zealand nurse who had obtained work in 1941 as a Sister at the Lautoka hospital. In 1943 she was transferred to the Colonial War Memorial hospital in Suva and, after six months there, was moved to the hospital on the northern tip of Taveuni Island. It was on one of these trips to the island that they met. Mum told us that the Captain of the *Yanawai* was a fellow called Percy (it was his surname) and that she and Tom first met over dinner on the ship with white table cloths and a few gins, perhaps with Captain Percy as chaperone.

The Taveuni hospital is just across the Somosomo straight from Buca bay, a short launch trip. They were married at the Catholic cathedral in Suva on 4th Jan. 1944, stayed that night at the Garrick and travelled the next day on the *Yanawai* to Savusavu and thence to Buca bay.

Mum was born on 4th June 1913 to a pioneering New Zealand farming family in what was then a tiny hamlet called Levin. As she came to the end of her teenage years, she became a nurse and eventually moved away from New Zealand. I suspect it was that strong, indomitable strength of character she always had that made her seek something different to farm life in New Zealand. She was a fine-looking

Sketches of Fiji

woman. I use the words 'fine looking' deliberately. Her face told of that strong, indomitable character and her blue eyes had a depth to them that made it hard to understand what she was thinking. It says a lot for both Dad and Mum that they would marry and she would travel with him to the isolation of a remote saw mill in Northern Fiji.

So Mum and Dad are married, living in Buca bay, and travelling frequently to stay at the Garrick hotel in Suva. The war is still on, the Japanese came quite close to Fiji but were pushed back from the lower end of the Gilbert and Ellis islands, the Coral sea, Solomon Islands and in New Guinea. As the war came to an end Mum and Dad decided to move to Melbourne and begin a new phase in their lives.

They first ran a hotel called the Limerick Castle in North Melbourne where I was born on 10th. August 1945 – the day after the Americans dropped the hydrogen bomb on Nagasaki. It was a rough place and the watering hole for some of the city's gangs including Redder Lewis, a known crime boss in that area of Melbourne, and a lady they called the 'angel of death'. She was a prostitute and what was known in those days as a 'gangster's moll'. A newspaper of the day summed up her career in crime thus: 'Dulcie Markham saw more violence and death than any other woman in Australia's history'. Dulcie and Nell were not compatible – to say the least! The upshot was that Mum felt this was not the place she wanted to raise her family and so we moved to a tiny country hamlet called Barmah on the banks of the Murray River near Echuca.

Tom and Nell Drysdale

They took over a hotel called by the somewhat elegant name of Hotel Barmah but known to one and all as the Barmah hotel. I was two and three quarters at this time (parents count these times carefully). Dad was licensee from 10 May 1948 to 25 September 1953. From there it was back to Melbourne for a while, and then to Fiji. Those formative years are important to setting what I am but are best told elsewhere.

But let me finish this by a few more words about my mother. After Dad died, she first went to live in Melbourne; and got there by signing on as nurse, and hence a member of the crew, on a tramp cargo steamer called MV *Capitaine Wallis*. Then she 'took off' to see the world. She stayed in youth hostels (yes, that's right), travelled by local bus and ferry; and over the next few years saw most of the UK, Europe and a lot of Canada, the USA and Africa.

She went up into Glacier bay in Alaska onboard a mail boat, sleeping on the bench seats. She celebrated her 80th. birthday by hot air ballooning across the Masai Mara in Kenya where, she later admitted, she'd told a very little white lie by saying she had just turned 70 – they had an age limit on who they would carry. She died in Melbourne at the age of 96. We took her ashes to Fiji and she lies buried now with her beloved Tommy.

Early days

My parents started a dry-cleaning business called Southern Press, the first dry-cleaning company in Fiji. We had two depots in Suva, one in Morris Hedstrom's and the other at Jenkins emporium opposite the post office. Clem and Annie Palmer ran Jenkins and they were very helpful, but dry cleaning alone simply wasn't enough. This was the tropics and most people wore cotton or linen which was washed and ironed by the house girls or the local Indian laundry. The business was eventually extended into commercial laundry and this was more successful; as was the subsequent linen hire service for the hotels.

Nevertheless, times were very tough in those first few years, and I recall clearly the time Westpac bank asked Dad to come in for a meeting. He knew that this was the end of the financial road and that they were going to call in their loans which would close the business. He and Mum spoke for a long time the night before over the dinner table. I didn't understand any of it, but it was clearly about money and was serious. The next day Westpac did as expected and gave the company four weeks to clear the commercial loan they had. Dad walked over the road (literally) to ANZ and spoke to one of the senior managers whom he had met through a mutual contact at the Yacht Club. ANZ agreed to extend him credit and this, coupled with the beginnings of what became a sustained growth in Fiji's Tourism industry, and consequently the need for a commercial laundry service, marked the financial turnaround for Mum and Dad.

In the early days of the business Dad recognized he knew nothing about dry cleaning and so employed a Dutchman who came to him

Early days

recommended by Ken Topliss, an icon of the Australian dry cleaning and laundry industry. It didn't work out; after a year or so Dad fired the Dutchman, and the Dutchman sued. He won his case in part because he argued that the Drysdale children (namely me) had kept taking his tools so he couldn't maintain the machinery. As much as I loved being around the machinery this simply was not true, but it seems the argument held up in court. Dad became a very quick learner. Not only about the laundry and dry- cleaning business, including stain removal and pressing, but he also studied for, and obtained, a boilerman's licence in order to operate the steam boilers that we used in the factory. I spent many happy hours with him on weekends, and sometimes at night, repairing the machinery. I learnt to change bearings on the huge spin dryers, dismantle, clean and reassemble steam pressure valves, pressure test the core pipes of the steam boiler, repair electrical irons, make wire coat hangers from fencing wire, and hundreds of other small maintenance jobs around the factory. We worked all of Saturday and most of Sunday on these jobs.

I remember Mother on her hands and knees scrubbing Persian carpets for the well-to-do of Suva. I've recently cleaned some of my own carpets and it really did bring back memories.

Dad ran the factory, maintained the machinery and did the 'spotting' to remove stains with an array of chemicals. This was an intriguing process to a young boy. Dad would spread the fabric on a stainless steel table similar to an ironing board, locate the stain over holes pierced in the

Sketches of Fiji

table, apply the chemical, beat (never scrub) lightly with a soft brush, and bingo the stain would disappear. Then he would remove the chemicals by squirting the area with a hand-held steam gun – magic stuff. Mum did the paperwork, receiving and dispatching the laundry and dry cleaning and driving the van for pickup and delivery. She ironed and starched and managed the ladies doing the ironing. The factory was incredibly hot with a big boiler, steam pipes running all over and the heat from irons and steam presses. But they stuck at it from early to very late, and often for seven days a week. Some days I would help by turning out the pockets and cuffs of the clothes before cleaning to find anything left behind. Sometimes small change, but usually just handkerchiefs, pens and penknives. These went into brown-paper bags and were always returned to their owners. After a ball at one of the clubs the tuxedos would often have left over drinks tickets in the pockets, but regrettably they were only good for the night of the ball!

The memories of this period are very mixed. They were painful times in many ways; Mum and Dad 'working their fingers to the bone', as one said in those days, and doing so in a factory full of heat and steam from the laundry. This was mixed with the strong chemical smell of the dry-cleaning processes and in a tropical climate. There was very little money and they hovered on bankruptcy for many years. From being welcomed and feted on arrival from Australia we moved to be the poor whites. There was no social life for my parents, brothers or me. While my parents worked, any daylight hours outside of school were spent hanging around the factory.

Early days

On those few occasions when I actually did homework, it was while sitting in the van waiting for Mum and Dad to finish delivering the cleaned laundry and picking up the next load. On occasion this was sitting on piles of dirty laundry in the back of the van. But we did make our own fun.

I made tin boats from sheets of old corrugated iron which were hammered reasonably flat on the lawn of the Returned Servicemen's clubhouse next to the factory. These were then nailed at bow and stern to blocks of wood. There was a knack to sloping this work to create a curve in the sides like a canoe. If that wasn't quite right you could place another piece of wood midships to hold the sides open; but if you had to do that it was a bit embarrassing. Then the holes and joints were sealed with the sap from breadfruit trees or tar pinched from the road. I paddled my little tin boats dangerously around Suva Harbour for hours on end.

I made fishing spears using reeds cut from nearby clumps on the creek bank near the gaol and wire from the factory's coat hangers, and got to know the creeks and mangroves around the Walu Bay area very well. I spent many hours spearing small mangrove fish and watching the incredible skippers walk on the slimy mud with their fins, where we would sink to our thighs. They seemed to me to be a prehistoric fish that proved we started in the swamps – and this was years before I had even heard of Charles Darwin or his theories. And listening to the millions of clicks per minute made by

Sketches of Fiji

the swarms of tiny crabs with bright yellow claws held defensively over their faces. I was fascinated by the black and white reef herons (Belo) and would try to emulate their ability to stand completely still for long periods, move a fraction, and then freeze again while they stalked their prey. They beat me every time. And fishing for tiny little 'tivi tivi' bait fish with a bent pin tied to cotton and 'jagging' them when they came to inspect the bright object.

Suva in the late 50's

Times were tough, there was little money, Mum and Dad were very worried about the finances and the business, and of course their children. We three boys really did run a little wild. In my case I took zero interest in school work, rarely did my homework, and was very rarely at home. But strangely, and in a way that's very difficult to describe, there was a sense of bonding and camaraderie in the family. We shared difficult times together and when there was occasion for happiness, we appreciated it all the more.

I remember the one occasion when we all went to the pictures. We dressed in our best clothes, Dad and we boys wearing ties, and drove in the van to the Regent theatre next door to the Suva fire brigade, and even had ice cream at interval. We all stood to attention, thumbs at trouser seam, for the national anthem (God Save the Queen – we were still a British Crown Colony). There was a newsreel with that unique scratchy BBC voice of the time and then the feature film. I know it was a famous cowboy film, but the name escapes me. In one scene the hero was down on the ground in a fight, being beaten to a pulp by the bad guy. Then he gained his feet and kicked the baddie in the whatnots. The scene was set so that we were looking at the back of the baddie at the time and, wondrously, as the kick landed out came a puff of dust from his trousers.

One of the more exciting things to do in Suva in those days was to go to the wharf to see the passenger ships arrive or depart. These were the P&O and Matson ships and they came quite regularly in those days as trans-Pacific aviation was still very much in its infancy. The

Sketches of Fiji

ships were greeted and farewelled by either the Police or Army bands who marched magnificently up and down the wharf in their ceremonial uniforms. The red tunics of the Army always seemed to me to be more dramatic and eye-catching than the navy police uniforms; but it didn't really matter, the whole event was exciting and noisy and bustling with people. And yes, there were the streamers that you see these days in the films, and all the drama of humanity that went with these magnificent cruise liners.

In teenage years my school mates and I would sometimes pretend we were tourists to get on board the ship during the day (we were the right colour you see) and wander wide eyed through the dining rooms, lounges, ballrooms and corridors, breathing in that unique smell of ships. In later years we would even sneak a drink at the bars. But eventually they tightened up what little security there was and, Suva being a small place, we were easily recognized.

As the ships moved away from the wharf the passengers would throw coins into the water and Fijian boys would dive to collect the coins. There was a Fijian man with no arms, often seen around the city, who we were told, had had had them bitten off by a shark at the wharf. He would ask you to read a note in his pocket which understandably was a request for money. Despite money always being very tight for us I did give him whatever I could, even on occasion forfeiting the Indian sweets or peanuts at the market and bus stand. It was my very first charitable donation and I'm pleased it was to him.

Suva in the late 50's

Because we did the laundry for some of the smaller tramp steamers that came through I often had the chance to board these special ships. They fascinated me with their cables and rigging, winches and chains that seemed to lie in a jumbled mess all over the deck. But after a while I began to see the organisation behind the design and layout of this machinery and would watch fascinated as they unloaded cargo in what seemed a smooth and effortless manner.

There were also the sugar ships in the days before the mill at Nausori closed and these were loaded manually. Hessian sacks full of sugar were brought to the wharf on trucks; men would back up to the truck, take a sack on their back, arms high above their heads, then bent over, run up a plank to the deck of the ship. They would drop the sacks on to a steel grating over the top of the hold and the ship's crew would undo the stitching at the top of the sack using a sharp knife in one smooth easy action. The sack would be upended, and the man would run back down a second plank to deliver it to a second truck before picking up another sack of sugar. Given the tropical heat these men needed a great deal of fluid and this was provided as a raw sugar/water mix in old kerosene drums. When they did get a break, they would gather around a bucket of 'yagona' as Kava, the traditional drink of the Pacific, is known in Fiji. This work went on 24 hours a day and watching it at night in the alternating light and dark of shadows as they ran, the noise and the nonstop movement is difficult to describe. The word 'weird' comes to mind.

Sketches of Fiji

The formal dress uniform for the police was the white serrated sulu and navy tunic. There is a photograph of a Fijian Policeman directing traffic outside Burns Philp that became a tourism image around the world. It wasn't a mock up, in my schooldays he really was there. His name was Sargeant Lesi, and in my later tourism career he accompanied us on some of the promotional trips. What intrigued me, at least for a while after our arrival, was to see huge, burly Fijian policemen, over six feet tall with 'big hair' and wearing sulus walking hand in hand down the streets of Suva. While I was still at school the Government introduced a regular police uniform of blue/grey slacks and shirt. There was something of an outcry, but it was argued the 'ovicers' could run faster in trousers to catch the bad guys than they could in sulus.

Samabula was very definitely an Indian Suburb. There were the Powells next to us and two part-European families in the nearby Fulaga street. Old man Check Kee had the small store on the corner down the road, and a tiny wood-fired bakery making 'long loves' in a nearby corrugated iron shed. He also had what was then a small (later to become a big) construction firm, and that was it. Everyone else was Indian – and Hindu at that. It is to my great regret that I did not learn more about this wonderful ancient religion. I think I did absorb a little through the skin though and believe I have at least some sensitivity to the culture.

We celebrated their festivals with our neighbours regardless of whether they were a public holiday or not (all but one was not). The music and colour remain vivid in my mind even if I didn't understand the story be-

Suva in the late 50's

hind the events at the time. One ceremony that stands out was the firewalking. On several occasions I went with the men to the river, usually just the Samabula creek, where they bathed and had the priest insert the long trident needles through their skin, cheeks, tongues, and ears. In particular, I remember the brilliant yellow of the turmeric paste the priest used and the bright red and yellow of the men's clothes.

There were marigolds everywhere. The sound of the endless, and unique, chanting comes back clearly, as does the mesmerising particular rhythm of the drums. It was a sound that travelled for many miles at night and I would lie in bed listening to it for a long time. I would also follow the men on their processional march at times, but obviously not throughout the long days and nights they did this for. By the time they got to the firewalking pit several days later their eyes were glazed, and they were clearly in a trance. One reads of the expression 'with glazed eyes' but until you've actually seen it, what this means is impossible to truly understand or describe.

The pit was about 20 feet long and full of white-hot cinders, and you could feel the heat from many feet away. Some ran, some walked, and some danced the length of the pit. What impressed me more than the actual fire walking though was the fact that mostly the men didn't bleed when the tridents were removed. Sometimes there was a little blood and the priest would press turmeric paste on the wound, but not a lot. I always found myself wound up in the ceremony and none of the grisly bits bothered me, but on one occasion my cousin Code was visiting from Australia and I took him along. I think it was the first time I saw someone shudder.

Primary school

My brothers and I went to Saint Felix College (now called Marist Brothers Primary school) which was located in the suburb of Toorak, on a ridge overlooking Suva harbour and the city. The Toorak name does come from the Melbourne suburb. It's a long story but it relates to a very controversial public company called the Polynesian Land Development Company set up by Melbourne businessmen to develop land in Fiji in the 1860s. This included the land that was later to become the capital, Suva. It failed. It's probable that our great, great grandfather was involved in that enterprise.

The views were impressive. From the school buildings you could see West across the bay to Josky's thumb, mount Korobaba, the Korobasabasaga ranges and South to the island of Bega with its adjacent islands. You could see the reef curving around from Nukulau to form the entrance to Suva Harbour, and then off in a Westerly direction around the bottom of Viti Levu towards Navua; not particularly conducive to keeping a young lad's mind focused on the niceties of arithmetic. The 1912 wooden building comprised two-stories with five classrooms on the ground floor. Upstairs was where the Marist brothers lived and had two more classrooms.

Next door was Saint Columbus School which was for the Indians. Because of a 1936 directive from the Colonial Education department the two were not allowed to mix. St. Felix College had been registered for Europeans and for 'those part Europeans being brought up as European' (*Kailoma*). Things were different then! Between the two was the chapel and handball court. The schools shared the same playing ground, but you could tell at a distance who was from which school because the St. Felix boys were dressed

Primary school

in starched whites, long socks held up with garters and policemen sandals made for us by the cobbler in Marks St. called Jack's Shoe Emporium; a 'hole in the wall' shop. The Fijian boys of course wore starched white sulus. The Saint Columbus Boys wore blue. At break times the St Columbus boys used the far end of the field and we used the end closer to the school.

For the outdoor part of our school curriculum we used cane knives to cut the grass on the banks leading from the school buildings to the playground. On one occasion the tractor-drawn lawnmower failed, so we had the 'pleasure' of cutting the grass in the playing field by hand using cane knives. This requires a special technique. One leans over, partly kneeling on one knee, with the free wrist propped on the upper thigh, and slashes away. There is a particular flick of the wrist to make a clean slice. Get it wrong and the blade flies over the grass or digs into the hard ground. Either way you were laughed at by the boys as being *va vulagi* (like a white man) or growled at by the supervising brother – or both.

Discipline was maintained by being made to write lines on the board (hundreds or thousands depending on how bad you'd been), making sasa brooms from the centre stem of a coconut leaf during the tea or lunch breaks, or getting the cane on your backside. For this latter you were called to the front, bent over, and got a whack or two, or four, on the bum with a cane. It was cane, not a birch as I believe they used in England. It hurt a bit, but not too bad. The problem for the teacher was that this made you the hero of the class. If you were very bad, you were summoned to the headmaster's office to be caned on the palm of the

Sketches of Fiji

hand. Now that did hurt, a lot, and as it was done in private with just the headmaster and your teacher present, the fame didn't attach quite as much as the show in the classroom. There was however a camaraderie among those who had recently had 'six of the best' from the headmaster. The fame didn't last long, but there were some who managed to renew the fame quite regularly.

Sport was rugby or soccer, generally rugby for us in Saint Felix and soccer for the Indian boys in Saint Columbus; cricket during the season, handball, marbles and tops. When we played marbles it was different to using the thumb as they do in Australia and New Zealand. We catapulted the marbles from the forefinger. The thumb was pressed to the ground to steady the hand and the fore finger pulled back towards the top of the wrist with the index and thumb of the other hand and with the marble squeezed in place between. The marble was then lobbed from the fore finger and traveled an enormous distance, far more than the thumb method. Some of the part-European boys were extraordinarily accurate over long distances and it was not uncommon for one marble to shatter the other on contact.

Top spinning was equally a very refined skill, particularly amongst the part European boys. In this game one top would be set spinning in the centre of a ring marked out in the dirt and the second player would throw his spinning top towards the first with the intention of knocking it out of the ring. This was done with great skill and force, and often resulted in chunks of wood being torn from the first top. I have even seen

Primary school

tops split entirely in two with the force of a blow. These tops were made of wood approximately three inches tall, two inches in diameter at the top, and tapering to a point where a steel peg was inserted. We had to buy these, so having a piece torn out was something of a financial blow. Thankfully when we started attending the Suva Technical College for one afternoon a week the teachers allowed us to make our own tops in addition to our kite rollers and the official set pieces of tea trays and pencil boxes inlaid with different timbers. In hindsight it was very good of our teachers to let us do this; all they asked was that we completed the exam pieces first – a great incentive really.

The Marist Brothers were wonderful men. Despite the tropical temperatures and humidity of Suva they wore heavy black gowns that were probably little changed from when the order was founded in 1817. They were each strong individuals whose character stood out despite the fact that they all were dressed the same. They taught us fairness, dignity, honesty, a sense of fair play and decency. One occasionally reads these days of sexual interference with boys at Catholic and other schools. Never at any time during primary or secondary school did I see, or even hear a rumour, of such things happening.

Most of them were new Zealanders, however we did have one, Brother Pricillian, whom we learnt had come from Spain where he lost a leg fighting in the Spanish Civil War. He got around on a crutch at very high speed and had a short temper, but clearly was deeply committed to his religion and to teaching.

Sketches of Fiji

The Principal was Brother Columbus who, although stern and forbidding, and the wielder of the cane on the palm of the hand, was also a father figure for many of us. He kept very strict personal discipline and could be seen at almost any spare moment walking briskly up and down the long wooden corridor outside the Brother's quarters on the second floor. He and Brother Pricillian spent their weekends walking all over Suva; indeed, they became part of the scene in Suva. People, whether they were Catholic or not, would pause in what they were doing to wave and call to these two men. They must have politely turned down hundreds of invitations to share a cup of tea *'Gunu ti'* or 'drink yagona', as kava is called in Fiji.

Even at that young age of 12 to 13 years we were a rough bunch. Some of my primary school mates were much older than I and already knew all about 'girls'. The names of Teddy Wilson and Butch Grant come to mind. They were members of the 'Black Eagle' gang whose headquarters was in an abandoned World War II bomb shelter carved out of the soapstone immediately below the school. The sign of being a member of this gang was that the hair at the back of the neck was shaved into what was called a 'duck's arse'. I remember sitting next to Teddy at the back of the class one day while he shaved Butch's hair to this shape with an old cutthroat razor - during a lesson. The alternative haircut was a 'Spanish' i.e. straight and square across the back. These guys were tough, but I don't believe they were bad, and their 'gang' was simply likeminded fellowship. I understand Teddy went on to become a senior officer in the British Special Forces serving with distinction in Germany and the Middle East.

Primary school

The class was mostly part-European boys with one or two Fijians and five Europeans; namely Grahame Southwick (of whom more later), Terry Litchfield (again more later), Garry Fagan whose father served at the New Zealand Air Force flying boat base at Laucala bay, Peter O'Connor whose father ran the Agriculture College at Koronivia near Nausori (Peter went to Australia at the end of primary, but we did renew acquaintance later in life when we were in Australia) and me. Many of the part-European boys had surnames that are famous in Fiji's post European contact era, Savage, Wilson, Mason, St Auburn, Eastgate, Beddows, Powell, Simpson, Pickering - it's a long list.

The suburb of Samabula North was quite a long way from Toorak. To get to school I would walk from our house over the crest of a hill at the back of our landlord's simple home and down to the main road in the little suburban township of Samabula itself, about 30 to 40 minutes. From there it was a bus to central Suva down Edinburgh drive, and then a walk up the hill to Toorak. The journy took well over an hour and that could be a problem in Suva's humid, rainy weather; but we just got wet and didn't think much about it. The walk up to the school took us past the Century and Lilac theatres and a shop opposite the Lilac selling naughty magazines. This was well before the then nascent Playboy reached the shores of Fiji and I expect the magazines would be considered rather mild today. They did however cause a certain amount of schoolboy interest as we walked past. Strangely they also sold religious books, Christian, Hindu and Muslim, and all were in the window together.

Sketches of Fiji

This was the time of the 'scary' movies: *It came from the deep* with posters showing a large beast with enormous arms complete with claws and with a dragon-like head and fangs; *Man eaters of the Congo* with posters showing a very scared young lady wearing very flimsy attire lying over a rock in the background, evil looking dark-skinned men with pointed teeth, and of course the inevitable blood-covered knife. But the most memorable one was *The corpse grinders*. It came back three times it was so popular. I didn't see any of these even though there was no age censorship – I just had no money.

Sometimes Mother would drop us at the school in the van if she was en-route to deliver some laundry. The Brothers respected her immensely and if they saw her, they would make a point of at least one of them coming down the steps to talk to her. In the usual schoolboy manner, I was teased about this and it caused schoolboy embarrassment at the time, but also a sense of pride deep inside.

This was still colonial Fiji with all the good and bad that this bought. I recall in those early days of walking to school and being surprised at having elderly Fijian and Indian men step out of my way. And here I was, barely teenage, and in school uniform. I felt, even in those young years, that this was not right, even if it was the norm.

I'll tell one rather bizarre example of this attitude. One morning when I arrived at school there was a large crowd gathered outside an old wooden house on the left- hand side halfway up the road towards the Empire

Primary school

cafe. Naturally I ran up to see what was going on. A young man had hanged himself in the house overnight and the crowd was trying to see the sight. I shoved my way towards the front, just as the police arrived and began pushing the crowd back. They courteously did not attempt to push me back, so I was able to catch a glimpse in the window. Like I said, a bizarre story but hopefully one that shows, at least in small part, the relationships that existed in a British Colonial environment.

Schoolwork and me were not compatible. The Brothers moved me from sitting next to one boy (we were two to a desk), then another and then another, in the hope that my seat companion might help. They also moved me from the back to the front of the class, again in the vain hope that this might stimulate some interest. Neither this nor the occasional 1000 lines, a tap on the backside, or even the dreaded visit to the headmaster's office did very much. But I came third in the class one year and managed to pass the high school entrance exam. It says a lot for those hardworking Marist Brothers.

Suva markets and bus stop

The Suva bus stop was immediately adjacent to the Suva markets, over the road from WR Carpenters and the Pacific Biscuit Company factory.

The markets themselves were wonderous to a young lad. Tropical fruit, green vegetables, the brilliant red of chilies, and huge root crops, together with great piles of acrid smelling dried yaqona, some in root form, some cut into lumps and some already pounded to powder. These sat alongside ropes of Fiji twist tobacco in huge balls almost two feet across. There were Fijian ladies sitting cross-legged on the concrete selling big flat wheels of dried pandanus leaves to make mats, and the mats themselves with end frills of bright wool, or just finely finished like an oriental rug; and big folded packs of Fijian bark cloth *'masi'.* There was stall after stall of them, jammed together with what seemed like hundreds of people all talking in what were to me, foreign languages. Fijians, Indians and Chinese all jumbled up together. People sitting and lying on the stalls, and under them. Talking, watching lazily, smoking rough Fiji twist tobacco *'saluka'* and occasionally selling it. The Bedford carrier trucks were lined up outside covered in the red dust of the interior from whence they had come, bringing the sellers and their goods.

And then there was the fish market! Strange fish lying on concrete slabs with water occasionally flicked over them; some huge, some tiny, some silver, some incredibly brightly coloured; woven green coconut leaf baskets of shellfish, sea urchins, bech de mer, seaweed, and octopus. There were long strings of crabs tied together with vines and blowing bubbles. And that pungent but vinegary clean smell of fresh

Suva markets and bus stop

seafood filled the air. There were ladies sitting on the floor silently and gently fanning the flies from their produce, and sometimes laughing at this naïve European *'kaivulagi'* kid in starched white Bombay bloomer shorts ogling the strange world of the Suva markets.

The buses in my primary school years were all built on Thames or Ford chassis and were the classic bus shape. The bodies were built, often by our neighbour Mr. P.A. Lal, using plywood and timber bolted on to the imported chassis. There were no glass windows for the passengers, just a canvas awning to roll down when it rained, which was often. The seats were simple planks, somewhat like a church pew; some were even upholstered, of sorts, with coconut fibre and bright shiny red vinyl. It was a real credit to the mechanics of those days that they very rarely broke down. In due course the old classic truck shape gave way to a square shape with a flat front to the bus. We called this the 'ice block' bus because of its shape.

The bus stop was always alive with people of all races, and mixes of races. The noise and fumes of the buses was one thing, but it was the cries of the peanut and 'bean' sellers that I remember the most. These were mostly old and somewhat bowed Indian or Chinese gentlemen who carried a woven wicker basket in the crook of one arm, the handle of which was always wound with a clean white cloth – well, clean in the mornings. The basket was lined with oil stained old newspaper and contained little paper bags of peanuts and soft or hard 'beans'. By the time we saw them the oil from the cooking would have soaked into the paper making it translucent. The 'beans' were actually dried peas

Sketches of Fiji

which had been cooked to make them salty and spicy, and, obviously, to a texture that was either hard or soft. The flavours of these beans were different from one seller to the other and different, hard to soft.

My favourite soft beans came from a fellow who looked as if he was a mix of Chinese and Indian. We all called him 'Snake'; I have no idea why, but even the Grammar school kids knew him by that name. He sold his stock in little cornets of newspaper to save the cost of paper bags. This would be frowned on these days because the ink is dangerous to consume – but this was the 1950s and '60s. These men were called the 'peanut-bean' men because they would walk up and down past the buses calling "penutbeeen, penutbeeen" in a particular pitch that I remember so clearly even today.

There was a little kiosk at each end of the bus station, one run by an Indian family at the main road end, and the other by a Chinese family at the wharf end. They sold milky tea in big enamel bowls called *pyala,* Cadbury chocolates, tins of Hellaby's corned bully beef from New Zealand (the only food product I know of that has had a popular song written about it) and cigarettes. The cigarettes were sold one at a time called a 'roll' – and lit for you at no extra cost. There was Fiji twist tobacco, matches, tins of Nestle condensed milk, tins of pilchards in brine, and ice blocks. Butter was sold cut into one-ounce slices and the Rewa dairy kindly printed the place to cut in dotted lines on the waxed paper package.

If there is one place in the world that speaks of my childhood in Fiji it is there at the Suva bus stand and markets.

Fiji food

Fiji food is unique; it is a blend of many races and cultures each adding their own flavours and culinary history to the mix.

Anyone who has grown up in the Pacific islands knows the 'Pacific Cracker' brand of hard biscuits. How I miss those teeth-breaking delights. They came packed tightly in an unlined cardboard box with a picture of a Fijian man with big hair and the world's widest smile on the front of the box. The 'Pacific Biscuit' factory was over the road from the bus stand and the smell of the roasting crackers would waft across. These were known throughout the Pacific simply as 'PBC'. Even now my mouth waters for an enamel *'pyala'* bowl of the hot, incredibly sweet tea, thick with condensed milk, and made into porridge by adding broken up PBC. Nothing in the world tastes like that!

There were two versions of the biscuits, standard PBC about two inches square, a quarter of an inch thick and as hard as, say, a gingernut. The other was the 'Cabin Cracker', almost three inches square and closer to half an inch thick. These were impenetrable, so you broke them over the edge of a table or hit them with something like a tin of pilchards or Hellaby's Bully beef, or more often simply soaked them in the pyala of tea to make that wonderful tea porridge. Alas they've gone now to be replaced by a much more genteel biscuit.

Lunch on most days at school was purchased. Mum and Dad were up and gone to work too early to think about making sandwiches before they left. I was given one shilling per day to cover the cost of the bus fare and lunch.

Sketches of Fiji

There was a small café near the school at the Lilac theatre end which sold a wonderful thing called a 'long loaf'. This was, as the name implies, a long, thin loaf of bread, of the classic shape and always very fresh. But the real delight came from hollowing out the loaf with your fingers and then pouring a small tin of pilchards or sardines into the hole. It might sound pretty ordinary today, but this was the height of dining to us boys.

The alternative was up the road directly in front of the school to the very famous Empire café. The 'Empire' made their own pies, sausage rolls, and cakes. Goodness knows what they contained. We could sometimes smell these cooking from the classroom and it made one's mouth water. The shop wasn't very big, but they seemed to be able to produce a huge volume of food which they sold all over Suva from the back of a van. It was a bit more expensive than the Chinese cafe up the other way, but occasionally we would treat ourselves to fresh pies straight from the oven. For me to be able to afford this meant I had to walk from Samabula North to the school, about one and a half hours each way – and past the Colonial War Memorial Hospital morgue! But it was worth it, and it allowed me to show that I had money to spend like the other boys.

There was a third even better than these two, and that was to walk down the hill past the Lilac theatre to Cumming Street. This was where the Indian curry shops were located. There were several along the street mixed in with the other fabric, sandal and hardware shops. For some reason they were all called a 'lodge'. So, we had the Indian lodge, the Rewa lodge, Navua lodge, Suva lodge, and a whole lot more. Our favourite was always the Rewa lodge

Fiji food

where for thruppence you could buy two rotis and a never-ending supply of curried vegetables. So long as you could eke out the roti, they would continue to put tablespoons of curry on your plate. Great for growing boys.

The food was served on aluminum dishes and came with an aluminum cup for drinking simple tap water *'pani'*. These were always greasy but that's just the way it was, and we didn't take much notice at the time. It wasn't until several years later that I learnt that Cumming Street doubled as the red-light district of Suva at night.

Anyone who has grown up in the tropics, or in the East, will tell you of the memories that flood back when you smell shops selling spices. And it's true. Walking down Mark's Street, Rodwell road, Cumming Street, or any of those backstreets in the centre of Suva, one would come across shop after shop selling spices, rice, dried fish and mushrooms, tinned foods, and all sorts of general knickknacks. The rice, Atta flour, and spices were stored in big wooden bins that pivoted forward from under the counter.

Not long after we moved to our home in Samabula North one of the Indian religious societies built a temple right next door. On the many religious festivals, they would welcome me to sit with them in the hall of the temple and eat the fried flatbread *'puri'*, vegetable curry, and an enormous range of chutneys and sauces. In the centre of Samabula Township was a Sikh temple (Gurdwara they call them) which served food to anyone who wanted to pass by. It was simple food, but I remember their unique spices and flavours even today.

Sketches of Fiji

And then there were the Indian weddings. They took place throughout the year, but there were special times of the year when it was the wedding season. Everyone who came past these extravagant affairs was invited to sit and eat at long wooden tables covered with newsprint, under a temporary shed made of mangrove sticks and corrugated iron. The food was pretty standard, but excellent: roti, puri, vegetable curry, and tomato, onion and mint chutney.

In the cane season the boys from Nausori, (there was a sugar mill there in those days) would bring molasses wrapped in newspaper from the mill. This was the first separation stuff, pitch black and still with bits of fibre and some dirt, even tiny bits of stone. But it tasted great. Then others would bring Fijian '*Madrai*', the slightly fermented rolls of starch about as thick as your finger made from dalo or cassava wrapped up in banana leaves, boiled, or cooked in an underground oven '*lovo*', and then stored underground. This was used in the old days as emergency supplies as it would keep for long periods. It was something of an acquired taste, but I acquired it.

And then there were the ice blocks. Imagine a bucket of warm water into which is poured a brown paper bag full of molasses-rich raw sugar from the mill, and a splash of vermillion red food dye with a slightly citrus artificial flavour. Stir the lot together and pour into tin-plate moulds to freeze. At first these ice-blocks were held in the hand and needed eating very fast as the sugary coloured water ran everywhere, but later they became very modern with sticks to hold them with. And

Fiji food

there you have it – a Fiji ice block. On a hot day, which was usual, a great deal of the sticky red mess would end up on your starched white school uniforms. Not something the mothers were particularly keen about, even if in my case we had the benefit of a commercial laundry.

These days I smile a little (quietly of course) when modern parents worry about giving their children sugar as it makes them 'hyper', and, heaven forbid the giving of red food colour. I just think of those frozen, sweet, red lollywater ice-blocks!

The food that stays strongest in my memory, and I know it's also true of my mother, brothers, wife and children, is the *roti* parcel. This was basically the working man's lunch. The wife would get up in the early hours of the morning to cook the flat bread which we called roti. I understand the word roti in Hindi simply means bread, and there is a very wide range served in India. But for Fiji there was only the one roti and I have not been able to duplicate it anywhere in India. It was unleavened flour called 'atta' mixed with a little salt and ghee and then kneaded into a dough. Round balls of this were rolled into flat circular rotis which were then placed on a hot steel plate that had been moistened with ghee. The plate was heated simply by firewood in the villages and the poorer areas, but I have also seen it on primus stoves. The roti was cooked quickly and throughout the cooking was dabbed with a pad of fabric dipped in ghee to flatten out the bubbles that formed. Liz and our daughter Jackie still cook these from time to time, and always they bring back memories.

Sketches of Fiji

The curry would almost always be vegetable – long beans, okra, tropical spinach '*bele*', dried peas, dhal, potato. Just occasionally a tiny trace of chicken or tinned mutton or pilchards. On very special days there would be goat, recently slaughtered by the men up the road. It is indisputable that the very best chicken curry is made from *Jungli Murgi*, called 'free range' today – but *really* free. Fiji curries are unique; there is nowhere in the world that makes a curry as good as Fiji. It is a simple homespun kind of flavour that one never forgets. In fact, *Kai Vitis* of all races crave their curries when absent from the country, even after many years. I think it's a kind of addiction; long may it live.

And then there were the Indian sweet sellers. There were lots of them, many congregated in a line between the markets and the bus stand, but all over Suva really. My favourite was at the back of the Garrick near the old Morris Hedstrom store and en-route to the Cathedral. The carts they used were a tray about five feet by three feet on two old bicycle wheels with handles for them to push. On top of the tray was a glass box with timber frames and lots of little windows. One larger window was hinged for the sweet seller to gain access from the top. Inside was Aladdin's magic. Sweets of all sizes and shapes piled up on enamel dishes – and the most amazingly gaudy, bright colours. My favourites were Gulab Jamun, Bhajia, and Gulagula, but the range was large. Some were spicy with local spinach or rourou, but most were just incredibly sweet and deep fried. Others were like (possibly were) solidified condensed milk – wonderful.

Fiji food

We would sometimes smuggle these into the classroom and eat them during class. It was a sort of test to see if we could get away with it. Usually we did, but sometimes the confiscation of the sweets hurt more than the cane. The sweets were very cheap, but even a penny or two was usually a difficulty. I admit that sometimes the church offering was diluted on the way. Only diluted, mind.

Then there were the Chinese lollies; dried plums with an acrid, salty flavour that made you just nibble at the edges. They came in various sizes and flavours but were always very strong. Others were scarlet discs somewhat like a church wafer in shape that you just laid on your tongue and let it melt. It took at least a day for the dye to fade from your tongue. And the ice blocks I spoke of earlier.

On special occasions Dad would order takeaway Chinese from the Golden Dragon or the Chungking in downtown Suva. We telephoned the restaurant and ordered from memory, usually by the item number, then drove into town with our own pots and waited while they filled the pots – we had no plastic in those days.

Marist Brothers High School

Then in 1959 it was to high school. The Marist Brothers high school, known to all as MBHS, was in another suburb called Flagstaff. There was a hill nearby with views across the Rewa delta and the approaches to Suva. It had been an observation post right up until the end of World War II and hence the reference to a Flagstaff. MBHS was a big school, built in 1937, and considered one of the best in the country with a very fine record of sporting and academic achievements. It was also run by the Marist brothers, however there were several lay teachers from both New Zealand and Fiji.

The principal was Brother Lambert who had been appointed in 1937 as the Marist school's first headmaster, and who was held in the highest regard by the political, commercial and educational society of Fiji. He was awarded an MBE by the Queen and I recall his very humble speech to us at assembly that week. He attributed his 'gong' entirely to the work of the former and current Marist brothers in Fiji – and he meant it. I think we all learnt a lesson that day.

While I was at school Brother Lambert retired as principal but stayed on to teach French. He was replaced by a Brother Cletus who was much more a disciplinarian. One thing that Brother Cletus did was to encourage debating and oratory at the school. It had always been something the MBHS was well known for, but Brother Cletus really placed a big emphasis on this. I'm pleased he did so because over the years I have given many hundreds of public speeches and lectures and believe I have a level of skill in this which I first learnt at high school.

Marist Brothers High School

Then there was Brother Felix who taught us, or at least taught the other students, singing and music. He told me one day that I was tone deaf. Oh joy! This was something I was very happy about as it meant I didn't have to spend time in the school choir on a Friday afternoon, and it gave me a special schoolboy status. The boys learnt all the usual schoolboy songs, *Men of Harlech*, *Gaudeamus Igitur*, the Maori farewell song, a Boer war lament *My Sari Marais*, and so on. One that always intrigued me was *There'll always be an England* – belted out at full volume by a group of newly pubescent boys (still a few squeaky voices) at a Catholic school, on an island in the middle of the Pacific, who had only the vaguest idea where England might be, and no idea at all why it should hang around that long. Still, the lyrics and chest-beating sound stirred the blood.

What we did *not* learn were songs in the Fijian or Hindi language. Speaking any language other than English, at any time, on the school grounds, or in uniform was frowned upon. Whilst this was not a formally promulgated policy of the Colonial Government at the time, it was real enough. I know it's denied by some, but I was there, and I experienced it firsthand. The logic behind this was that the Colonial Government could see that independence was fast approaching for Fiji and they wanted to ensure that the Fijian people held a good command of the English language as that day approached. This was not some egotistical British pride, but rather a recognition that if the Fijian people were to advance in what was essentially a Western world of business and culture, then they would need to speak English well.

Sketches of Fiji

Brother Anthony taught us English literature and poetry. To this day I have a love of reading and books which I attribute to his nurturing. The school library was extensive, and I spent many happy hours just browsing. I also took a large number of books home and lay on my bed reading for many hours; no particular style (or as it's known today, 'genre') but generally about history and people. I still dislike novels and prefer to read about historical events and the people who have shaped our civilisation.

In the grounds at the back of the school was an incredible botanic garden. In addition to his teaching duties, Brother Anthony also looked after these gardens. We were each allocated a plot in the garden and Brother Anthony spent many hours, not only showing us what to do, but also talking to us about the plants. On one occasion he also showed us how to build a ramjet water pump in the stream leading to the lily pond. I was a lot more interested in the mechanics of this pump than the cell structure of a frangipani leaf.

Speaking of discipline, by now it was not the 'done thing' to use the cane except for really serious matters. There was however the occasional 'clip behind the ear' when we were overly frustrating. Detention became the official alternative, and many long hours were so spent! Some of the teachers devised other innovative ways to maintain discipline. One, a lay teacher, made us stand in a wastepaper basket facing the class and holding our ears. It worked, but I suspect would not be politically correct these days.

I did well at chemistry, physics, English language, literature, and religion. French was okay (Brother Lambert taught this) but I completely

Marist Brothers High School

failed to understand the mysteries of algebra and trigonometry. I was also hopeless at Latin, scoring around eleven per cent in the final exams. Given my deep interest in language, reading and debate this is a little strange and I'll try to rationalise why this was so. The teacher was a New Zealander whose method of instruction was to have us parrot the verbs and vocabulary over, and over again. I objected strenuously to sitting there repeatedly chanting 'amo, amas, amat'. I guess I just switched off, something I now regret. Anyway, my little rebellion resulted in my repeating Form three before subsequently going on to pass the Cambridge University entrance exam at the end of high school years.

Chemistry was my favourite subject and by securing samples from the school, buying small items from the chemists, some of Dad's spotting chemicals, and scrounging from Grahame Southwick's optometrist and pharmacist father, I put together quite a little chemistry set. I kept it in a World War II wooden ammunition box. It was painted green with the word 'chemicals' painted, not very well, on the top in white. I still have the box although the lid has gone. Today it is a toy box in the cubby at our home for the grandkids to tidy up their toys. My laboratory was the space under the concrete front steps of our house. It was a tiny little area and I suspect that if anything went wrong I would not have had time to get out before something dramatic happened.

Sports at MBHS were the usual cricket, rugby, soccer, and athletics. I found that I had the 'wind' to do quite well at long distance and cross-country races, although I could never win against some of the

Sketches of Fiji

Fijian boys who were such fine athletes. I noticed this ability also in bush walking where I usually had more stamina than the others, and certainly in my spear fishing days, where I could stay longer under the surface than most. I did not like team sports and so never made it to any of the soccer or rugby teams, I did however play cricket reasonably well.

During later high school years I worked sometimes for 'Lectric limited' during the school holidays. One of our jobs was rewiring the electrical circuitry for the buses I spoke of earlier. Given the heat, humidity and rain of Suva, and the fact that the cables were exposed under the bus, this was a regular job. There was no question of attempting repairs, we simply ripped out all the old wiring and completely rebuilt the loom. Another job I did was to make transformer/rectifiers to install in houses in the old part of Suva. These homes had originally been wired for 110 volts DC and the transformer/rectifiers allowed them to use 240 volts AC. I also rewound and repaired electrical motors. Some of these were very large, and others as small as Singer sewing machine motors. The rest of the work was usually repairing fans, toasters, and electric irons.

My foreman was an elderly Indian Sikh gentleman (Mr Singh of course) who had learned his trade on the job. He had no understanding of the theory behind what he did, but he was a master of his trade nevertheless. He taught me a great deal about electrical wiring, machinery and appliances and added greatly to the foundation for my later engineering life. And he lectured me soundly on the dangers of electricity when one day I got a very heavy 'belt' from one of the transformers.

Dispensing cures

Boils, head lice (*Kutus* we called them) intestinal worms and ringworm were the order of the day. Boils simply saw their painful life through assisted by hot compresses and Iodine or Mercurochrome. Sometimes they became carbuncles. The worst were the carbuncles under the armpit called '*Bekas*' because they kept you awake all night walking around with your elbow held out like a flying fox (*Beka* in Fijian). Lice responded to kerosene and the use of a Kutu comb. But occasionally people shaved the kids' heads. This caused some confusion at times because of the Hindu custom of shaving the eldest son's head when the father died.

Ringworm was treated with Gentian Violet, so you could tell from the red or purple if it was boils or ringworm. Intestinal worms were fun. You knew you had them, or at least that they had got to major infestation stage, when you became very tired all day, irritable, itchy bum and the bowels did funny things. The treatment was to drink flowers of sulphur. This was basically yellow sulphur powder, stirred into water and drunk very quickly. The sulphur didn't dissolve, the water just helped get it down. The smell and taste were unbelievably bad. Often the mixture just came straight back up again, necessitating another shot. Then the parents got the idea that you should do it every six months regardless of symptoms! Thankfully Combantrin came on the market and that was easier to take.

When I was 13 there was an outbreak of polio. The schools were closed and several kids died, others were crippled. A close friend at the time, Edward Stork, was one of those who was paralysed. His father was the Governor of Suva Gaol and they lived over the road from the gaol near

Sketches of Fiji

our factory. I was staying with him the night they took him to the hospital, so Mum and Dad were very worried. When we returned to school we were all vaccinated – very painful as I recall. The oral vaccination used these days was a later invention.

We were given annual medical check-ups and inoculations by students from the Tamavua medical college. This was overseen by senior nursing sisters. Sister Ram Samuj was a terror who brooked no nonsense about not wanting the anti-typhoid needle. In fact, getting the needle was far better than having her yell at you in front of the whole school. The interns would look down your throat, in your ears with a kind of torch (same one, no disposable tips), feel behind your ears and listen to your chest with a stethoscope. Sometimes they would get you to lift your arms up above your head. In high school the male medical students would feel your balls and say 'cough'. No rubber gloves in those days. I never knew, and still don't know what they were checking for, but at 13 and 14 it was not a nice experience. They stopped it after a couple of years, presumably because of some misunderstandings. Think of a thin, small, medical student feeling the balls of a six foot six, 16-year-old Fijian rugby player in full view of his mates – oh boy what fun!

In the early days we went to Dr. George Hemming as our GP. George was also the pastor at the small Anglican Church at Suva Point, but spent his days tending to the poor at the JP Bailey clinic near the wharf in downtown Suva. Bailey was a wealthy merchant and landowner, and a recluse, who before his death established the JP Bailey Trust to help look after

Dispensing cures

Fiji's poor. George charged two shillings per visit, but if you couldn't pay, then anything or nothing would be okay. We would sit on hard wooden benches outside his consulting room and it was strictly first come first served. As one person was attended to we would all slide up along the seat until it was our turn. There was a fabric screen set at 90 degrees to his desk and you would take your place on one side while he dealt with a patient on the other side. Given you went in immediately after that patient you would often learn who they were, and what ailed them!

George was brusque to say the least, and if he thought you were malingering, he would have you out of his little office quick smart with a firm word rather than a medical certificate. But he also had an enormous depth of compassion and humanity. He must have seen hundreds of people every day in that little clinic and dispensed wise words as much as he did the medicines. He had an Indian nurse who assisted him, and she had full measure of his brusqueness, compassion, and efficiency.

Once you had your prescription you then walked over the road to Southwick's pharmacy (a second outlet to the Samabula one) to get your pills or whatnot. This pharmacy was *air conditioned*, a brand-new technology for Fiji in those days. Grahame's father advertised this fact in the newspapers. On one occasion, we were holidaying at Deuba with the McAllister's and their Grandmother Mrs. Mac Caig when I developed a rash of boils. Mum drove me back to see Dr. Hemming because I also developed a quite large abscess in the groin. Not good for a young lad at 14 years of age! George and his nurse had a look, got me on to the table, lanced the abscess without

Sketches of Fiji

anesthetic, and had me out of there in less than 10 minutes with a prescription for penicillin. It all happened so fast I had no time to be concerned about people fiddling around with that part of my body.

George continued to treat the poor people of Suva until well into his eighties when he retired to New Zealand and I believe continued his pastoral work.

Later, as money became a bit more available, and as I began to work, we used Dr. Duncan who had a surgery in the Victoria Arcade. The problem here was that Suva was a very small place and anybody who was anybody was treated by Dr. Duncan. As you sat in the surgery, unless you were clearly sneezing and sniffling, there were lots of sideways looks to wonder what you were there for. But that's okay you looked sideways at them as well. It would be a room full of fixed, forward-looking stares, and awkward, embarrassed, little grins.

Early Teenage years

Around the end of my first year of high school the Southern Press business began to improve slowly, and we moved from Samabula North to an apartment on Prince's road in Tamavua. This was in the next suburb, and one that was a little more up-market. It was a pleasant flat in a block of two, one above the other. Downstairs was an elderly lady called Mary Edwell Burke who was a very well-known painter and her paintings are now quite valuable. For the first time we had a view, and what a view it was. We could see the reef from Nasese round more than 180° and up to the head of the Wailoku valley. Below us was the Wailoku river, Suva harbour and Lami Township. Beyond that lay mount Korobaba and the Rewa and Korobasabasaga Ranges. Sunsets were dramatic.

Grahame Southwick and I spent a lot of time together. He had comics, *Mad* magazine and a synthetic orange drink called *Tang*. On one occasion he was sent a pair of Levi jeans by a relative living overseas. This was 1958/9 and I had never even heard of Levis - and it was the first time I ever saw a zip in trousers. We listened and laughed loudly to the BBC's *Goon Show* and roamed the bush towards the sea from his house, now location of the new parliament buildings. Grahame's mother, Maureen, had a large tropical garden out the back where she would entertain the cruise ship passengers with her wonderful sense of humour when they visited in their sightseeing buses from the ships. She would serve them her famous banana cake, and they all praised it greatly. Further out the back, beyond her garden, was a big guava patch and we would have great fun playing guava fights – pelting each other with the hundreds of slightly overripe fruit that were everywhere during the season. Some of these were full of maggot size worms – even more fun.

Sketches of Fiji

I said that Grahame's father was an optometrist and pharmacist; his pharmacy was on the hill near the little township of Samabula North. Sometimes on Saturday evenings Grahame and I would hang around in the shop (I refrain from suggesting we 'assisted'). It was a great joke for us when we saw a gentleman sidle discreetly into the shop and move to the far end of the counter. We would go up to them knowing full well that they were there to buy condoms, quite unusual in those days and only dispensed from chemists. After they had mumbled their order we would repeat in a very loud voice 'Oh, a pack of three' so that the rest of the shop could hear. Bloody good thing others didn't do the same to other people we know later in life!

There were sometimes parties at various homes in the 'Domain' where the Colonial Government wallahs lived. These were large homes set on beautiful lawns, and in manicured gardens, that were maintained by groups of prisoners overseen by a single warder armed only with his swagger stick. In the early teenage years, the parties were organised by the parents (you know, little dahling's birthday party). I sometimes felt that I was invited as a token local European but that's probably being unfair. There were never any Fijian or Indian guests.

Usually I had no idea who the others, especially the girls, were. Many were back on holiday from boarding school. It would go something like this: we would get a formal invitation in the mail 'Mr. and Mrs. Everhard Blowfly invites Master Andrew Drysdale etc. etc.'. My father would then reply on special paper in his copper-

Early Teenage years

plate handwriting with his gold Parker fountain pen 'Mr and Mrs. Thomas Drysdale are pleased to accept your kind invitation for our son, Andrew etc. etc.'.

I would be dressed in my one pair of long pants salvaged from the non-claimed dry-cleaning and adjusted to size by my mother, in a starched white long-sleeved shirt, and wearing one of Dad's ties as per the invitation's instructions. Mum would drop me off in the van but would not come in. I would stand at the doorstep until the mother of the birthday girl saw me; then would come the introductions. 'Oh, you must be young Andrew – Drysdale, isn't it? Rosie, darling, do come and say hello to Andy.' Puke. And then to the pipe-smoking father of the house, 'Dear, this is young Andy Drysdale, you know, his parents run the dry-cleaning business in town.' Puke.

And then there were the boys, all wearing Levi jeans (with zips) and open neck shirts, despite the explicit instructions on the invitation regarding dress. The record player would be playing Buddy Holly alternated with slow songs to cover all angles. The couples would jive or foxtrot, neither of which I knew how to do despite the hours spent at the Girl Guides hall supposedly learning. One first needs to want to learn.

So, it was stand in the corner drinking lemonade (the only time I had that opportunity) and eating sausage rolls or asparagus rolled in a slice of bread, till the mother would drag darling Rosie over with instructions to dance with 'Andy'. Extreme embarrassment, mental blank, feet

Sketches of Fiji

sticking to the floor with some early form of blue tack, we would both shuffle around a bit until the record stopped, then mumble something and go back to our respective corners. Thankfully the appointed time to end would eventually come and the cars would roll up to collect us. This was normally 10 pm, but in more risqué houses it would be 10.30 or even 11.00. The parents would have whiled away the intervening hours at their club and be feeling somewhat social on arrival, which meant long farewells – by the adults. Mum would come in the van and I would be very pleased to see her. Later, when the parties were organised by the girlies themselves the mood was rather different, as were the events. Somewhat rollicking actually!

I sometimes wondered what would have happened if my parents had invited the daughters to a party at our tiny home in Samabula North, next to the Hindu temple, surrounded by clumps of wild guava, overgrown Para grass, and what were euphemistically known as 'wood and iron dwellings'.

As I recount all of this I don't intend to be rude to the Colonial Civil Service families, but know I am being so. It's just that that's the way it was. There were however many who became close friends to Mum and Dad and who were genuine and wonderful people. Let me name two for now: Ian (later Sir Ian) Thompson and his wife Nancy (a 'local European') were wonderful people, respected by all nationalities and deeply committed to the betterment of Fiji and its people, especially the indigenous Fijians.

Early Teenage years

One fun thing to do, especially to celebrate New Year, was to make a 'bamboo cannon' from the thick walled, short node bamboos – as opposed to the thin walled, long node ones used for making kites. The best bamboo would be still slightly green and about five feet long. We used a crowbar to break out all the nodes except the last at one end. Just ahead of this we cut a small hole about three quarters of an inch in diameter. A rag soaked in kerosene was stuffed down to the bottom and lit. It was kept alight by blowing into the hole. When we judged the interior of the bamboo was hot enough, we would snuff out the flame by blocking the hole with a cloth, wait a few moments for the interior to fill with hot kerosene fumes, blow into the hole a few times to add oxygen, then apply a flame to the hole. The kerosene gas would flash and boom very loudly. Then we'd snuff out the interior flame by closing off the hole with a cloth, wait a moment, blow into the hole, and again apply the ignition flame. This would be repeated until eventually the bamboo would split, and we would have to stop. A variation was to place an empty jam tin into the mouth of the cannon to see how far it would be thrown when the hot kero gas was ignited. This was all great fun.

However, there was a danger that sometimes, as you blew into the hole, the gas would self-ignite and blow back into your face. The result was, at the best, a loss of eyebrows and front hair, but it could also cause quite severe facial burns. But hey, what fun!

Scouting about

It was at about this time (1958) that Southwick and I became involved in the Boy Scouts movement. The New Zealand Air force base at Laucala bay had a hall at the very back of their extensive grounds off Sukuna road that was lent to the Scouting movement for the 2nd. Laucala Air Scouts. I enjoyed scouting and did reasonably well with the badges and promotions, ending up as a troop leader. But I didn't get to Southwick's top award of Queen's Scout. I read a great deal about Lord Baden Powell and his exploits during the Boer war in South Africa and was extremely interested in him as a person in addition to the work he did with the Scouting movement. We met every Friday night and Mum would drop me off in the van at Sukuna road where I would walk through the guava patch to the Scout hall. I think she probably then joined Dad at the Yacht Club for a couple (?) of drinks before they both returned to pick me up at around 9.00 PM.

We went camping on several weekends and I guess this, plus Barmah, was where my love of the bush began. These were pretty mild camps by comparison to what we did later, but they formed the basis of the discipline that is necessary for bush work. One Easter we were camped by the stream at Wainadoi when there was a flash flood in the middle of the night which caused us to scramble to higher ground, losing most of our equipment in the process. Talk about fun! This was the stuff we read about in the comics. However, as might be imagined, we had some rather excited parents who had heard in the news of the flash flood and knew that's where the little darlings were camped. Nevertheless no one was hurt.

Scouting about

Wainadoi is interesting from our family's perspective as it was here that my wife's grandfather had mined for gold. On one of our camping expeditions (long before meeting Liz) I found an old hand-worked goldmine near the bank of the river quite high up in the valley. There may have been other mines in the area, but I like to think that this was her grandfather's one. My father-in-law used to joke that the only gold the old man ever got out of this mine was enough to make the wedding ring for his wife. It was in this valley also that he planted rubber trees, many of which are still standing today. Unfortunately, the climate was not right for rubber and the enterprise was not successful.

After a while I left the Air Scouts and transferred to the Suva Sea Scouts where my other mate Terry Litchfield was active. Their meeting hall was at the back of the old Boys' Grammar School hostel in central Suva, on the edge of the sea wall. It was still there when I last visited in 2016. I found the Sea Scouts more interesting as we had lectures from several old sea captains and from Captain Huff who was at that time the Director of Marine and the Harbour Master for Suva. We also had an 18 foot clinker built wooden skiff which we repaired, sailed and rowed all over Suva harbour and up into the Rewa delta area near Nukulau Island. This was still the days of timber ships and Fiji had a large fleet of inter-island sailing cutters (single masted, fore and aft rigged sailing ships), so the hardware stores, particularly Millers and Carpenters, still stocked all the magical gear that was needed to repair these ships. I learnt to rivet timber planks together using copper nails and the cupped washer called a rove, to stitch canvas us-

Sketches of Fiji

ing a sailmakers needle and 'palm', splice ropes and tie a huge variety of working and decorative knots.

Our camps were almost invariably at Nukulau Island and we would sail there in the trusty *Sea Eagle* at least once a month. I have a photograph of me standing alongside the 'goat shed' on the island in full patrol leader uniform. In the British system the Navy was always considered the first service, so when the Scout's annual Queen's Birthday parade took place in Suva we were the first troop. On one occasion I had the honour of carrying the flag and marching at the head of the column.

Around 1959 Commander Stan Brown purchased a wooden hulled, twin masted ketch, MY *Maroro* (flying fish) and began an 'outward-bound' sailing school. Stan and his wife Jean were wonderful people who contributed a huge amount to the development of Fiji and its people in many ways. He was a mentor to many of Fiji's leading military officers and Jean was personal assistant to Ratu Mara all through his years as Prime Minister, and then as President. What stories she could tell; but won't. She helped Ratu Mara write his memoirs. But, back to the ship and training.

Terry Litchfield and I were on the very first of these sailings. We didn't go far, only to Bega, but this was about developing character and skills, not long-distance cruising. We worked very hard on navigation, sailing instruction in the skiffs, rowing drill, knots and what they were used for, and orienteering onshore. We scoured the tiny islet called Storm Island using a World War II military hand-held compass and British

Early Teenage years

1:50000 maps to find clues left by Cdr. Brown. I'm pleased to say Litch and I did quite well at this. One evening we went ashore in Malumu bay to the village for a dance called a *'tralala'*. Dancing with the local girls dressed up in their finest, wearing flowers and smelling of scented coconut oil. My goodness, at 14 years of age!

Eventually in 2004 Storm Island became Royal Davui, Grahame Southwick's luxury, and exclusive resort. How the world turns.

Tamavua home

Around the time I turned 15 another family friend, the Corbetts, who were one of the three local butchers (the other two were Leylands and Wah Lees, spelt Wahleys) offered Mum and Dad the rental of their old family home about a half mile further up the road and opposite the well-known shop, Kundan Singh's. This was a wonderful old timber home that must have stood for at least 100 years. At the time it was built this area would very much have been 'in the bush'. It sat on the very edge of the soapstone cliff that fell away more than 500 feet vertically down to the Wainibokasi valley and river.

There was a large oval mahogany dining table which had a hole through the top. Mr. Corbett told us that hole had been made by a musket ball at a time when one of his ancestors had been fighting off the Fijians from Colo-I- Suva. True or not it was a good story; the hole was the right size, and there are many records of problems with the Fijian tribes of that area in the early days.

I had my own room for the first time in my life. It was under the house at the back and with its own rear entrance. Here I moved my chemistry set and all the other bits and pieces that I had accumulated, including a basic toolkit. I built and installed a pressure switch under the carpet at the top of the steps leading to my room and connected this to an alarm in the room which was powered by an old car battery. This in turn was charged by a transformer/rectifier that I had built. The door to the outside was fitted with a solenoid-operated locking mechanism, again powered from the battery. The solenoid came from one of the early car

Tamavua home

turning indicator arms. To open this door from the outside one pressed on what looked like a nail head in the wood of the wall; this operated a micro switch which in turn retracted the electronic lock. Clever stuff!

Immediately outside my room and down the slope towards the cliff were some enormous old breadfruit trees of the Samoan variety – small, very sweet fruit. The flying foxes (*Bekas*) love these fruit and during the season the whole night would be filled with the noises of their flopping about and eating and screeching. Great targets for the shang-eye.

Beyond the slope the ground fell almost 400 feet vertically down into the Wailoku valley. Standing on the cliff edge I could see the river directly below, and the abattoir and night-cart building of my early tin boat days. Naturally I tried to climb down the cliff, but soapstone is slippery at the best of times, and after rain very much so – that's why it's called soapstone I guess – so progress was not good and eventually commonsense overcame schoolboy heroics.

Now, for the first time Mum and Dad could afford a house-girl. She lived with her husband in a small, one room, corrugated iron home out the back. He had a job with the Public Works Department (PWD) but also did the gardening because my parents simply didn't have time for this.

In the bush

In time I grew out of the Scouting movement and began to develop an even greater interest in bush walking. Terry Lichfield and I joined the British Rucksack club. This was run as part of the British Council, albeit to this day I'm not sure I fully understand what the British Council actually did. Some sort of Colonial Office export of British culture I suspect. We met in the British Council chambers which had a lecture room and a large library (this did interest me) and watched slides of other people's adventures.

The club had been founded a short while before by Commander Brown and now was chaired by a fellow called Terry Oliver who worked for Cable and Wireless. He was assisted by a young Fijian man called Peter Naituva who helped with the local knowledge and who worked for the Native Land Trust Board. I was pleased to see a little while ago that the club has undergone a revival in recent times. That's good; I have many happy memories of those days.

So, cheaply kitted out, Litch and I went on several rather genteel bush walks with the Club over the next few months. In due course we realised that we wanted to do more than the Club was doing, so we began to organise our own trips. I also did a lot of these bushwalks with Grahame Southwick, and sometimes with other lads.

The centre of our bush walking was the ravines and jungle of the Rewa ranges behind Mount Korobaba, and from there into the Wainibokasi valley, or across into the Navua valley via the Rewa or Korobasabasaga ranges.

In the bush

Sometimes we climbed to the Nadrau plateau, but these trips took several days and were logistically more difficult. Mount Korobaba was our starting point for most of these journeys and we climbed it so often that, as a challenge, Litch and I began to time ourselves from the base to the summit; and slept on top for more nights than I can remember. It was magical to sit at 1428 feet looking at the city lights and the harbour of Suva, and then back across to the blackness of the heavy jungle behind us.

As my family knows, I am absolutely hopeless at navigation in a city, but I do seem to have a knack for finding my way through the jungle. Never at any time was I lost, although the terrain where we were walking was some of the toughest one can imagine. Extraordinarily heavy jungle and thick red mud was the order of the day. Starting from the top of one ridge we would slip and slide from tree to tree through the mud and undergrowth to the stream that inevitably ran at the bottom of these ravines. Then we would pull ourselves from tree to tree, vine to vine, up the ridge on the other side. In places we would travel all day and be less than five miles forward from the starting point. We would camp at night, usually by a stream, so that we had water, but this posed another problem. The area was always extremely wet making it difficult to collect fire wood that was not already soaked through. As a result, we tended to rely on small primus stoves that burnt methylated spirits.

We did not carry tents, mostly because we couldn't afford them, but also because we needed to keep the bulk of our rucksacks as small as possible. The large rucksacks I see people using these days would have

Sketches of Fiji

made travel through the jungle extremely difficult. Instead we would use whatever materials were available to build a shelter for the night, or would use a rock overhang, and there was usually one nearby if you followed the stream for a while. The usual materials for these bivouacs were the large leaves of the wild ginger. These plants often stood more than 20 feet high, with leaves at least a yard long and 12 to 20 inches wide. Nature was very good to supply these for us. Our groundsheet, when we had one, was just a small rectangle of canvas.

Strangely, given this was the tropics, it was usually cold; perhaps because we were wet from head to foot all day and there was little opportunity to dry out. We did what we could to keep a change of clothes dry for the nighttime, but this was rarely possible. There was no plastic then and the best we could do was to wrap things in waterproof canvas. The trick was to at least keep a dry pair of woollen socks and a head cover of some sort. Sometimes we would comment that we were shivering in our jungle paradise, and not more than a few miles away the citizens of some township or village would be tossing and turning, perspiring under their mosquito net.

Sometimes the jungle was very quiet except for our breathing and tramping in the mud and undergrowth. Other times there were noises everywhere, pigeons, doves, parrots and streams bubbling through rocks and undergrowth. But always it was wet, soaking through everything we were wearing, through our rucksacks, and unless we had been very careful, our food. Fortunately, Fiji has no venomous snakes or spiders in the jungle, nor does it have the leeches that I remember from the Murray River in

In the bush

Australia. We sometimes came across the marks of wild pigs digging in the mud, and occasionally heard them running away, but never saw one up close, fortunately, as they can be dangerous. It was not unusual to see villagers in the Colo area with wild pigs they have speared though.

The Fiji jungle has a smell which is quite unique; musty, decaying vegetation, and the smell of stagnant water that has become a form of tea with leaves long soaked into a puddle or rock pool. But somehow that smell is equally crisp and clean, it doesn't clog your nostrils or throat; in fact, if anything it clears the lethargy that the heat and humidity might otherwise have caused. I've been into jungle areas in Asia and into dense Australian bush; neither smell anything even vaguely like that tropical Fiji jungle.

Food consisted of an unleavened damper made from flour, water, and salt; sometimes with a tin of Hellaby's bully beef or sardines and toasted in the morning with a scraping of butter and Vegemite. Occasionally, when we had saved a few pennies, there would be PBC. And then of course there was the TEA! Made with fresh water from the stream, boiled in a billy, thick and black, and made almost into the constituency of treacle by adding Nestle condensed milk from a jar. One of the ceremonies of packing before leaving for a trip was decanting tins of condensed milk into small screw top jars. For longer trips we had to use powdered milk in order to save weight and I can remember the lumps of grey gunk stuck to the sides of the enamel tin mugs because we simply stirred the powder direct into the tea.

Sketches of Fiji

Our tools were a cane knife, sharpening stone (I still have mine), spoon and sheath knife. I made my own sheath knives from old industrial hacksaw blades that I ground roughly to shape on the grinding wheel at Tom Pickering's United Engineers and finished off by hand on an oilstone. This took hours but was, I guess, a labour of love. The handles were of Fiji hardwood held on with the ubiquitous binding wire; the sheaths were made from leather bought from the Indian cobblers near St. Felix College. I had one of these until we moved to Australia – I guess it was lost in the move – pity, they were great knives.

One of the games we played was *'vidi vidi'*. I have no idea where the game or the name came from, but it seemed to be Fijian, and I've heard it given other names as well. We balanced a sheath knife on the tip of a forefinger, held vertically by the forefinger of the other hand, and then with a quick flick, spun the knife to the ground to try to spear a small stick. The knife had to touch the stick and end up vertical in the ground. Once you had been successful from the finger you then moved on to spin the knife from the wrist, elbow, shoulder and finally nose! We got quite good at this, but one day Southwick managed to stick his knife right into his elbow joint and we got into trouble with the parents.

A variation on this was a bit later when being macho, as they say these days, was the thing young lads did. The variation was for you to stand with bare feet spread a little apart, your mate would stand at right angles to you and place the tip of the knife on his raised elbow, then flick the knife to stick in the ground between your feet. The slightest flinch

In the bush

would result in humiliation and laughter. We must have been pretty good at it – never had to go to the hospital once. I guess the medical fraternity would have a fancy name for this.

We ate from British or American Army mess tins. The British ones were grey enameled steel and the American, pressed aluminum. Both had a steel handle that folded over. I still have the American one. We relied on water from the streams that we crossed with more frequency than we would have liked, but also carried one-pint water bottles. Again, the British were enameled steel wrapped in felt, and the American ones were aluminum - you will have seen them in the American war movies.

In the early days our 'boots' were Dunlop tennis shoes. Thankfully it became the thing for the boys around town to wear jungle boots as a sign of their manhood and as a result the BATA shop imported them for sale. This suited us perfectly as they were exactly what we needed for genuine jungle walking – not a manhood thing at all of course. Our backpacks came discreetly from the New Zealand Air Force and later, when this low-cost source dried up, we found we could buy them direct from Farmers store in Auckland and have them sent to us. They were heavy canvas but didn't last long in the wet clay jungle of the Suva area.

Joske's Thumb

There was one challenge that Grahame Southwick and I were determined to overcome, and that was to climb Joskie's Thumb on the far side of Suva harbour. This is a dramatic 1450-foot volcanic plug shaped, as the story goes, like the deformed thumb of one of Suva's leading, and very controversial, merchants of the late 1800s and early 1900s. The Fijians call it '*Rama*'.

Sir Edmund Hillary had tried twice, and failed, to climb the thumb when he was stationed in Fiji during the war. This is from his autobiography. 'We had come up the wrong side — underneath the ball of the thumb. Bitterly disappointed at being rebuffed I was much too conscious of the 400- foot (120-metre) drop below me to take any more risks... The thumb had beaten us again.'

Ironically the ball of the thumb is exactly where you do start the climb.

So naturally, at sixteen years of age, and believing we were indestructible, we decided to beat him and to climb to the top. And we did, twice, without any fancy climbing gear, not even ropes. On the second trip we slept on top in what was foul weather and returned home to find our panicked parents yelling at us about the tropical depression that had passed by during the night.

The climb began by walking in from Vesari on the South coast of the island through very boggy fields, then into the jungle at a gradual climb until we reached a deep volcanic rock overhang at the base of the mountain where we spent the night. This was a significant shel-

Joske's Thumb

ter and I feel sure that if anybody was to engage in an archaeological examination, they would surely find remains of early Fijian campers. Not something that bothered us I'm afraid.

Then the next day it was a very steep climb to the base of the volcanic plug itself, and then hand over hand from ledge, to knob of rock, to small bush, to clump of grass, to the next ledge and so on – with no rope or safety gear at all. Much of the volcanic rock was soft and crumbled when held or stood on, so great care was needed. Just below the actual summit was a small ledge with some scraggly bushes. Here we rested for a while before climbing the last 30 feet which was bare rock and almost vertical. The summit itself was completely bare rock approximately 12 feet in circumference and not very comfortable, but at that age who cared.

One did not look down during the climb; the sight was probably breath-taking but presumably also unnerving. At one point I decided to get rid of a stick I had been using for support and threw it out into the void – the same abyss that Edmund Hillary refers to. Rather pretty really. It spun, then slowed gracefully to horizontal, and then drifted away down out of sight. I wondered for a moment if I would do the same if I fell – but hey, onward and upward.

As I said in the 'What Fiji means to me' essay at the beginning of these notes, someone had been there before us because on the summit was a little Ponds face cream jar, and inside a scrap of paper and small

Sketches of Fiji

stub of pencil. There were three names written on the paper, but we couldn't decipher what they were. We added our names to the list.

In 1983, more than 20 years after Southwick and I had climbed the thumb, the Fiji Rucksack club escorted Sir Edmund Hillary to the top at long last. I hope that the Pond's jar was still there. Presumably it would be a bit strange for him to find a lady's face cream jar on the top of a volcanic plug in Fiji, especially if you thought you may be the first to reach the summit.

Grahame Southwick has written an extraordinary book of his life's experiences called *A hard day in the office*. In the book he also tells this story – probably a lot better than me.

Nukulau crabs

On another occasion Southwick, the Stork boys, and a whole bunch of our friends spent several days camping at Nukulau Island (more shortly) during the school holidays. We didn't have any money, so we subsisted on what we could catch or commandeer. As a result, Peter the caretaker, found he was short a few chickens from time to time. During the day we went fishing with spear guns and at night would take a hurricane lantern and Fijian handheld fishing spears on to the reef at half tide. This is a form of fishing the Fijians call *Cina* 'torchlight'. There were pools where the fish would lie dormant and therefore easy to spear; and the reef in those days was alive with crabs and prawns.

We carried sacks of these back with us each night. They were promptly dumped into a big pot of boiling water, cooked, and a feast was had by all. These were gloriously happy days but on this occasion I managed to eat a poisonous crab. The species is called a 'painted crab' because its shell looks somewhat like an artist's palette, but when cooked it turns red the same as every other crab. They are unique to the area around the Rewa delta and the islands offshore Suva and are often lethal. They're not common, but each year we would hear cases of at least one person dying from having eaten one of these crabs. But I was 16, fit and healthy. I remember collapsing around sunrise and vomiting continuously.

It was obvious to the boys that I was not well, and so they lit signal fires and flashed a mirror borrowed from Peter in the hope that the New Zealand Air Force base on the shore adjacent the island would

Sketches of Fiji

notice. In due course they did and sent a crash boat to see what was going on. They took me back to the flying boat base where I was checked by their medical team and promptly put into the base's hospital. They didn't want to wait to take me to the Colonial War Memorial hospital. I was there for three days and then released to home where it took several weeks before I regained strength.

As a result, I developed an allergy to crustaceans. In the early years, if I inadvertently ate a prawn, crab, or crayfish, in fact anything that crawled on the ocean bed, I would shortly thereafter begin to vomit violently, lose my sense of balance and fall to the floor. In later years however, whilst I'm still allergic to crustaceans, the reaction is nowhere near as intense. On occasion I have inadvertently eaten small amounts of crab and prawn, particularly when living in Asia, and, whilst I know I've done it, I can usually continue with the dinner. I guess it would be pretty stupid to try to eat a whole crab though.

The symptoms resemble being drunk and some years later we celebrated a mate's (Brian Jefferson) 21st. birthday with champagne (well, Great Western sparkling in shallow dish-like glasses) and later that night I was terribly ill. The next day I thought with great dread that I must be allergic to champagne until I was asked if I had eaten the curry. We'd had a long day in the Yacht Club bar that day, and things had been a little confused that night, even before the champagne drinking had started, but I seemed to remember doing so. It turned out to have been prawn curry. Ah, the relief that I was not allergic to champagne.

Royal Suva Yacht Club and Nukulau

As high school years came to an end I joined the Royal Suva Yacht Club and became involved in the life of the club that had been, and still was, central to the social world of my parents. The clubhouse sat on a small promontory near the gaol, enroute to the cemetery. It was a simple wooden building with a dance hall and attached bar, a veranda, and a small restaurant. There was a large boatshed to one side, launching ramp, and a small jetty. The fleet consisted of 'P class' sailing dinghies, Javelin racing yachts, a handful of larger yachts, and quite a few power boats ranging from 'runabouts' to large launches. My interest was primarily in the power boats and water skiing.

Weekends were often spent camping at the tiny island of Nukulau, you can walk around it in less than 30 minutes, and these eventually became officially organised events for the Club. Now when I say camping don't imagine tents. In fact, except for the time I was in the Air Scouts, I have never slept in a proper tent. At Nukulau we either slept on the boats, under a tree, or more often in what was called the 'goat shed'. This was simply a tin roof held up on posts with no walls and a dirt floor. It could indeed have been used as a goat shed at some time because there were lots of fleas, but that didn't bother us.

At the back of the island, facing the reef and the open sea, was what we called 'the doctor's house'. Nukulau had been a quarantine station for the indentured Indian labourers in the late 1800s and early 1900s, so presumably this was the doctor's house from that time. By now it was abandoned, derelict, and the ever-shifting sands had brought the water right to the foundations of the house. I believe it's gone now. Nevertheless, it gave us some shelter if we needed it in bad weather.

Sketches of Fiji

The eastern corner of the island remained overgrown and we were told this was where the bodies of those who did not survive were laid to rest. If so there were no headstones at all. I know this because we boys gleefully roamed through this area hoping to find human bones in order to scare the girls but had no success. Still, the very large '*dadakulaci*' sea snakes under the pier would always bring the girls to life.

Just across a narrow passage was another tiny island called Makaluva that was exclusively for the Government Colonial Service wallahs. It had sophisticated (for the time) guest houses and was out of bounds to us locals. We didn't mind; and I bet we had more fun than they did in their splendid privacy. Nevertheless, therein lay the divide. For all the good the Colonial service did, they were after-all the representatives of the 'Raj' in Fiji; and Makaluva was the classic example of that divide. For some locals, Makaluva, and the fine Colonial residences in the manicured Domain, were the visible manifestation of an attitude that the Colonial Service people felt they were in some way different and superior.

We grew up fully accepting that there were people who had more perks in life than we did. It didn't bother us, it was just the way things were. And just as we accepted there were people with more than us, we understood there were others with less than us. It was just the way things were. Time unfortunately has judged the Colonial Service, not by the good that they did, but in part by this cocoon they drew around themselves. They've gone now, and I hope that the future will

Royal Suva Yacht Club and Nukulau

be a little kinder to them for the legacy of decency, fair play, honour and good Governance that they instilled, rather than for their perks.

As I understand the history, Nukulau was the quarantine Island in the Indian indentured labour or 'Girmit' days, and Makaluva was where the Government wallahs lived. They would come across to Nukulau to carry out their duties and return to their comforts on Makaluva. The only Government officer on Nukulau was the doctor who lived at the back of the island. Anyway, storms and hurricanes moved the sand on Makaluva and the homes fell down. It was little more than a sandbar last time I saw it, with a large concrete water tank standing forlornly on what had become the beach. Somewhat poetically reminiscent of the Raj itself.

One of the strongest memories of Nukulau was the sound of the surf on the reef. Lying at night under the stars, in the derelict doctor's house, or under a skimpy shelter, it fills your head with its power. Nothing sounds quite like it, and after a while you begin to recognise that different reefs sound different, even allowing for the tide and weather conditions. It's almost as if they are tuned differently. The reef outside Nukulau has a distinct, sharp crack to it. Along the Sigatoka coast it is a slow, rolling, boom. The outer edge of the reef at Bau waters is more of a crackle. West of the Yasawas it curls on itself and becomes confused.

Later-on these Nukulau weekends became such a popular event for the Club that they built a clubhouse and many a roaring night was had by all.

Sketches of Fiji

What a sight it must have been with the yachts, motor launches, and ski boats anchored at the island's gorgeous white beach. And what a sight it must have been in the mornings to see the wonderfully hung-over Yacht Club members! We sang along together and drank most of the night, pausing for one or two hours of sleep, then eating and drinking throughout the day. Camaraderie, stories and relaxation the likes of which would be very difficult to replicate anywhere else today. Sailing or cruising back to the Club on a Sunday evening, sunburnt, happy, and slightly worse for the wear is a memory that remains extraordinarily clear in my mind.

In the early 2000s Nukulau was for a time a temporary prison for failed coup aspirant George Speight. From its days during Fijian tribal history, as the home of the American Consul who played a controversial part in Fiji being ceded to Queen Victoria, to being the indentured labourers quarantine station, to wartime lookout, to our days, and then to Speight's time; what stories the spirits of that Island could tell. On our bedroom wall we have a very old black and white photo entitled 'Nukulau Palms'. The scene is taken from the centre of the island looking West. There are old design yachts moored near the beach and a family sitting on a mat under the coconut trees. That is Nukulau for me. More recently there was a photo circulating of a bandaged George Speight sitting on a chair at the centre of the island looking to the West. The photo is almost exactly from the same spot.

Suva in the late '60's

During my final year at school I became convinced that I wanted to join the Australian navy. I wrote away for the papers which duly arrived, and I filled them out. The next step was that I had to discuss this with my parents as I was legally still too young to make this commitment by myself. All hell broke loose! Dad's view on it was that sailors ultimately led an unhappy life and achieved very little for the sacrifice. Mum's view related more to boozing, brothels and brawls; and a generally disreputable life. What to do? Dad spoke of his conundrum to a friend at the Yacht Club called Ken Boehm. Ken was the chief engineer for Fiji Airways at the time. The upshot was that Ken invited me to spend the August school holidays of 1963 helping out at Nausori Airport, just to see if I might like it. I did, and of course a whole new world opened up for me. I'll come back to that shortly.

By the time I started work, bush walking had given way to the Royal Suva Yacht Club and water-skiing.

Lichfield had joined his two older brothers in the Australian Army. Grahame Southwick had worked in the insurance business for a while, and then went to Australia, eventually to go abalone diving near Adelaide. I had a new set of friends, most of whom were 'bank boys'. Each of the major Australasian Banks had branches in Fiji which they staffed at both senior and mid-level with expatriates, the locals did the drudge work. It would be very good if someone wrote a book one day about these remarkable young men and the work they did in both the urban and rural communities. And about the 'bank girls', for there were several of them as well - thank goodness! The

Sketches of Fiji

Bank of New South Wales provided a house for the girls in Waimanu Road between the CWM Hospital and Saint Joseph's school which was known far and wide as the 'Virgin's Perch' – I'll not comment on the adjective!

Alex Hancock, or 'sexy' as he was known, was the closest of my friends at this time and eventually became best man at my wedding. He was a slight fellow with glasses and bright red hair who drank a lot; but then so did we all. He was one of the BNZ bank boys. His father was a senior executive at Morris Hedstrom Ltd. and as a result always had the latest in cars. 'Sexy' got to borrow the cars and that helped his popularity enormously. One of these was a white Falcon Futura soft top, the only one in Fiji. Very visible, which at times was good, and at other times not so good. Then there was 'Speedy' from the Bank of New South Wales and a whole raft of others. All, I admit, hard-drinking, hard-playing, but also hard-working fellows.

Some of the other friends were the local offspring of the long-term expatriate community; Brian Jefferson (his father worked in Government), Carl Bay whose father was the head of the education department, and many others. Aside from the bank girls who were withdrawn by the late '60s, the girls were mostly daughters of local European families. There were also several part-European girls; one of whom, Sandra A'Costa we will speak of shortly.

It was a large circle of friends and acquaintances and the social life was hectic to say the least; most of this centred on the Royal Suva Yacht Club. The head barman was a wonderful Fijian man called Kali and there are many hundreds, nay thousands, of Yacht Club members who will remem-

Suva in the late '60's

ber him with great affection. I'm afraid that on more than one morning I woke still sitting in a chair near the bar, knowing that Kali had positioned me carefully the night before so that I did not end up on the floor.

Oh, and yes, we did even sometimes go boating. In my case this was mostly 'Nukulau weekends', water skiing at Mosquito island and spearfishing. The head 'boat- boy' (terrible term these days I know) was another Fijian man called Kini. He has a place in the hearts of many RSYC boys and girls for the way he so politely and quietly helped their early boating days; and seemed to always be there while they waited for their parents to finish at the bar. It was a wonderful life at that time, and I remember it with many fond memories.

One thing the Club was famous for was its rum. It was called simply and logically 'Yacht Club rum' and it was a powerful brew. The whole process of importing, checking and bottling the rum was overseen by a small group of Yacht Club elders led by Rob Wright. It arrived in enormous hogshead wooden barrels from Bundaberg in Queensland. After arrival it would be allowed to sit for a few days in the Yacht Club boat shed to get over the trip, being watched carefully by the Elders and the staff. Then on the appointed day, usually a Saturday morning, the Elders would gather, surrounded by the Yacht Club kids and several of the future patrons of the stuff. The bung would be carefully removed, and a sample drawn using a chemistry pipette. This would be placed into a long thin beaker and a special hydrometer would be lowered gently into the rum. Then the Elders would go into conclave around the sample and mutter weird words amongst themselves.

Sketches of Fiji

Finally, when they were satisfied, the bottling would commence. There were boxes and boxes and boxes of empty dark brown beer bottles. Occasionally, when there were not enough of these, clear glass was used, but this was not preferred. The bottling was done one of two ways; either a small tap was screwed into the bunghole in the head and the rum drained through a funnel into the bottles, or else a rubber surgical tube was used to siphon the rum from the barrel. It was remarkable how many preferred this latter process and would volunteer to do the sucking to start the syphon going. The bottles were then sealed either with a crown cap or, when they were available, corks. The final step was to glue the Yacht Club label onto the bottle and escort the cases to the storage area at the rear of the bar. Ah, no, that wasn't the final step. The final step was to sacrifice a bottle or two in the interests of ensuring quality.

There were also parties at people's homes, mainly the Hawthorns' which was *the* party place, Maybins', Sellers', Hancocks', and the Boultons'. Mrs Bolton made the best chicken curry you ever tasted; it was also the best morning-after remedy in the world. They had the first commercial 'chook' farm in Fiji. Don and Nancy Aidney had a continuous open house, but usually the parents were there so we didn't spend long – it was good to know where the 'olds' were though.

These parents were our parents; we looked on them as part of our extended Yacht Club family and knew we could turn to any one of them if we needed help. And we knew the advice would range from

Suva in the late '60's

worldly wisdom and understanding to a clip behind the ear together with a comment like 'don't give me that bullshit'.

Under the Hawthorne's place was a huge black 1930s Armstrong Siddeley car with a pre-select gearbox. Old man Hawthorne wouldn't say where he got it from. He had boxes and boxes of spares and I wanted very much to restore it, but he wasn't interested. Sometimes, late and long into the party I would wander down there to look at the beast; perhaps a bit misty eyed.

Don't know what made me think of this, but I didn't get my first pair of Levis till I was around 18 and working. They were white, and I wore them constantly – at least getting them cleaned wasn't a problem. I wore them so often they became my signature 'look'.

And then there were visits to the only nightclub in town, the Golden Dragon; and other activities outside of the Yacht Club that we will draw a veil of discretion over.

One of the more interesting things we did in those days was to drive to Koro Levu beach hotel, Fiji's first tourism resort, to seek out conversations with female tourists. This was a three to four-hour drive over very dusty gravel roads. Sometimes we would do this midweek, returning in the early hours of the morning and going straight to work. There were several logistical problems in this which I will leave to your imagination, but one of these was finding a shower at each end of the journey to clean up and wash off the thick dust before moving

Sketches of Fiji

on the to the task ahead. I'm going to come back to Fiji Airways and the fact that I had to actually go to work as well in a moment.

When we weren't doing all of this we listened to the wireless and occasionally LPs. This was the era of rock'n'roll and all the famous names of the Beatles, Presley and Co were in their heyday. On Sunday afternoon we listened to 'Casey's Top 100' from the US, or an hour of what we nicknamed 'sad songs'. These were Connie Francis, Pat Boone and others; cowboy wailings of lost love, people being hanged for killing their lovers and so on ad nauseum. The program was called 'listener's favourites' and people would write in to request the songs, dedicating them to family and friends; so presumably that's what appealed. The other program was a local announcer Hugh Leonard who hosted a Fiji version of 'top of the pops' every Thursday evening. He always closed his program with the words 'well that wraps it up, and ties it with a ribbon for yet another week'.

Cars

I had a fascination with things mechanical and was never happier than when I was tinkering with spanners and screwdrivers, oil and muck. When I turned sixteen I took the examination and was given a driving licence.

My parents went through the usual terrifying few months prior to that; and I can tell you that learning to drive in a flat front, column shift, manual gearbox Ford Thames laundry van made life interesting. By then Dad also had a Volkswagen 1600 car. It was the large fastback version of the classic Volkswagen of those days. I got to drive it a bit, but clearly needed wheels of my own, so I found a second-hand motor bike that was within my very nominal price range. When Mum and Dad got to hear of this enterprise there were some rather stern discussions, references to my father's missing lower limb (the result of his youthful engagement between a tram and car when riding his Norton motorbike in Melbourne) and much 'what to do'. The upshot was that Mum and Dad agreed to match the amount of money I had for the motorbike on the understanding that I would buy a car. Oh joy, oh bliss, sixteen years of age and able to have a car.

One of Dad's friends, Mr. Pickering, not the one of United Engineers, they are a big family in Fiji, had a Rover 90. This was a straight six-cylinder English car with twin SU carburetors. It needed a lot of work and that's exactly what I enjoyed doing. Dad negotiated a good deal with Miller's car paint shop, and we split the cost of a repaint; dark bottle green it was – very elegant.

If any of you reading these notes know how delicate and sensitive twin SU carburetors can be, you will understand the hours I spent tuning

Sketches of Fiji

that engine and getting the two carburetors in balance. Presumably I became reasonably good at doing this because after a while other people would sometimes bring their cars to me for tuning. Dad's measure of a well-tuned car engine was to sit a full glass of water on the top of the rocker cover and if the engine idled without spilling a drop it was okay. To this day that remains my measure.

As part of this I quickly learned how to set the distributor points gap using feeler gauges. Those of you who know how to do this will understand when I say the gauge slides like silk between the points when the setting is exactly right. If it catches, they are too close, and if you don't get that silken feel, they are too wide.

I stripped and reassembled that car and its engine more times than I can possibly imagine now. In doing so I learned a huge amount, at my own expense, about using the right grease in bearings and joints, and in sticking to the maintenance manual when making adjustments. Also, that there are two types of brake fluid, vegetable and petroleum-based. If you use the wrong one you will have no brakes. This is exciting and expensive to learn! Anyway, this work gave me many hours of pleasure and a good grounding for my future in aviation engineering and the need to do things right.

At the end of my first year with Fiji Airways (more shortly) I flew to Australia for a holiday on the very first of what would become thousands of flights and stayed with my cousin John Code and his parents in Moonee Ponds. It was a wonderful time. We had a car, I have no idea where from,

Cars

and drove to Barmah, then all over Victoria. We slept in the car and drank rough Victorian wine (and it *was* rough in those days) out of a four-gallon tin drum that we filled from time to time at the then nascent vineyards. It was on this trip that I tasted Coca Cola for the first time – strange the things you remember!

I had left my car parked at Nausori Airport and returned a month later to find there had been one of the numerous floods that occurred in that delta area. There was, literally, a rice paddy growing inside the car. I cleaned it up, got it operational again, ran it for another few months, and then sold it.

In late 1965 I bought a Wolseley six/eighty. This was, and is, my all-time favourite car. She was nicknamed 'Matilda' from the Harry Belafonte song of the same name which has the line 'She takes me money and run' (to Venezuela). The body lines were a bit different to my father's Wolseley of the Barmah years, and the built-in hydraulic jacks had gone, but boy, what a car! Again, the engine was a straight six-cylinder with twin SU carburetors, but with an overhead cam. To adjust the valve clearance, you screwed a cap down into the valve stem; an ingenious design. Being typically British engineering, to do this meant you had to have special tools, and of course only the agents had these tools. Not to worry, I made the tools in the Fiji Airways workshop at Nausori Airport.

The distributor sat vertically above the front of the overhead camshaft cover and was particularly sensitive to adjustment – but by then I was

Sketches of Fiji

the expert in these things. The parts were expensive when purchased from Millers who were the agents, but I found I could buy them reasonably cheaply and import them myself from Dominion motors in Auckland. When I did eventually sell the car it was to a fellow engineer who gave me a cheque for £30.00. The cheque bounced!

Paying for petrol was a bit of a problem, so after a while I began to use 100 octane aviation petrol from the fuel drains that we took from the tanks on the aircraft. This is standard aircraft practice, done to ensure that there is no condensate water lying in the bottom of the tanks. The fuel was normally discarded as it could not be returned to an aircraft once it had been drained, so it ended up in my car. Now ordinary car fuel is dyed red and 100 octane is dyed green, so the carburetors and fuel system on the Wolseley assumed a mix somewhere between red and green that looked rather unusual. The other problem was that the engine was designed for eighty octane fuel. I could overcome the spark timing problem by resetting the distributor, so the engine ran beautifully, but it also ran much hotter than designed. The upshot of this was that the exhaust valves continued to burn out, and so did the exhaust system; an expensive problem. In fact, if I costed this properly it would probably have been better for me to stick with the regular petrol.

There were a few incidents with these cars. My first accident was during one of our 'tourist conversation' trips to Korolevu beach hotel when, on the return leg, the car 'left the road', as the officers of the law would say. No problem, this was a British car; men from the nearby Malevu village simply helped me lift it out of the ditch and we were on our way.

Cars

Another was when we were attending a fire at the Lami dump and my car skidded sideways in the muck and into the Chief Fire Officer's Volkswagen. This was a real ooops! The British car was virtually unmarked; the VW was more than a little creased. Harry le Vesconte was very good about it but was heard muttering about insurance premiums.

Once, coming home in the early hours of the morning after working more than 30 hours at the airport, I sideswiped an oncoming car. My fault, and I paid for it.

The car of Suva belonged to a rich old man called Mr. Snell who lived in a wonderful old wooden home opposite the Home of Compassion in Tamavua. It was a Humber Super Snipe, black of course. It would cruise silently by with its automatic gearbox a mystery to me; something that I really wanted to see up close. The old man drove with that slightly nose-in-the-air look that one associates with the word snob, but perhaps he was just peering through his glasses. I never met him.

As an aside, much later on after several other owners, Mr. Snell's house was purchased by friends of ours, Leslie and Bruce Philip who turned it into a B&B. We stayed there several times. The views across the valley are spectacular and took me back to my young days living in Tamavua just a little way down the road. The only other car of note was the Governor's Bentley, but you only ever saw that on official occasions. I believe it's still parked in the garage of Government House.

Spearfishing

Throughout my teenage years and well into married life, spear fishing was a passion that I alternated with cars, work and social life. It started in the tin boat days when the spear gun was what the Fijians called a *gilivati* (Gilbert Islands) presumably because that's where the idea came from. It consisted of approximately eighteen inches of bicycle tube with the ends connected by a small piece of galvanised binding wire. The spear was a length of number eight fencing wire, flattened at one end, which was then notched with the file to take the binding wire; and the other end sharpened to a point. The centre of the rubber strip went around the thumb of one hand and the flat end of the spear went into the binding wire drawn back by the other hand. To see underwater we used simple swimming goggles. Given that we had never seen diving masks these were considered excellent, although at depth they would either leak, or hurt like hell around the eye socket.

One day I read Jacques Cousteau's book *The Silent World* and was instantly captivated. Breathing gear was way, way beyond my means and I don't think any existed in Fiji at that time, except for the brass helmet diving suits the Public Works Department had. I was particularly interested in his diving mask though and managed to make one of my own from a piece of oval glass bought from the Suva Glass and Mirror company just near our factory, a piece of thick truck tube and some sandal buckles. The glass was sealed in place with black Bostik. It worked – sort of. There were no fins, although I did try to make some using fencing wire and canvas, not successfully I'm afraid. I spent hours diving with this primitive gear from my tin boat un-

Spearfishing

der the newly built PWD wharf, on the reefs around the inner lighthouse, and the passages near Mosquito Island.

In the last year of high school Burns Philp imported a shipment of Australian-made 'Undersea' spear guns, and Cressi diving masks and fins. I spent a long time just ogling that gear, but it was way beyond my schoolboy finances. As soon as I started work, this was one of my very first purchases. The guns of those days were aluminum tubes, a head which held the surgical rubbers, and a pistol grip that contained the trigger mechanism. The spears were 1/4 inch steel rod and had a removable barbed head – wonderful technology.

During high school years I had no boat and would swim across the narrow 'double bunger' passage at Nassese to that reef; or hire a punt from Suvavou village to fish on the main Suva reef. Money to pay for the punt came from selling the fish so there was a considerable incentive to success. The punt owner would pole across the shallow reef, then row across the passage. If money was tight, and it usually was, I'd have them drop me (or us, because sometimes the others would join me) at the reef as the tide began to fall so we could rest on the reef. They would then come back to pick us up later. I heard stories of the pickup not happening which would have made for a long swim, but never experienced this myself. When we did not have a boat waiting, we would tie the fish to a piece of bamboo which we anchored to a rock or towed behind us. Sometimes the local white tipped reef sharks would help themselves, but the reefs were so prolific in those days that it didn't bother us a great deal.

Sketches of Fiji

Gradually the spear guns got bigger and made of wood. We moved further afield to Namuka Island near the passage to Bega, and the area around Naselai and Tomberua passages using hired punts. There were sharks, and at times they became inquisitive, but we got to understand their movements and when they were obviously jittery, we simply got out of the water and went somewhere else. We also learnt to stop towing the fish with us, particularly around Naselai where sharks were more frequent than we would have liked. Instead, the practice was to leave one person in the boat with the motor running and the moment you speared a fish you returned to the surface, held it out of the water until the boat arrived, and the driver took the fish from the spear.

We quickly grew out of the shop-bought guns and made our own, albeit using the purchased trigger mechanism and the spear heads. I made all my own spears, and these became bigger and bigger, as did the guns, until we got to a 3/8 inch stainless rod about five to six foot long. We also added a reel for the cord so that we could head to the surface for a breath whilst still fighting a large fish. Some of these were very large indeed, especially the cod. Trevally '*Saqa*' fought strongly, sometimes tearing themselves off the spear, and we learnt to shoot accurately to avoid losing them. I still have three of the guns that I made, but its many years since they smelt salt-water.

We speared many very large fish in those early days but gradually they got smaller and smaller. From several sacks gathered in a morning we

Spearfishing

went to one sack in a day. This was in part because we became a lot more selective in the fish we speared. In the early days it was anything edible, but later we preferred good-eating, and good-sized, fish such as donu, cod and saqa. We didn't ever shoot for the sake of it. We shot fish for food or money to cover our costs. Any surplus we sold to the Lami Chinese store or the Indian store at Nasesse and used the money to help pay for our trips. At best this would cover the cost of fuel, but at least that was something to cash-strapped young lads.

There was quite a large group of us that went spear fishing, sometimes particular groups would form then move on depending usually on the availability of boats. Grahame Southwick was an expert shot, Tiko Eastgate was an extraordinarily powerful underwater swimmer and a very good overall spear fisherman. I found I could hold my breath longer than many and this helped improve my catch totals.

I hear people decry spear fishing as an unfair sport, and there may well be people who simply bang away at anything that moves, but we never did that. In fact, I would argue that our method of selecting specific fish was far better than netting, or the use of poisons and dynamite that was prevalent in Fiji at the time.

Incidentally if you cut yourself on coral it can very easily become infected and very painful. There's an easy fix – simply dab raw 'Condy's crystals' on the wet cut. Works like magic even if it hurts like hell and covers the boat in pink stains.

Sketches of Fiji

As most people know, sharks are majestic. I recall on one occasion drifting over the edge of the reef in Mokogai passage and looking down to a sandy bottom where easily more than 20 sharks lay sleeping with their gills open in the current. I watched them for almost ten minutes before getting back into the boat and going elsewhere to fish. This is also the place I saw my first Tiger shark. He was anxious (not alone in that), twitching and stiff in the body – time to go Drysdale.

I only ever shot one shark and that was on a day when we had caught almost nothing and were very short on cash. He was cruising along the sandy bottom at Tomberua passage in about 20 feet. I unscrewed the barbed head from the spear in case things went wrong, dived to approach from behind, and hit him square on the top of the head slightly behind the eyes. He shivered momentarily and sank to the bottom - thank goodness. We sold him to the Chinese shop and got reasonably good money.

It wasn't all about spearing fish. There were many times when I would simply pause and look at the drama and beauty of the reefs. Sometimes, on a calm day, I would simply lie on the surface on the outside of the reef edge and watch what was going on below in the extraordinarily clear Fiji water. On the other hand, being down 30 feet or so, holding your breath, and looking up to see a school of hundreds of large pelagic barracuda circling above is, to say the least, an adrenalin pumping experience. On one occasion a pod of dolphins joined us and, holding our breath for as long as possible, we watched the ballet of these beautiful mammals.

Suva fire brigade

I guess I still had a hankering for some sort of disciplined forces experience so in 1965 I joined the Suva Fire Brigade as an auxiliary fireman. This was a part-time group set up to support the permanent firemen. I would come home from work at Nausori (more shortly), change into my 'dress' uniform, and report for duty at the station.

The Chief Fire Officer was Harry Le Vesconte who had served in the Manchester fire brigade in England throughout World War II, including the terrible German blitz. Harry ran a 'spit and polish' brigade; everything in its place, everything sparkling and polished, and the firemen trained to the highest degree of discipline.

I spent one or two evenings per week on watch-room duty to allow the permanent staff time for a break and a meal. Then there was the seven a.m. Sunday morning drill! Sometimes coming straight from the Yacht Club, this was not a nice experience. Harry was also a member of the Club and knew full well if I had been there late. The drill would start with a parade where Harry checked our uniforms, then we conducted an exercise in teams to see how quickly we could locate the equipment on the appliances, as the fire engines were called, and then moved on to fire drill. For this, wooden targets were set up in the distance and, working in teams of four, we would run out the hoses and connect the branch (as the nozzle was called). Man #1 and #2 would hold the branch in a fireman's grip. Man #3 ran back to the hydrant man #4 and ordered "water on". The first team to knock the target down won the drill. Then when it was all over we had to clean

Sketches of Fiji

up the mess, hang up the hoses to dry, wipe down, and sometimes polish, the brass-work before a final parade and sign off.

When we were on duty in the watch-room there was really nothing to do except answer the phone if it rang. The duty was four hours starting at 6.00 p.m. and I used this time to study for my aircraft engineering licences. Given the hectic social life there was no other time available. It must have worked because I did quite well in my licence exams.

The brigade was divided into the permanent staff, who in turn had two crews called 'watches', and we part-time auxiliary firemen – about 14 of us. The permanents were paid a full-time salary and we part timers were paid by the hour. We received payment for the regular watch-room duties and then extra call-out pay when we attended a fire. On average I would be paid about £12.00 per month. This was quite good money considering that my first-year apprenticeship salary was £26.00 per month.

Our home telephone lines were connected to the brigade watch-room. When a fire call came in, the watch-room officer would telephone a special number and simply keep repeating the address of the fire over the phone for about five minutes. Our phones at home would ring with a particular triple pitch ring, quite different from the normal telephone call. We would take the call, then leap into our fireman's outfit and drive directly to the address. We were trained in what to do if we got there first, but generally the fire

Suva fire brigade

appliances arrived before us because the watch-room would turn out the appliances and the permanent staff before calling the auxiliaries.

We had a khaki dress uniform with a navy peaked cap and epaulettes to show our rank. The actual fire-fighting uniform consisted of a black pith helmet (no more brass helmets since the advent of electricity in homes), heavy felt wool coat and trousers and rubber boots. We also wore a wide leather belt which carried a fireman's axe in a holster. This was double headed: blade on one side, spike the other. Looking back on this now, it seems strange that we did not have gloves.

Both uniforms had brass buttons and, yes, they were always kept shining bright, as were the fire axe, boots and brass belt buckle – or Harry would have you on the mat. A few years ago, we were in the small New South Wales town of Temora and I visited the local fire brigade museum. There in a glass case was the exact uniform we used to wear!

Most of the fires that we attended were grass fires, or fires caused when curtains blew on to kerosene lamps or candles. None of these were particularly dramatic but during the Indian festival of Diwali it was non-stop call-outs because of the oil lamps used to celebrate this Hindu festival of light. There were some serious fires and some loss of life, although I was fortunate enough to not be present at those call-outs.

There were two particularly dirty jobs. One was when the rubbish dump at Lami would ignite through spontaneous combustion (it hap-

Sketches of Fiji

pened several times) and it would cover Suva or Lami with a pall of thick, black smoke. Putting it out would take days of stinking, dirty work in the company of rats and mongrel dogs. I had to bath in Dettol after each shift to feel even reasonably clean.

The biggest and immediate danger was falling through the crust into a hollowed-out fire zone below. We kept a close watch on each other in case that was to happen, but we knew the chances of surviving such an event would be a bit slim. On one occasion the fire started to get away from us, so Harry called in the Army explosives experts to blow a hole in the crust to allow us access to the burning core. Given the captive methane underground we expected pyrotechnics, but all that happened was a 'crump' and a small display of crud. They were good those Army boys. We got to the fire and put it out quickly.

The other was once when WR Carpenter's copra shed in Walu bay caught fire, again spontaneous combustion within the copra. Putting this out meant physically carrying literally tons of greasy, stinking, copra out of the building in sacks before we could get to the burning copra buried deep within the pile. It was hot, dirty, hard work in choking smoke over several days; and with no breathing apparatus, not even a face mask. The smell of burning copra will remain with me forever. I dislike cooking that has coconut in it!

There is a story that combines my cars and the fire brigade. Suva had only four motorcycle policemen, one of whom was a long skinny fellow

Suva fire brigade

whom we nicknamed 'Belo' (as in reef heron). He was the scourge of us young lads. He would wait for us outside the Yacht Club and would regularly follow us in the hope of catching us speeding or doing something wrong. Maybe we were paranoid, but we really felt that this guy had it in for us. There were no drink/driving laws in those days.

One night I was called to a fire at Suva Point near the cemetery. The area was a squatter settlement and the homes were what were called 'wood and iron dwellings'. One of them had burnt completely to the ground by the time we got there, but fortunately no one was injured. Now, when a fire is still burning the fire brigade is in charge; once the fire is extinguished control then passes to the police - at least that's the way it was in Fiji. Belo was there and was making a complete nuisance of himself while we tried to extinguish the fire. This got on everybody's nerves, but eventually the fire was extinguished, and we handed control to him. He immediately began stomping around the fire scene, not what he was supposed to do, and then disappeared from sight, literally. He had fallen into the pit latrine! Having determined he wasn't drowning, we began laughing.

Picture the scene: late at night, destroyed home, anguished homeowners, fire brigade officers bent over double laughing their heads off, and a policeman up to his waist in you-know-what, yelling very loudly. We happily lent a rope to his fellow policeman and suggested that they might like to get him out of the hole as it was now a police command. They did so, and he disappeared down the hill and into the sea at Suva Point. Much hilarity followed him!

Sketches of Fiji

I served for five years in the brigade and was honoured at the end of that time to be presented with a meritorious service medal. By this time Harry Le Vesconte had retired and had been replaced by a New Zealander. On one occasion both Harry and the new Chief, Brian Henderson, known as 'Mc Wirter the squirter' to his bowling club friends, approached me to see if I would sign on as a permanent on the understanding that I would receive training overseas, with the intention of becoming the Chief Officer in due course. I was thoroughly enjoying my work at Nausori Airport as an apprentice aircraft engineer and, with some regret, said no.

In later years I realised I had no photos of this time and went to the new station in Walu bay, which had been opened during Harry's/my time, but they had them put away and the man in charge was out. They suggested I check with the local Mc Donald's restaurant as this was in the converted old fire station where I had served for most of my time. I did, and sure enough there on a wall at the back was a photo of the entire brigade lined up, including one very fine young fellow. Thankfully on a subsequent trip I found the man with the photos and was able to get some copies. As it happened their PR guy was there at the time, so I did an interview and they got some publicity on the TV and in the Press.

It's time now to go back to 1964 and to my life as an Aircraft engineer.

Sketches of Fiji

RIGHT:
Tom and Andrew, 1948

BELOW:
Self at 7 years,

BELOW RIGHT:
Nell – indominable lady

Sketches of Fiji

ABOVE:
Cousin Code and self 1958

ABOVE RIGHT:
The Wolseley

RIGHT:
Indian sweet seller. His grandson, Bernard Chandra, was a classmate

Sketches of Fiji

ABOVE LEFT:
Self and Litch MV
Maroro off Bega Island,

ABOVE RIGHT:
Patrol leader
Nukulau Island,

LEFT:
Still pontificating at 70

Sketches of Fiji

RIGHT:
Nukulau Island
palms circa 1930

Sketches of Fiji

LEFT:
Exit one crayfish,

BELOW:
Mosquito Island

Sketches of Fiji

Sketches of Fiji

Fiji Airways
1964 - 1978

The Apprenticeship

To set the scene: in 1957 Qantas bought a pioneering little Fiji Airline from the estate of famous aviator Harold Gatty; and in November of 1958 changed the company name to 'Fiji Airways Ltd.'. In 1964 the Qantas shareholding was reduced to one third when BOAC (British Airways) and TEAL (Air New Zealand) also bought shares by subscribing $120,000 each. Qantas provided management on secondment from Sydney. In 1965 the Fiji Government bought into the company in equal shareholding to the other three.

When this story starts in 1963, the General Manager was Captain Ritchie and the Chief Engineer was Ken Boehm.

Boehm invited me to spend the August school holidays of my last year in high school (1963) working at Nausori Airport to see if I might like aircraft engineering. This was a ploy by my parents to get me to change my mind about joining the Navy - and it worked! Those two weeks determined the future path of my working life. All thoughts of the Navy disappeared, and I agreed to start work at the end of the year as Fiji Airway's first apprentice.

I was completely fascinated with the sights, smells and sounds of the aircraft and their engines. They were real aeroplanes, just fabric and plywood in some cases. This was still a time when the engineers repaired aircraft by taking them to pieces, checking, reassembling, and adjusting everything from zero. When I first saw Gypsy Queen 30 and Gipsy Major 10 engines stripped completely to their component

Sketches of Fiji

parts, reassembled, and tested in a homemade engine test bed I knew I was hooked. The smell of hundred octane fuel, cellulose nitrate dope in the fabric shop, that special smell of hot engine oil, and of duralumin when you're working it by hand, really got me. But more than that was the quiet humour and professionalism of the engineers, both expatriate and local, who had these wonderful machines in their care.

Although I was officially the first apprentice there were three others already employed as trainees and we were all signed up at the same time. The others were 'Og' Ogilvy, Michael Egan, and a part European man named Robert Southey who had been at school with me for most of the high school years. After a few months Reggie Palmer (a son of Clem's) joined, and a little later, Sisa Rasaku, Inoke Sukulu, Albert Murray, Umendra Chaudhary, Atu Waga, and Maka Noti Afu from Tonga.

The apprenticeship contracts were formal documents printed on large, light blue, sheets of heavy paper. They were full of legal terminology that I had no hope of understanding and tied with government tape. Yes, the term 'red tape' is real. They required a three-way signature: Fiji Airways, myself (and my parents as I was still under age) and the Fiji Apprenticeship Council. The contract was for five years which seemed an unbelievably long time, but in hindsight went very quickly. We signed on 2 January 1964.

Reggie Palmer and I met each other again many years later when we were both living in Singapore and he showed me his copy of

The Apprenticeship

that original contract. Mine was misplaced many years ago, although I do still have my apprenticeship book and certificate. I'm very proud of these and have the certificate on the wall in front of me now. The interesting thing in the contract was the pay rate; two shillings and sixpence per hour.

I was first assigned to engine overhaul work – exactly what I had been hoping for. The engine overhaul shed was in fact a World War II Nissen hut that had been converted for the purpose. The foreman was Charles Ogilvy, a large man whom I discovered later at the Christmas party had a very fine, trained baritone voice. What bought him to a little engine overhaul shed in Fiji I don't know, and I would never have imagined asking - he was the foreman! I remember Charlie's words as he handed me a pair of second-hand grey overalls (supervisors wore white overalls) 'if you put these on, you'll never really take them off. This business gets into your blood' – how prophetic.

At the time the company had just retired the wood and fabric de Havilland Rapides and was now operating two de Havilland Drovers (a three-engine Australian-built aircraft), three of the four-engine Mk.1 de Havilland Heron aircraft and one Mk 2 with retractable undercarriage. Three more Mk 2s were to arrive during 1965. The advent of the Heron in 1959 meant that for the first time Fiji Airways could fly regionally to Tonga, Samoa and then to the New Hebrides (now Vanuatu), the Solomon Islands and the Gilbert and Ellis (now Kiribati and Tuvalu) Islands.

Sketches of Fiji

My first job was to strip the Gipsy Major 10 and Gipsy Queen 30 engines down to their component parts, clean these parts in a bath of kerosene (bare hands, no protective gloves in those days), and present them to the licensed overhaul engineers for inspection. I would then watch fascinated while these highly skilled men would measure the parts with internal and external micrometers down to 1000th. of an inch. Some components were treated with a special dye-penetrant to test for cracks under ultraviolet light; amazing stuff to this young lad.

The parts then went through a doorway into the assembly area. Each of the stripping/cleaning, the inspection, and the assembly areas were kept completely separate. Despite it being an old wartime corrugated iron shed the assembly and inspection areas were surgically clean.

The aircraft themselves were maintained in a nearby hangar attached to the original passenger terminal. A new hangar was built in 1966, and a new terminal shortly after.

We were to receive our theory training at what was then the R. A. Derrick technical school that had recently been built in Samabula. Problem was they had no aviation instructors, so we enrolled in the automotive course taught by Humphrey Chang. I wasn't altogether unhappy at this as it certainly helped keep the Rover, and then the Wolseley, on the road. But clearly, other than for the basics, it wasn't going to get us licensed as engineers in the aviation industry.

The Apprenticeship

Then the British government sent an instructor from the UK to teach us. It seems the Colonial Service had one of its well-known glitches because the well-meaning young man who arrived came from the English engineering file manufacturer 'Wilshire files' and knew absolutely nothing about aviation. But we did learn an awful lot about handling tools, including filing a complex shape from a block of cast iron; all by hand, accurately true, and square on all sides.

After a year of this, and with some heavy protests by Fiji Airways, a second British instructor arrived. What a difference! Forester Lindsay had been part of the design team for the famous Spitfire aircraft and had been responsible for the fuel system and later modifications to the flying control surfaces. Now we really did begin to learn theory of flight, aircraft engines and the standards, and regulatory regime of aircraft engineering.

Forester was a bad asthmatic but even on the days when he was particularly unwell he would still come to class and gasp his way through the lesson. We admired him greatly, but being boys quickly found that his real love in life was sailing. When we got bored one of us would ask a question about sailing, and off we went on that subject. But, as my dear wife has pointed out, Forrester was not that silly – his explanation of fluid dynamics around a yacht hull and airflow over a yacht's sail just happened to be the same principles as those used in aircraft design! I learned a huge amount from that man and will forever be grateful to him for that sound and pragmatic founding in aircraft engineering that he gave us.

Sketches of Fiji

As study materials we used a book called *The Theory of Flight,* another on aircraft engines, but most importantly, volume 1 and volume 2 of the British Civil Air Registration Board (ARB, precursor to the UK CAA) Regulations. Each book was a large burgundy coloured lever arch file about four inches thick. In these two volumes was contained the entire subject matter needed to pass the ARB exams to become a Licensed Aircraft Maintenance Engineer (LAME). Once you had this basic licence it was then necessary to be examined on each of the aircraft and engine types and to be issued a specific licence on them before you could certify. I kept my copies of the BCAR regs until we left Fiji to move to Australia in late 1998. I regret having thrown them out, but I guess it's too late now.

Looking back at that time, we were pushed very hard by our engineering manager, Grahame Marriot, who replaced Ken Boehm at the end of the first year of our apprenticeship. I believe this was because he had a vision and determination to build a team of local licensed engineers as his legacy to his time in Fiji; and because he saw it as the right thing to do. He argued, and gained approval for, five to six apprentices to be contracted each year so that by the end of my term there were almost 30 apprentices – that's more than the company had in licensed engineers. That the regulator went along with that unusual ratio is probably an indication that they also shared his vision.

Grahame Marriott was something special. He took an enormous interest in the apprentices and it was largely through his efforts that we finally got Forester Lindsay as a lecturer. He was adamant that before

The Apprenticeship

he finished his term the Fiji citizens under his control would have advanced significantly in qualifications, experience, and responsibility. There were several people in Fiji who felt like this, but they were outweighed by the cynics who said it could never be done. There was only one local licensed engineer at the time, Ken Christofferson, who had trained under a previous Chief Engineer, Len Dobbin.

Grahame also insisted that the company include another experienced, but unqualified, Fijian engineer Nimilote Verebasaga in our training programs. Basaga became the first indigenous Fijian to be granted an aircraft maintenance engineers licence, and every one of that first cohort of apprentices ultimately became licensed.

He was a workaholic and demanded that we develop the same work ethic. I remember him working through lunch, eating a meat pie from the airport canteen and dripping the juices on to the papers in front of him, while giving me directions on something or other. Many years later there was a function in Sydney to welcome me as the new CEO of what had by then become Air Pacific and I was pleased to invite Grahame to join me. I hope that what we achieved with that company in the following ten years was vindication of his work and efforts.

The Test Truck

After my first few apprenticeship months spent stripping engines and cleaning the parts, I graduated into overhauling the cylinder heads. The main skills here were in using a special dye penetrate to detect cracks, heat shrinking new steel valve seats into the alloy cylinder heads, and then lapping the valves to a perfect seal. Engineers amongst you will know exactly what I mean. But this was a small shop and I was also allowed to assist in the measuring and assembly areas, albeit under strict supervision. The second six months took me into those areas officially and I delighted in the professional accuracy that was needed. Then, joy of joys, I was allowed into the home-made test truck to 'run in', and then 'power run' these engines.

The test truck was simply an old truck chassis on wheels with a steel frame made of galvanised water pipe on one end to mount the engine, and an enclosed galvanised iron cab at the other end that was, partially at least, soundproofed. On top of the cabin was a 44-gallon drum of hundred octane fuel with pipes running to a fuel control panel in the cabin. From there the 100 octane went through fuel flow gauges and on to the engine.

There was a panel of other gauges to measure RPM, cylinder head temperature, manifold pressure, oil pressure and temperature, and control levers for throttle and fuel mixture. The test propeller was fixed to a course pitch to load up the engine, and then reset manually to various finer settings during the tests. The exhaust pipes were open stub pipes cut to different lengths to tune the exhaust – very loud and with amazing red/blue flames. These we watched carefully through the glass window for length and colour.

The Test Truck

From our position in the cabin we ran these piston engines no more than four feet away for hours on end at maximum power, at rich and lean mixtures, and through acceleration and deceleration tests trying to stress the engine into failure there and not on the aircraft. Looking back now I hate to think what might have happened if an engine had, for instance, broken a conrod or crankshaft. We would have been very exposed to hot flying metal parts and possibly burning hundred octane fuel from the drum above us. Nevertheless, it didn't happen so here we are.

This test truck was famously the centre of a rather funny event that occurred in December of 1965. We needed to overhaul the instrumentation, electric circuitry, and fuel pumping system for the truck, so Grahame Marriot submitted a capital expenditure request to the Board for their consideration at the mid December meeting. Being good fellows, the Board decided that they would take the opportunity to visit the troops at Nausori Airport, shake a few hands, issue some Christmas wishes, and inspect the test truck before making their decision. This was fine in principle, but when they opened the door of the test truck there inside, bubbling quietly away in four-gallon drums, were several mixes of home brew. This was known at the time as 'raisin jack' and my fellow apprentice Atu Waga was the chief brewer on behalf of the staff Christmas party. He had found that the hot, stable temperature inside the truck cabin was ideal for this purpose. Grahame Marriott was aghast. There he was, fresh on secondment from Qantas, and arguing the case for his first ever Board paper. The Board quickly left the scene leaving Grahame to invoke hellfire and damnation on those involved. Still, they did approve the expenditure, so I guess all was well.

Sketches of Fiji

There was an irony in this; the reason for the brew was that, following a riotous Christmas party the previous year, the Board had reduced the budget for booze, so necessitating the raisin jack. And there was a sequel. Grahame's instructions to destroy the brew resulted in only a token gesture and at an appropriate moment during the following week's party the brew was produced with much fanfare by Atu and his fellow brewers. It wasn't long before Charlie Ogilvy broke into song and stilled us all with the quality of his baritone voice. Naturally after a while someone asked for *Ol' man River* and we all joined in and, arms around each other, moist eyes in some, sang at the top of our voices.

The last I recall of that party was seeing Grahame Marriott driving his company-provided Holden station wagon down the grass cross strip of the airport to the village at the far end. The car was packed with bodies and there were people lying on the roof and on the bonnet. In the best tradition of Japanese company drinking parties, the next day discipline returned to normal, no one spoke of what had happened, and Grahame had endeared himself to his staff.

Dornier Libelle

One of the things we apprentices did was to start the restoration of a Dornier Libelle aircraft that Forrester tracked down. It was in a shed at Marlow's saw mill at the back of Morris Hedstrom Ltd in the centre of the old part of Suva. The Libelle was a sponson float plane that old man (Alf) Marlow had imported into Fiji in 1929 to get himself and others between Suva, Lautoka and Labasa, but it had been badly damaged in a 1930s hurricane. Maurice Mc Grael refers to it in his book *Fiji's Aviation Story*. Despite very limited resources we tried to fix it up. My part was to overhaul the engine and we got it to turn over with enough compression to fire, but we didn't get it to run – the magnetos were corroded beyond repair. It was a four- cylinder air-cooled upright engine.

Before we could finish the work, Dr Dornier himself came to Fiji and bought it from old Alf to place in their museum. It seems this was the last remaining Libelle in the world. The one they had in their company museum had been destroyed during the War. We had mixed feelings about this but had to accept that we couldn't complete the work properly– we just didn't have the money; and they undertook to return the aircraft to almost as new.

During this work, the Fiji government Department of Civil Aviation and the government Public Relations Unit became interested in what we were doing and came to photograph us. Years later (around 2000) Forrester sent me a copy of that photo. Sure enough, there we were proudly standing around her in a very 'smile for the camera' stance. Rob Wright senior took the photo.

Sketches of Fiji

More recently Reggie Palmer and his wife were in Germany and visited the museum - there the Libelle was, fully restored and suspended from the ceiling for all to see. I very much appreciated the photos he sent. This year I saw an old photo of the aircraft afloat in Suva harbour which had been copied from the Fiji Museum records. The photo was dated 1930, just before the hurricane that wrecked her. Weirdly, the photo was in a real estate agent's window at the Denarau marina. I bought the photo for F$10. So now I have a photo of it in its operational days, of us repairing it (courtesy of the Forrester, and the government archives) and of its final resting place.

Years two and three of the apprenticeship

In year two (1965) I was transferred to the main hangar to work on the aircraft engines during maintenance checks, plus the beginning of airframe work. These were the days when it was not uncommon to remove the air-cooled cylinders, separate the cylinder heads, replace the piston rings in situ and even remove the front or rear bearing housing of the crankcase to carry out repairs. Real engineering.

The Gipsy Queen 30s fitted to the Herons were six- cylinder, inline, inverted, air-cooled engines. It says a great deal for the engineering skill, and the skill of our pilots in handling these engines, that we were able to get the overhaul life up to 2000 hours, which in those days was extraordinary. The GQ30s had a weakness though. They had a long magnesium alloy crankcase which was prone to cracking because of the torque around the midsection. This would understandably require the engine to be replaced and we got to the point where we could do this in approximately four hours.

The Gipsy Major engines fitted to the Drovers were of a vintage that powered the Tiger Moth albeit by now a more powerful 'Major 10' version. I lecture at the University of New South Wales where there is a Gipsy Major set up in the lobby as a museum piece. I delight in telling my new students that I held a licence on that engine.

The task I was assigned most often was to check the timing and the points gaps on the twin magnetos and to set the valve rocker clearances. Yes, that's right, both jobs requiring a sensitivity with

Sketches of Fiji

the feeler gauge and an understanding of that silky feel I learnt in tuning the Wolseley and the Rover.

In those early years we used a hangar attached to the old terminal building. It was okay for Drover aircraft but rather small for the Herons. To get the Herons into the hangar we jacked them up on the tarmac outside the hangar and rested each wheel on a small steel trolley fitted with castor wheels. These enabled us to then push the aircraft by hand into the hangar.

In March 1965 we introduced the famous DC3 to the fleet. They were used on the Suva to Nadi flights and to Tonga; occasionally to the other Island ports. These had been modified to have large rectangular 'viewmaster' windows and were very much appreciated by the passengers. The first came from Qantas and they sent their own engineers to do the certification - and provided flight attendants! We did the work. Then in June 1966 we leased our own DC3 from New Zealand's National Airways Corporation (NAC). We did all the maintenance on that aircraft and at the end of my apprenticeship I obtained licences on the airframe and on the Pratt and Whitney R1830 engines. I used to smile at the 'pilots relief tube' - a funnel with a length of hose to the outside. It had its own part number.

One memorable evening on tarmac duty we had to replace the big rubber seal on the dome of the propeller holding the mechanism that actuated the variable pitch. The aircraft then departed with

Years two and three of the apprenticeship

a full load of passengers and freight right on maximum take-off weight. The night was dark and stormy, as they say, and over the Serua mountains the new seal blew, and the engine lost all its oil. The pilots shut down the engine and proceeded to Nadi; but a fully loaded DC3 in tropical heat conditions, together with the humidity and intense rain, had difficulty holding altitude over the mountains on one engine. Thankfully they did manage to clear the top of the Nausori highlands and descend to land safely at Nadi. After it was all over we found we had been delivered a dodgy shipment of seals. Still, it was an interesting evening for us and for the pilots; and presumably the passengers.

Early 1966 we found serious corrosion in the belly of one of the Herons. These aircraft were built using a pioneering technology of the day called 'redux bonding'. Put simply the longitudinal fuselage stringers were glued to the outer skin. This reduced the number of rivets needed, and hence the time to construct, and Redux bonded joints were much stronger than riveting alone. The problem was that these joints were prone to corrosion; a fact not known when the technology was first developed.

It was decided to replace the skin and stringers. This was a very big job and beyond the sheet metal-working skills of our engineers. A Qantas 'sheetie' called 'Mouse' Mc Dermott (if you saw him, you'd know why) was sent from Sydney. To my great delight I was assigned to work with him for the next several months while we completed the repair.

Sketches of Fiji

I learnt a great deal from Mouse and was very pleased when, at the end of the work, he accepted a permanent job with the company. One thing Mouse did was to help me design and make my own tool box from galvanised iron 'left over' from when we built the passenger boarding steps. That toolbox has travelled with me for more than 50 years and I still have it today.

I didn't find the airframe work anywhere near as interesting, but did enjoy the complex process of rigging the aircraft to fly straight and true. We would annually strip the aircraft to their constituent parts, including removing the wings, all flying control surfaces and the undercarriage. The flight controls were alloy frames with fabric surfaces. I took an interest in this fabric work and in due course was granted an approval by the Air Registration Board to carry out fabric repairs; I guess a rare approval these days. This included hand stitching the linen fabric to the ribs and frames with a thick, waxed cotton thread using special stitches unique to the industry; then shrinking the fabric until it was taut with a cellulose nitrate 'dope'. Some of the guys claimed I liked the work because of the smell of the dope. I deny this vehemently.

By year three (1967) I was allowed pretty much to work on my own. The licensed engineers (LAMEs) would check critical points in the work and were ultimately responsible for the safety of the aircraft. We took our work extremely seriously and signed our name to every task we completed. That year I also began to work on the tarmac, or 'ramp' as it was called, where the aircraft were turned around. This meant shift work, and this in turn had a disruptive effect on my social life.

Years two and three of the apprenticeship

Spearfishing became a rare event – I just couldn't ever be sure I would be there when the boys wanted to go. Thankfully water-skiing was at Mosquito Island, only a few minutes from the Yacht Club, and even if I missed the departure, I could go to Lami and be picked up from the shore, or simply walk across if the tide was low.

Nevertheless, the ramp work was exciting, and I was learning a huge amount, both from doing the work and from watching the LAMEs. This was the pointy end of aircraft engineering work. Here on the ramp everything we learnt in the overhaul shop and the hangar went into quickly diagnosing faults, fixing them, and getting the aircraft out on time. We would never compromise on safety, but equally there was a strong professional drive to keep those aircraft on time. We thought nothing of working through the night and well into the next day to change engines and faulty components, re-rig the aircraft, and do all the things that might be necessary to ensure our passengers got away on time. There was only one flight a week to some of our destinations and therefore the need was critical.

Years four and five of the apprenticeship

By 1967 the company had acquired several more series 2 Heron aircraft with retractable undercarriage, bringing the fleet to seven Herons. The Drovers were retired. My roster moved me between shift work on the ramp and to the hangar depending on where the need was greatest. I very much preferred working on the ramp. There we were rostered as a small team of one LAME and four Aircraft Maintenance Engineers (AME's i.e. skilled and experienced but unlicensed) and usually one apprentice. Our work ranged from boredom between flights to high intensity when the aircraft was on the ground. Only in exceptional circumstances would the pilots relay a problem to us through the control tower. There was no aircraft-to-ground company radio frequency in those days. Having marshalled an aircraft in, one of us fixed the chocks and undercarriage pins in place, another positioned the passenger steps and opened the door. The shift leader would go straight to the cockpit direct vision (DV) window and grab the flight log from the pilot to see if there were any 'snags'. These would be quickly discussed, diagnosis made, people dispatched for tools and spares, and the pilots interrogated to try to determine any finer details beyond that written in the logbook.

While all this was happening, Air BP and one of our team would have received the outbound fuel load for the next flight and would commence fueling the aircraft, checking the engines, and topping up the oil. It was high adrenalin from there until the aircraft again taxied out.

The last thing we did was to conduct the 'walk around' inspection prior to handing the aircraft log book, and hence control of the air-

Years four and five of the apprenticeship

craft, to the pilot. This was done with great concentration and focus as it was our hand- over point and we were very proud of our profession and the need to ensure we missed nothing. The pilot would then conduct his own 'walk around' and we would be mortified if he found anything that we had missed. I can remember only two occasions in many thousands of departures where this occurred. Neither were critical, but it does show how important many eyes are.

There was great camaraderie on the ramp, and I enjoyed the company of the porters and cleaners, traffic officers, pilots, air traffic controllers, the firemen and all those people so important to these operations. Between aircraft departures we would drink yagona (still allowed today I believe, but not for the pilots) and just generally talk amongst ourselves of nothing in particular *'talanoa'* as it was known. Then the control tower would ring the bell in the fire brigade shed to alert them to the approach of an aircraft, and we would all of us swing into action.

Generally, unless the defects were serious, the pilots would carry the snags over till the last inbound flight and then write up the log book. This meant that for the afternoon shift who started around 2.00 p.m. work really began around 6.00 p.m. that evening. It was perfectly normal for at least one of those five-day shifts to result in working throughout the night and well into the following day. The morning shift arrived at 5.30am but would not relieve us from our duties repairing a particular aircraft as it was difficult to hand over complicated maintenance procedures part way through; and in any

Sketches of Fiji

case, they had their own job to do in dispatching the flights for that day. When the hangar crew arrived at 8.00 a.m. we would sometimes be given extra hands to help, but the duty to get that job finished, and the aircraft serviceable, remained ours. As a result, there were many times when I worked more than 24 hours straight with only a short break for meals. This was okay so long as the adrenalin kept pumping, but eventually you would hit a wall and it was time to go home.

To keep us nourished, if that is the word, throughout these long hours the company provided what was known as 'emergency rations'. These comprised hard PBC biscuits and tins of Hellaby's corned beef. You have no idea how good this can taste at 4.00 a.m. when you have been on duty since 2.00 p.m. the previous day; and especially when washed down with tea made milky and sweet with tinned condensed milk. It was at the end of one of these sessions that I had an accident with the Rover that I referred to earlier.

Most of my study was done in the watch-room at the fire brigade and this, plus what I learnt on the job at the airport, was enough to cause me to come first in the exams every year. Indeed, I won the Fiji Apprenticeship Council 'Apprentice of the Year' Award early in 1969, much to the delight of my parents, and me too I might add. It was for the top apprentice, Fiji- wide, and all trades. I remember attending the final interview with the Board of the Fiji Apprenticeship Council dressed in a clean white shirt, Dad's tie and carrying a briefcase that was empty - but impressions count.

Years four and five of the apprenticeship

The presentation evening was a very formal affair in the town hall with lots of parents, teachers, government officials and the Minister for Education at the time, Muhammad Ramzan. Fiji Airways General Manager Ron Duffield attended as well because the Apprentice of the Year's employers were also given a cup. I still have the miniature of the cup and presume the original larger version is somewhere in what has now been renamed the Fiji Institute of Technology.

Now, Ron liked his drink, a characteristic of the Airline's CEOs you will find, and the evening dragged on and on, with speech after speech after speech, so once he had the cup in hand, Ron "took off" out of the building, presumably en-route to the nearest Johnnie Walker.

Engineering licences

Fiji at that time was still a British Crown Colony. The Air Regulations were basically a clone of the then British Air Registration Board (ARB) requirements and were overseen in Fiji by a representative of the ARB. In the first half of my apprenticeship this was a man called Reg Warren. He was a martinet, extremely good at his job and completely unforgiving of error. Any time he appeared in the hangar we became somewhat nervous, and when we saw him pull on his white overalls the 'somewhat' became 'very'. He would spend hours crawling under the floor of an aircraft looking for corrosion near the toilets or along the redux bonded stringers in the bottom of the fuselage. He would also spend hours poring over every signature and detail written in the aircraft log books and maintenance records. But boy, we respected him. He set a standard for us, and indeed for the expatriate engineers as well, that played a very large part in the extraordinary safety record we achieved during those pioneering, bush flying, days. He was a man of few words, but if ever one of us apprentices asked him a question he would reply in a careful, clear, detailed manner and question us in turn to ensure we understood.

Reg was replaced about halfway through my apprenticeship by Ron Cooper. A very different personality, but equally a true professional. Ron took us apprentices under his wing and would encourage us to read books on aviation, some of which he lent to us. He would also pause to spend time with us to talk about aircraft engineering, aviation generally, and to ask how we were faring in our studies. He could see that we were gaining the practical experience but was concerned to ensure that we kept up our theory studies. Often, he would ask what

Engineering licences

section I was studying and then question me on that subject. He created an environment where we really did put in the effort on our studies.

Then the day finally came at the end of our training (17th. February 1969 to be precise) when I and my fellow apprentices finished our five-year 'time' and went to sit the licence exam. That we all passed is a testimony to Grahame Marriott, Forester Lindsay, Reg Warren and Ron Cooper. This gave us what was known as a 'basic licence'. It came with the admonishment that we had met the minimum standard to certify aircraft, but we still needed to pass what was known as the 'type' examinations for specific aircraft and engines.

I decided to do the HS 748 airframe and engine first, followed by the Heron, and then the DC3. Each of these was separate and comprised a written paper and then a one and a half hour oral exam. The oral exam was the worst. If you wavered even a tiny amount in your first reply, Ron would dig deeper and deeper until he satisfied himself as to the depth of your knowledge on that subject. It was grueling, but in hindsight indicative of the very high standards set by the ARB. But there I was, at long last, a Licensed Aircraft Maintenance Engineer, or LAME as we were called.

This was a really big event, not only for us, but for the company, I suspect Ron himself, and the Ministry of Transport. So much so that we were presented with our licences by the Minister, Charles (later Sir Charles) Stinson. Again, the Government's public relations department was on hand to photograph the event.

Sketches of Fiji

One of the things I became qualified to do was to compass swing the aircraft. This was to calibrate the aircraft magnetic compass and to record any deviations; rather important given the distances we flew over water. We normally did this at the Southern end of the grass cross strip. On one occasion however, there was maintenance work going on, so we went to the other end of the strip. Try as I might, I simply could not get standardised readings. Then Inoke, one of the old Rewa Fijians with me, said quietly 'boss, what about the iron?', 'What iron?' 'Oh, the one down below'. It turned out that the strip at this point was over muddy ground and during the War the American engineers had used 'Marsden' matting to stabilise the area. These were perforated sheets of interlocking steel, now under nearly a foot of grass; not good when you're trying to swing a compass. Learn a lesson Drysdale – compass swing only in approved areas. Incidentally you will still find Marsden matting all over the Pacific, often used to make pig pens.

While on the subject of navigation tools, I was also approved to overhaul and calibrate the periscopic sextants we used in the Herons. The calibration was a bit basic. We had a series of black dots marked at increasing vertical angles from a point on the wall, up the wall and over the ceiling of the electrical shop. We mounted the sextant in a frame we had built from water pipe and then 'read off' the dots. To initially find the right position for the dots on the wall and ceiling we used a new sextant that had been calibrated by the manufacturer. These days it's probably called 'reverse engineering'. Basic or not, it worked and, provided we re-checked our calibration with a manufacturer's calibrated sextant once per year, the ARB surveyors were happy.

Pioneering flying in the Pacific

I can tell many stories of these pioneering days and of the truly professional people, both on the ground and in the air, who saw to it that we never lost an aircraft, or a passenger – except for one who died of a heart attack.

By 1965 we had a total of seven Herons and flew them throughout the Pacific. It was pioneering flying; navigation was by non-directional beacon (NDB), a World War II bomber drift sight stuck through a hole in the side of the fuselage, and a periscopic sextant mounted in the forward roof escape hatch. The first officer, who doubled as navigator, sat on the front right-hand passenger seat crosswise across the aisle. To allow him to do this, we had cut away the inboard armrest of the seat. The seat opposite was removed, and a navigation table installed. No calculations on 'G' forces in those days; and don't get the idea this was sophisticated. It was a piece of plywood screwed to the cockpit bulkhead and supported from the hat rack at the rear by alloy hooks. Note: hat rack – not overhead bin. At one time when the company was short on cash the Chief Pilot issued an instruction to the navigators to use soft lead pencils and to use them very lightly on the charts so that the marks could be rubbed out and the charts reused.

My role was what we called a Travelling Ground Engineer (TGE). The engineer carried a box of spares and his own toolbox - note my earlier comment about the distances my toolbox has travelled. But he was also the flight hostess. When the aircraft landed at an outstation he would rush out, check the engines, dip the oil, supervise the refueling of the aircraft with a hand pump from 44-gallon drums of fuel,

Sketches of Fiji

take a fuel drain and check it, organize a change of the toilet (which was a tin can in a little cubby hole at the back of the aircraft) and do the engineering walk-around inspection. He would give the clearances to start the engines and climb in though the back door trying not to be blown away by the slipstream.

After takeoff the engineer then morphed into being the flight attendant. We served sandwiches and soup, and occasionally milky coffee. Trays of sandwiches were stored in the hat rack and the coffee and soup were in thermoses jammed behind the last seat in the aircraft next to the toilet. The 'catering' was prepared by whatever local hotel was en-route to the airport. The crew would pick up the sandwiches, soup and coffee, then carry on to the aircraft. We also attended to the sick bags; and there were plenty of those in use when we were flying through the tropical cloudbase.

The airfields we flew into were all World War II fighter or bomber strips. In the case of the Gilbert and Ellis islands these were simply coral dredged from the lagoon and laid on the sandy surface of an atoll. This worked quite well because the coral was crushed and, as it dried, it bound itself together almost like concrete - except for a continuous surface dust like talcum powder. Because of the horseshoe shape of these atolls both the approach and departure would be over water.

The airstrips were only a foot or so above high-water mark and were regularly affected by the wind and waves of passing storms. Funafuti

Pioneering flying in the Pacific

was interesting because at spring tide you could dig your heel into the grass runway surface and watch water well up into the hole. This in turn gave rise to an algae growth on the surface of the runway that could be slippery at times. Great fun!

Notwithstanding the local airfield manager, we would always do a low fly-past over these fields before landing to chase away the pigs, dogs, chickens, and kids who used the runway as their playground. The passenger terminals ranged from reasonably sophisticated buildings to World War II sheds. I regret now not photographing the terminal at Funafuti which was a small corrugated iron roof mounted on coconut posts, with no walls, proudly bearing a large sign, longer than the building, saying 'Funafuti International Airport'. I see they have quite a nice terminal now.

Several of these strips had no electrical lighting for the runway, and sometimes the lighting failed on those that did. On occasion we were caught out and had to land after dark. The airports had stocks of World War II 'gooseneck' lamps that burnt kerosene. These would be placed down each side of the runway and the cotton wicks lit. Quite exciting, especially for the passengers!

Sometimes, we would send two Herons in tandem to accommodate the number of passengers our reservations people had booked and still be able to stick to the published schedule. When that happened, we carried a traffic officer in one aircraft with the TGE in

Sketches of Fiji

the other. That way we could turn the aircraft around in the outer ports on time – and of course had a 'hostie' for both aircraft.

Ernie Dutta, from the commercial and reservations team, and Tony Wong, from the 'Traffic' department (as the airport passenger handling staff were called), often flew with us, but there were several others, most of whom, like Ernie and Tony, went on to become senior executives for the airline. Many of these were still with the company when I became CEO and they deserve recognition for what they achieved.

I can also tell of the camaraderie amongst the crews overnighting in rather basic hotels around the Pacific after extremely long days. We were feted by those tiny communities that we served; and it was often difficult to leave the parties at anything like a reasonable hour in order to be ready for duty in the morning. Neil Ganley, Gordon Shearer, Barry Rankin, the highly memorable George Crutchfield, the names go on and on. But I must admit we were not always pure. One engineer, who shall not be named, had a nice little business carrying French perfume from Port Vila back to Fiji in a little cubby hole in the leading edge of the Heron wing. I recall seeing a very well-known pilot being seriously ill under the wing of the aircraft one morning after a night at the British Ex Serviceman's Club in Vila (presumably from something he ate). Thank goodness it was on the far side of the aircraft and the passengers in the little shed that acted as the terminal did not see it. The refuellers did though and laughed out loud.

Pioneering flying in the Pacific

There was another interesting little trick: Fiji's customs laws allowed passengers to bring in one bottle of wine duty free on each trip. We quickly cottoned on to the fact that in Vila and Noumea one could buy five-gallon bottles of rough Spanish red wine – 'one bottle Sir'. Customs, being spoilsports, introduced a regulation that stopped us doing this after a few months, but not before there were many very sore heads after barbecues in Suva; it really was a very rough wine.

One story that still makes me smile now was that early one morning we were dispatching a Heron from Nausori to the Solomons via New Hebrides. The aircraft was a charter flight carrying American returned servicemen and their wives who were revisiting the battlefields of Honiara. Now, when the Heron operated domestically it did so with one pilot – ah, the good old days – but for the regional flights we installed the second control column in the first officer's position. This was not unusual and was a design feature of the aircraft. However, on that morning I had forgotten to install the second control column, and nobody noticed until after the engines had started. This was presumably because the first officer realized that he couldn't do the 'full and free' flying control checks because he didn't have a control column! No problem, he opened the little direct vision window in the cockpit and called out. I got the column from the engineer's hut and handed it through the window to him. Whereupon the back door of the aircraft opened and out jumped a reasonably elderly lady exclaiming in a loud voice that there was no way she was going to travel on that aircraft. Looking at it from her point of view I guess one can understand and sympathise.

Sketches of Fiji

We shut the engines down, disembarked the passengers, and then I gave the first of what subsequently became many engineering lectures on how the control systems on this aircraft worked. I took the lady to the cockpit and showed her physically how the control column was inserted and locked into place. It took a while, but we did get them convinced and the aircraft departed. How on earth do you write up that event in the delay report?

There were other aircraft that I was licenced on; a Grumman Mallard, a Beaver and a Piper Caribbean Tri- pacer from Korolevu Air Transport which we managed for Bill Clarke who owned the Korolevu beach hotel. Charlie Stinson (sorry, Sir Charles Stinson) and Tom French also had Cessna 172s, but I'll move on.

Hawker Siddeley 748

By 1967 the passenger numbers and growth in the airline were accelerating and in September of that year we introduced the Hawker Siddeley HS 748 aircraft. This was big news as these were what we would call today 'state- of-the- art' pressurised turbo-prop aircraft.

The introduction of the HS748 gave me the opportunity in October '68 to spend three months in England at the Hawker Siddeley, Manchester, and the Rolls-Royce, Derby, training schools. Despite the best efforts of Forester Lindsay and others, my practical training had been limited by the realities of Fiji's aircraft fleet. At Hawker Siddeley and Rolls-Royce I was exposed to the latest training techniques and was given the opportunity to see aircraft and turbine engines assembled and tested for the first time. I guess I was like a kid in a candy store and spent long hours on the factory floor after training was over trying to absorb as much as I possibly could. I also did quite well at the formal exams and was very proud to achieve 96 per cent in the Rolls-Royce exam. I remember sending an excited telegram to Fiji (for those of you who remember telegrams) saying 'Roycar exam 96%'. Roycar was Rolls-Royce's telegraphic address and every letter counted as cost in a telegram. That didn't stop my father-in-law John Gilmore later teasing me about the missing four per cent.

When one speaks of Rolls Royce it is almost synonymous with engineering professionalism, so I was delighted to have the opportunity to visit the factories in Derby and Glasgow. I found everything to be as expected, with one notable exception. The large alloy centrifugal compressor blades on the Rolls-Royce

Sketches of Fiji

Dart needed to be balanced to extremely fine tolerances, so I went along to see how this was done. You might imagine my surprise when I saw an elderly gentleman perform this delicate function using an 18-inch Bastard (yes, that's its proper name) file! Och, but he had the manual skill you see.

I finished my training in time to be part of the team doing what is called the 'acceptance' of the aircraft destined for Fiji Airways. This is where every line of the paperwork is checked for accuracy and 'completeness', every inch of the aircraft inspected for defects, and application made for the issue of the 'Certificate of Airworthiness'. We found a few defects, but not many.

We departed Manchester on 5th. December 1968 and arrived into Suva on 17th. That was one day after my first wedding anniversary – not a good thing to do!

Enroute we overnighted in Sanur, Bali which was little more than rice paddies and mangrove swamps. We stayed in the then brand new Sanur beach hotel as it was the only hotel in the area. There were no tourist souvenir shacks, but several wood carvers came to wait on the road outside the hotel each day. I bought a carved ebony lamp-stand which we still have. The carving is very fine and quite different from the tourist stuff of today.

The decision to introduce the larger HS748 aircraft also meant we had to build a new hangar. The existing one attached to the old terminal

Hawker Siddeley 748

building was already too small for the Herons. Not far away were the remains of a World War II hangar; basically, some heavy buttresses that could be used to support a roof, and a concrete floor.

There was some of the original roofing still in place at the rear – amazing trusses built of Oregon pine during the War. It was big enough, just, to house a single 748. A new roof was built over the buttresses, store rooms at the back for the spares and a separate administrative block down one side. The floor had to be overlaid with new concrete to achieve a level surface. As a result, the entrance to the hangar was up quite a steep slope and there was about 18 inches clearance each side of the wingtip once the aircraft was in place. To get the aircraft into the hangar we used an ordinary Massey Ferguson tractor at the end of a long tow bar, so it was a double-jointed action. It required considerable skill to push the aircraft, in reverse, up the slope and into the hangar without rearranging the wingtips. I was one of the few authorized to do so but wouldn't have a hope in hell of being able to do it now.

We pioneered many passenger routes throughout the Pacific and one of these was to the tiny island nation of Nauru. I was engineer on board the first scheduled (if you call one flight a week scheduled) HS 748 passenger service to Nauru in June of '69. The island is roughly 12 miles in circumference and basically circular. It is nothing more than a coral pinnacle poking above the Pacific Ocean hundreds of miles from anywhere else. As a result, it is the refuge of thousands of seabirds who over the years have left their droppings and these became 'guano' phosphate which is

Sketches of Fiji

used for fertilizer. This was pretty well the only source of income for the country; but it was very valuable. There were about 8000 Nauruan's at the time, and they were very wealthy on a per capita basis. Where the phosphate had been extracted from around the sharp limestone pinnacles in the centre of the island it looked like a dramatic moonscape.

This scheduled service meant a great deal to the Nauruan's and so, on arrival there was much pomp and ceremony. We were welcomed by President Hammar De Robert with a brass band of six, speeches, island dances, food and of course drink. After the ceremonies were over we were driven to the single men's quarters as there was no hotel at that time. We left our bags in the entrance and were taken straight to the sports club. This was basically a bar in a shed, but the expats had also built a go-kart track, so we had a few drinks and watched grown men pretending they were children again.

We then went to the phosphate company manager's home for dinner and drinks, and in due course were driven back to our quarters. We were assigned our rooms and told everything in the room was available to us at no charge. We didn't know what this meant until we opened the fridge in the room and found it stacked bottom to top with bottles of nicely chilled black label scotch.

Then there was the famous skinny-dipping story; okay, bet that got your attention! First, I need to explain some technology. The intercom system in the HS748 was somewhat basic. You selected transmit, intercom, or PA (public address) from a single switch. The first

Hawker Siddeley 748

officer's system was directly connected to the spare used by the third person in the cockpit, in this case me. Thus, anything the first officer was doing was also live with the spare headset and microphone. One day I was travelling from Honiara and for some reason was in civvies and sitting next to a middle-aged lady. We got chatting during the flight and at one point she said to me 'Did you hear that the crew were skinny-dipping in the hotel pool last night?'. Now it was true that we had had a late night at the Honiara club and on the way home had decided to take a dip in the brand-new pool at the Mendana hotel – but as it happened, we did so properly clothed.

Anyway, after a while I went up to the cockpit still chuckling about this story, put on the headset, and said 'Did you hear the Air Pacific crew went skinny-dipping at the Mendana last night?'. Unfortunately, and unbeknown to me, the first officer was transmitting on High Frequency (HF) at the time, so my little message was transmitted across the entire Pacific Basin. There was no response, and we breathed a sigh of relief until, on descent into Nadi, the control tower gave us clearance to land and finished the message by saying 'How was the swim?'. Thankfully we heard nothing more of the event.

I say 'we' because with the introduction of the DC 3s the company began to employ flight attendants. In the early days the girls received their emergency training in Suva from Australian flight attendant training staff. These Fiji hosties were very good at their job and the quality of service on Fiji Airways improved dramatically from the engineer's soup and

Sketches of Fiji

stale sandwiches of the Heron days. Adi Litia Cakobau, Bridget Singh, Elesi Quroya, Litia Dewa, Peggy Wilson, Tute Cooper and many others.

I've commented a couple of times about the professionalism of the Fiji Airways flight and ground crews; these girls were the same, incredibly good at their job, and wonderful people. The training was basic but their intelligence and commitment to the job ensured that they handled both the technical and hostess aspects of their work in the most exemplary manner.

There were several people who contributed to the training and motivation of these flight attendants, but without a doubt the man who really made it all happen was Bob Kennedy. Bob was of an old Fiji European family from Nadi (the airport land actually) and became mentor and trainer for these ladies. He defined, set, and insisted upon, the very high standards that became the hallmark of our passenger service. Somewhere on my bookshelf you will find a pictorial book produced by Bob called *Harold Gatty's legacy*. It's largely a photographic record of the history of Air Pacific and with a focus, naturally, on the in-flight service. It makes a very interesting read. Bob kindly mentions me in his dedication in the book and for this I thank him greatly.

Regional flying and engine changes

As engineers we were very proud of our on-time dispatch record and, considering the pioneering environment with very limited resources, there is probably some justification in this pride. The one thing that got us every time though, was those pesky Gypsy Queen 30 crankcase cracks. They occurred completely at random, sometimes even with new crankcases. When that happened it was quite spectacular, especially if on the inboard engine and some two to three hundred miles from the nearest island. The cracks would occur between cylinders three and four, midway along the case, which then allowed all the engine oil to leak away very quickly. Given the slipstream of the propeller, the oil would spread rapidly over the engine cowlings, fuselage, wing and flaps. This usually caused quite a lot of excitement for the passengers sitting adjacent to the engine line. We carried enough spares and ingenuity to get us home on almost every occasion, but there was simply no repair for these cracks, and it meant an engine change.

The pilot would radio Nausori control tower and the engineers on tarmac duty would be given the message. Sometimes it was simply shouted down from the little veranda that ran around the top of the tower. This was then relayed to the hangar crews, in person, on a bicycle. The hangar engineers would quickly load a spare engine (kept fully rigged for this purpose) into a relief aircraft and a specially selected 'engine change team' would head off as soon as the pilots could get there. Sometimes within an hour or so of receiving the engine failure message we were airborne. I was one of those on the team and many are the times when I went to work in the morning and didn't

Sketches of Fiji

come home for several days. Sometimes the departures were so rapid that one of my colleagues would be designated to phone home to tell my wife. She eventually got used to it – I think!

Heron engine changes in the field were relatively easy, and we did enough of them to have the whole process down to a fine art. The lifting gantry, spare engine, parts and extra engineers all fitted easily into the relief aircraft and we could have the unserviceable aircraft airborne within four or five hours of the spare engine arriving. It usually meant only one extra overnight in the field for passengers and crew; and, given we typically only carried twelve to sixteen passengers and three crew, this could usually be managed.

The RR Dart engines on the HS 748s that we introduced in 1968 were an entirely different kettle of fish. One of the more difficult in-field engine changes on the 748s was in June '74 at Funafuti in the Ellis islands (now Tuvalu).

Accommodating fourty passengers, two pilots, two hostesses and the engineer at that tiny place was not easy as it had only one hotel of seven rooms. But several opted to stay with local families and we managed.

At that time the company had only three 748s and this meant that two were out of service for several days as we had to use one of these to ferry the spare engine to Funafuti. As you might imagine this was a major scheduling problem for our reservations people and our passengers.

Regional flying and engine changes

One of the problems was trying to fit two 748s on the runway together at Funafuti. This is truly a very small atoll and the runway at that time was a World War II grass strip. It starts at the bottom corner of the island and ends almost at the other; and it is the local playing field when we were not there. We got the islanders to help us push the unserviceable aircraft off to one side of the field and into an area we cleared near the tiny shed that was the Funafuti International Airport terminal.

There were several other logistical problems: how to get the spare engine out of the hold, how to lift it into place, and how to lift off, and hold, the prop. We had the special Dart gantry to haul the engine out of the forward hold of the relief aircraft, but this was on small steel castor wheels and these immediately sank into the grass strip. The only machinery on that atoll were a few motorbikes, outboard engines and a single flatbed truck. What we did was to cut down the 2.5 inch galvanised water pipe flagpole at the terminal, the one at the school, and another one at the Government offices.

From this we fashioned a tripod. Then, by using this, a block and tackle, the engine gantry, and an awful lot of manpower, we could move the spare engine out of the aircraft onto the flatbed. We removed the prop from the unserviceable engine using our gantry, and then got some hefty locals to carry it to one side to rest on some old tyres. Then we lowered the failed engine on to some tyres, pushed the aircraft to a new position by hand, lifted the serviceable engine off the back of the flat bed, drove the flat bed away and pushed the aircraft to the engine. Then we carried

Sketches of Fiji

the prop to the new engine, picked it up with our gantry and finished the work. Rolls-Royce produced a book on the Dart engine and a photograph of this exercise is in that book. The job was a success, but before leaving the island we had to weld the flagpoles back in place!

Angry young man

Towards the end of the fourth year of my apprenticeship, stupidly, suddenly, and without any discussion with those affected, management put a notice on the board at Nausori to say that our working week would increase from 40 to 44 hours and that the extra hours would require us to travel to Nausori on Saturdays to work. The notice also advised that in future we would be required to clock on and clock off. There was to be no increase in pay for these extra hours, and there was absolutely no explanation as to the reasons.

Equally stupidly, the expatriate engineers were to continue at 40 hours per week, would not work Saturdays, and would not be asked to clock on and off. The directions were signed by the General Manager, Ron Duffield, but it was obvious that it had come from the new Human Resources manager seconded from Qantas. He was the first HR guy we had, prior to this we dealt directly with our own managers. I spoke with Grahame Marriott who, although clearly embarrassed at the situation, had instructions to follow.

Perhaps the Qantas management in Sydney, seeing the trade union movement in Fiji beginning to gain momentum, and experiencing their own industrial problems at the time (and still) thought they would get a head start by tightening up the existing conditions before the battle commenced. What they did in fact, was to declare war on the local staff. Over the years Qantas has done many things to the benefit of Fiji Airways and Air Pacific, but this was not one of them. It was the dumbest thing I have ever seen in industrial relations. It turned well-meaning young local leaders, with a genuine commitment to the

Sketches of Fiji

company, away from mature and responsible debate to a militant form of trade unionism that has haunted the company ever since.

I guess I became what in those days was called an 'angry young man' and was receptive when, after those new rules were forced upon us, a few of the local staff from the commercial side of the company began to agitate to form a trade union. At first I had no idea what a trade union was, but the principles seemed right, so I attended a few meetings at the Fiji Trade Union Congress headquarters at the bottom of Edinburgh drive in Suva. Subsequently, Kit Naidu, Bernard Lal, Bill Narhrun, Lorenti Morris, several others and I began to organize meetings amongst the company's staff. The trade union movement in Fiji at that time had, and still has, a strong political agenda but I did not allow myself to get drawn into that discussion. My concern was for my workmates at Nausori.

The upshot was that, although still an apprentice and under twenty-one, I assisted in the formation of the Fiji Airways Workers Association (FAWA). I wrote the Union's constitution, and the first log of claims, on our dining room table and proceeded to negotiate on behalf of my colleagues. The reality was that I did this whilst not being a member of the Union. The apprenticeship contract specifically stated that apprentices could not join the trade union movement. But that didn't stop me doing the writing, organising, speeches and negotiations. There were moves within the company to have my apprenticeship contract terminated because of these actions, however the Fiji Apprenticeship Council and Grahame Marriott intervened to prevent this happening.

Angry young man

These were in many ways, heady days for a young man; standing in front of the assembled workers spewing forth the usual trade union phrases (though I never used the expressions 'comrade' or 'brother', others did), having access to the highest ranks of the company, and being both feted and looked on with nervousness. I was also viewed as something of an oddity by people on both sides of the fence because I was the only European in the entire Fiji trade union movement. Grahame Marriott was most concerned at what this might do to my future career and spoke privately to my father, who in turn spoke to me, but I was determined to make a change.

Even some of the men at the Yacht Club bar would 'have a chat' in great seriousness late at night, arm around shoulder, beer mug a bit askew and with that slow, considered speech that comes when it takes a while to think of the next word. They were well meaning, but I was on a mission.

Early on in my trade union days the bus drivers went on strike and as a de facto executive member of the Fiji Trade Union Congress I attended many of the meetings where they set the strategy for the Transport Workers' Union. It quickly became clear to me that the inner sanctum of the Congress was really pursuing a political agenda and had very little concern for the bus drivers.

We were summoned one evening to a meeting of the Congress executive in their headquarters at the bottom of Edinburgh drive to meet with the

Sketches of Fiji

then Minister of Labour, Ratu Edward Cakobau. I have never forgotten his opening words. He said, 'you are the *Turaga* (chiefly leader) here tonight, we all have a baby in our arms, that baby is the people of Fiji, we are parents and like all parents we must do what is best for our child'. He said very little more but listened carefully to the statements from the union leaders, asking a question here and there, but basically listening. His bearing was as a leader and high Chief of Fiji '*vakaturaga*'; respectful of the people he was meeting and of their concerns. I was horrified, indeed disgusted when, after he left, that little core of Trade Union Congress executives made jokes and laughed about him. They then issued instructions to the Transport Workers Union to proceed with the strike regardless of its impact on the people and schoolchildren of Fiji. This was done without any discussion with the rest of the executive - or a vote. I won't name names here; this document is not intended for that purpose.

I immediately distanced myself from all organized labour activities in Fiji other than my immediate concern for the Fiji Airways members; and resigned from the Union after we concluded the second award negotiations. Years later, when I returned as CEO of Air Pacific, I was saddened to see that the attitudes displayed at that Congress meeting so many years earlier were still prevalent in the trade union movement, and in what had become the Air Pacific Employees Association. They were past masters at building aspirations amongst their members and using this to create a synthetic anger based on greed. They fuel an industrial relations environment based on conflict and adversarial militancy. It is one thing to adopt

Angry young man

hard, and at times strongly worded, negotiating positions, but quite another to cynically manipulate the union membership for political ground – much of that for personal gain.

I can say in complete honesty I believed then, and still believe today, that the first negotiated set of conditions for Fiji Airways engineers, flight attendants and other staff was a fair and responsible one. Indeed, when I returned as CEO in 1988, I smiled quietly to myself when I saw how little the structure and wording of the then current agreement had changed from the original that I had written on our kitchen table and negotiated 20 years earlier.

It also made me smile a little when, after the announcement that I would become CEO was made, a fellow apprentice from all those years ago told the journalists that he doubted I would be an effective Chief Executive because I had very little industrial relations experience. When the journalists asked me to comment about this I simply said, 'tell him to look at the signatures on the bottom of his Union's constitution'.

But I've got ahead of myself again.

The 'Raro' Charter

There was a period when Air Pacific operated a HS748 charter service on behalf of Air New Zealand from Nadi to Rarotonga. The main island of Avarua had a short wartime runway which needed to be extended and upgraded to cater for jet aircraft. To do this meant it had to be closed completely for several months. There was a road running parallel to the runway, adjacent to the sea wall, and that was strengthened to be able to take HS748 aircraft. This became our landing strip. At each end of the 'runway' was a boom gate that was lowered to stop cars when we were due to land, and a World War II air-raid siren was sounded to warn people of our approach. Nevertheless, we always did a low fly-past to ensure various children, dogs, pigs, cows and goats were not present.

Air New Zealand would fly the passengers from Auckland to Nadi of an evening in their DC 8, and we would then carry them overnight to Pago Pago in American Samoa where we would give them breakfast at the airport café while the aircraft was refueled. Then on to Rarotonga arriving about 9.00am. Now any of you who know the Cook Islanders will know that they love a party, so they sometimes got well primed enroute to Nadi, carried on the party throughout the rest of the night to Samoa on duty free booze, and were well and truly happy by the time they left the aircraft at Avarua. In fairness though, at no time did we have to discipline any of our happy passengers. On one flight Premier Henry led the singing and dancing up and down the aisle for most of the night.

We were accommodated in the single men's quarters which were comfortable enough; but those hospitable Cook Islanders took us to

The 'Raro' Charter

their hearts, and it was rare that we got to eat a quiet meal or get to bed early. We were taken on the back of trucks around the island, and on motorbikes all through the little back roads of the township, invited to play rugby and cricket and to go fishing.

Now the Cook Islands are famous for their *Tamure* dancing and regularly beat the Tahitians at the annual Bastille Day celebrations. This event is taken very seriously, and a great deal of attention is paid to the detail and craftsmanship of the 'grass' skirts that are worn by the girls. These are actually made from the fibres of the Pandanus leaf and are extremely fine.

The vigour of the men, and graceful movements of the women (graceful until they speed up that is) is incredible. The girls wore bras made of coconut shells held in place with a single, thin, woven cord of Pandanus. I never did find out if these were padded inside but given that an important part of the skill in the girl's dance was their ability to keep the upper body relatively still whilst the hips moved at either blurred speed, or the slow lascivious (wonderful word) roll of the dance, perhaps they weren't. What I do know was that there were some very large coconuts. These are unashamedly sensual dances and the girls of the Cook Islands knew exactly how to win that competition.

Because of the short runway length at Avarua, on the return leg we carried 'minimum fuel' for the take-off, and then topped up at the nearby Aitutaki atoll. This is probably the most beautiful atoll and lagoon in

Sketches of Fiji

the world, certainly that I have ever seen, and I've seen many of them. In those days there was just a simple village shop and a small ramshackle village. I understand there is a tourist hotel on the island now.

The runway was long enough for our operations and was the classic Pacific Island wartime strip made of crushed coral. Uplifting the water methanol needed to boost power for take-off here was often a problem because of our infrequent stops. Water methanol would go 'off specification' very easily. As a result, there were several occasions where we had to stay overnight while a boat bought new supplies from Avarua.

On one of these stopovers I met a strange fellow. He was an American who had been based on the island during the War and had returned after the War to marry his local island girl. He ran the little shop and was de- facto the chief of the island. He was probably also a complete alcoholic. On rising in the morning, he would pour a cup of very black tea into an enamel mug, then pour a Vegemite glass full of straight whisky as well. He would then proceed to drink both, after which he was ready to face the day. His choice of whisky was Ballantynes because, he said, the flat shape of the bottle meant it would lie securely on the coaming in front of him when he was at sea in his launch.

He was however very resourceful. On one occasion I found that the water methanol hand pump had been used by somebody to pump outboard fuel. This meant it could not be used. No problem, this ex GI put Drysdale and a 44-gallon drum of water methanol into the

The 'Raro' Charter

bucket of a front-end loader, lifted both up, and I simply siphoned the water meth out of the 44 into the tanks.

Perhaps a fitting end to this little story of our 'Raro' time: Air New Zealand required us to place a sticker by the door of the aircraft for each flight. This we did not like to do as it spoilt our paintwork, but it was a requirement of the charter. The sign proudly said 'Operated on behalf of Air New Zealand'. I mounted one of these on a piece of aircraft sheet metal and hung it on our toilet door at home.

Hurricanes, aircraft and rescues

Hurricanes are a fact of life in Fiji, and with them is the torrential rain beyond anything that people in temperate climates could imagine. This of course gives rise to flooding. The Fijian name for the area where Nausori Airport is located is *Luvu Luvu* which means flooded land. It is in the delta area of the Rewa River and floods were a regular occurrence during my engineering days. I doubt that anyone has the records now, but I believe I hold the record for swimming between the hangar and the terminal at the height of one of these floods.

We had two tractors for towing aircraft at the time; a very old David Brown, and a Massey Ferguson. I remember during one of these floods seeing Atu Waga driving the David Brown through muddy water up to his waist and with no sight of the tractor except for the very top of the rear wheels, the exhaust and air inlet pipes, both of which fortunately went up vertically from the engine. They made them strong in those days!

We developed a regular routine once a hurricane warning had been received. Where possible the aircraft were flown out to Tonga or Samoa. The alternative was to stake them to the ground in the open using a system developed during World War II. This was two six-inch- long pieces of galvanised water pipe welded to form a cross. Through each of these we drove long spikes of steel into the ground and the tie-down ropes went around the cross of pipe. They were very effective. The alternative 'dead-man' system was the one described in the DC3 maintenance manual. This was to bury a block of wood tied to the end of a rope deep into the ground. This latter didn't work in the sandy, muddy, flooded Nausori ground.

Hurricanes, aircraft and rescues

We developed another trick as well, and that was to use long thin bags of sand, some made from old canvas fire hoses, which we laid along the top of the wings just at the point of lift. This broke the airflow over the aerofoil section and prevented the aircraft getting airborne while stationary in winds of over 120 miles per hour. All very clever except sometimes they got blown off.

In all those years at Nausori the only aircraft we ever lost were a Tiger Moth (during Hurricane Bebe in October '72 when the hangar roof fell on it!) and a Cessna 172 that was privately owned and not properly staked down by its owner. It says something for the ingenuity, planning, and resourcefulness of the traffic officers, engineers, pilots and other staff of Fiji Airways that we could be operational again within a few hours of the hurricane passing. This was particularly important as on several occasions our aircraft were used to carry relief supplies to areas that had been affected.

When a hurricane was imminent, we would prepare the aircraft, lift everything we could on to the work benches and get ready for both the wind and the inevitable flood. We then sent most of the staff home, leaving a handful to stand by and see out the hurricane at the airport. The emergency rations of Pacific Biscuits and tinned meat became the only source of food, sometimes for two or more days. Believe me, you were ready for a change, and a change of clothes, at the end of that time. We joked that the biscuits would make you fart dust.

Sketches of Fiji

That same hurricane Bebe that destroyed the Tiger Moth in 1972 gave me the opportunity to observe a side of human nature that is not nice. My, by then, father-in-law John Gilmore and I volunteered along with the rest of the Yacht Club to carry emergency relief supplies to the flooded villages in the Rewa delta. We were one of the first launches into the delta and found entire villages washed away. Sometimes the only evidence that the village had been there was thatching piled up against trees, some house posts poking above the flood waters, and occasionally the village church that had been made from concrete blocks and set on a slight rise.

We found people huddled together in small punts amongst the mangrove trees and towed them back to Nausori. It would have been impossible for them to pole or paddle against the flood currents. Finding these villages amongst the mangroves was often difficult as the maps showed waterways and channels that simply no longer existed; and new ones had been created. By the time we got to the emergency services headquarters at the Nausori police station on the first trip the floodwater was still so high that we tied the boat to the railings of the first floor of the building. Whenever I drive past that building and see it perched high on the banks of the river it is difficult to imagine we were able to do so.

In addition to bringing people to the rescue centres, our job was to carry relief supplies to those villages that did still exist. And it was here that I learnt something about human nature that was not nice. The govern-

Hurricanes, aircraft and rescues

ment officials, army and police were handing out rations of corned beef, Pacific Biscuits, rice, milk powder, and cooking oil. Whilst there were many genuine families who were thankful to receive the supplies, there were also people taking the rations and selling them to the shopkeepers as far away as Samabula North. I know this because I saw a shopkeeper from near where I lived as a child paying individuals for these supplies. I was also present when the police arrested a shopkeeper from Suva who was claiming supplies in the name of a cousin of his from the Nausori area. The cousin had already been issued his supplies and was in fact sitting in the shopkeeper's boat at the time.

What struck me most about this was that there were many people from the relief agencies, Yacht Club, Defence Club and just ordinary civilians who were placing their lives in danger to bring help to those who had been affected; and the contrast of this to the avarice that I saw still shocks me today. It made me quite cynical I'm afraid, and I think carefully before supporting aid programs to areas devastated by nature. Much later in life when I was working in Asia I became involved in facilitating relief supplies to the hundreds of thousands of people affected by the Indonesian tsunami. Regrettably there were reports of the same practices.

Hurricanes, homes and boats

When a hurricane was imminent government officers would raise a yellow warning flag on the mast at the Colonial War Memorial hospital (CWM as we called it) situated high on a ridge above Suva. Then a black flag as final warning. But in any-case we listened carefully to Radio Fiji and plotted the hurricane's movements on marine charts. Everyone of course was an expert on what it would do next and reminded anyone who would listen of the year that hurricane X did the 'blah, blah, so I'm telling you this one will blah, blah'. Much learned discussion, but also much activity. Checking that we had tinned food, water, candles, kerosene for the primus stove and benzene for the lamps, matches, batteries for the torch and transistor radio; and of course, Johnny Walker whisky and Yacht Club rum.

All the houses and buildings had hurricane shutters. These were usually made of timber slats but occasionally were solid plywood panels. There were galvanised iron brackets either side of the windows and the horizontal beams holding the slats would drop into these brackets. It didn't take very long to get these up; provided they had been put away carefully, the painted numbers showing where they went were still legible, and the brackets still securely fastened to the wall. The prudent amongst us would check all of this at the beginning of each hurricane season.

We also had to worry about the boats and the Yacht Club elders would make a judgement call at a certain point to take the boats up the river. This was the Vesari River. Once there we would simply tie the boats to the mangroves, and someone would stay on board.

Hurricanes, homes and boats

Hopefully the tide would be low when the hurricane hit so we would have the extra protection of the sand bar at the mouth. It was quite a sight seeing the Yacht Club fleet moving en-masse across the harbour in already heavy conditions; and then to see them in the river at first light after the 'blow' had passed. By then of course the watchmen would be well underway on the rum and whisky.

Once all preparations were done it was then just a matter of waiting; and of course, having the odd drink, and pontificating on the next move the blow would make.

There are two things about a hurricane that those who have experienced one will remember. Firstly, the sky in the days leading up to the blow takes on an eerie colour. It's hard to describe but try thinking of a day-old bruise. Lilac and purple shot through with pink on the underside of the clouds. The air is still and heavy; even the birds are quiet. It looks and feels ominous, as indeed it is.

The other thing is the almost unreal feeling that exists when in the eye of the storm. Now people speak a lot about the eye of a storm, but the reality is that it is rarely experienced – but we did. The centre is quite small, perhaps 50 miles across, and you must be directly in the hurricane's path to experience it. Nevertheless, when you do it is unforgettable. You will have been hunkered down for several hours listening to the screeching wind, incredible rain and occasionally the crack of tree branches falling, or a piece of sheet metal crashing around the house. Then quite quickly the sound and

Sketches of Fiji

wind die away, the rain stops, and a watery sun comes out. So, you emerge from your bunker and look around at the devastation. Leaves stripped from trees, branches down, on occasion damage to buildings and cars, and grass blown flat as if it had been ironed. There would be flooding in low lying lands and sometimes dead animals. But above all, a weird silence. Then you start to move, rushing around the house re-securing ropes and cables, re-nailing boards where they have come loose, or over broken windows, and generally preparing for the repeat run. Quickly the wind begins to pick up, this time from the opposite direction, and the torrential rain starts again. Then it's back inside for another four to six hours. Finally, it's over and you emerge to look at the destruction around. The clean-up starts.

There were no chainsaws in those days, so it was axes and cane knives and hard labour. Clearing access to the main road was an early priority. Hurricane shutters were taken down and stored carefully away in their correct positions (usually). Temporary repairs were made where damage had been experienced, and all the while the transistor radio was on as you listened to the progress of the hurricane away from you, thankful that you were able to do so, but fearful for those still in its path.

Then a day or so later, usually after repairs to the Yacht Club pontoons, it was time to bring the boats back. I can't recall a single occasion when the boats that had been securely moored well up the river sustained any damage other than small branches and lots of leaves stuck to the paintwork. Sometimes owners left it too late to move their boats, just didn't care, or were away. We each helped the others

Hurricanes, homes and boats

as much as possible but sometimes there simply wasn't time to move all the boats, and inevitably some ended up sunk at their moorings. Strangely this wasn't always a bad thing, the bottom around the Yacht Club was soft mangrove mud and the hulls would sustain relatively little damage. Different story for machinery and electrics of course.

In all of this though there was a camaraderie that existed amongst the club members, each of whom would do all they could to assist the others once their own boat was safe and secure. Indeed, sharing the experience of being through a hurricane creates a bond between people that lasts for many months after the blow has passed.

As an aside, this was the tropics, and if you didn't clear away the branches and twigs lying on the ground within a few days, they would start to grow, put out roots, and make the removal more difficult.

And a bit of waffle

Let's step back from aeroplanes and hurricanes and return to the life of a young man in Suva in the late sixties and early seventies. The Yacht Club remained the centre of my life, largely based around the horseshoe bar, parties, a little water skiing at Mosquito Island, and still occasionally some bush walking or spear fishing. There were several other clubs in Suva such as the Defence Club, the Fiji Club and the United Club. Some people belonged to more than one, but typically you tended to have your favourite, if only to avoid duplicated membership charges – certainly the reason in my case. The expatriates came and went, and we locals became used to meeting the new ones and farewelling the old as a regular part of life. Usually a great reason for parties. The bank boys, and girls, would become friends and then move on.

Then as Fiji moved towards independence in 1970 the locals increasingly began to take on more senior positions in government, commerce and industry. Post- independence, the government and Nation of Fiji were keen to do away with the old British Colonial system and engaged in an understandable drive to 'localise'. This had substantially more success than many would have you believe – which in some ways is a measure of the Colonial government's forward thinking and planning. Where they did have expatriates, the Civil Service moved away from the Poms to more regional recruitment. Equally in commerce, probably because of cost rather than a burning desire by Fiji's business houses to localise, the number of expatriates began to reduce. Those that did arrive typically came as senior executives, usually from Australia or New Zealand.

And a bit of waffle

I'm going to generalise here for a moment, but please bear with me. The men and women of the British Colonial Service were trained professionals and, whilst the elitism and bureaucracy was painfully obvious to us locals, they knew their business and, for the most part, applied themselves with extremely high levels of diligence. Whilst this was true also to many of the Aussies and Kiwis who came in the later stages of the Colonial era, and on into independence, there were some who were plucked from middle management within their firms, given promotion and transferred to Fiji without sufficient training, or any real understanding of the environment they were going to. Others applied for jobs in Fiji, without a full understanding of what life in a tropical developing nation was like.

I hope not to offend those who did contribute tremendously to the development of Fiji, and for whom the following hat doesn't fit, but some were not good representatives of either their companies or their countries. Many came from relatively junior management levels and now found themselves as General Managers or Chief Executives, albeit in a small pond. They also suddenly found themselves in a fine house with servants and large entertainment allowances. In some cases, their activities did great disservice to those who did contribute well. It was also rather obvious that some came carrying the baggage of marriages in trouble.

Thus, on one hand we had Fiji citizens now being promoted to levels of government and commerce denied to them before, and on the other hand a new wave of expatriates less trained or experienced to handle

Sketches of Fiji

the challenges of working in a newly independent developing nation. Here for the first time I began to see bitterness towards the expatriate developing. That is not to suggest that a level of resentment had not existed in the past, but now it began to crystallise and become more visible. Fortunately, as time went on and the locals could prove their worth, the number of expatriates reduced and this feeling lessened.

One could speak at great length and engage in heated debate on the pros and cons of Colonialism, but one of the things that became obvious to me post-independence was the rapid polarisation between the Fijian and Indian people. Sadly, this ultimately led to the political coups in the mid '80s and 2000. Now I'm not for one minute suggesting things were pure and light in the Colonial days, far from it, but the Whitehall government was in some ways a neutral referee. We lost that at independence.

A nation typically comprises three things being held in common by the majority of those living in the country: land, race and language. Sometimes religion. Whilst Fiji could point to its land policies, and for the most part, clarity of boundaries and ownership as one of the legacies of the British government, regrettably there was insufficient commonality in the balance of the equation. What is more, the 1970 Constitution specifically categorised our people into racial boxes.

Prior to independence I received significant advantage from being a local European. At the time I didn't even see it happening, and in hind-

And a bit of waffle

sight I'm very uncomfortable about this, but it was a fact of life in the late sixties and early seventies. Put simply, I was pushed hard to perform because the expatriate management were more comfortable with a local European as a potential future leader than with one of the Fijian or Indian people. One only has to look at the line- up of that first year of apprentices to see what I mean. In the first cohort were three local Europeans and one part European. It wasn't until later in the year that a group of Fijian and Indian apprentices were signed up. It took men like Grahame Marriott, Reg Warren and Ron Cooper to shift the momentum and to encourage the Fijians and Indians to take their place as well.

One of the things that gave me great pride in later years when my time as CEO of Air Pacific came to an end, was that every one of my senior executives was local. Yes, we had some expatriates in the technical areas of the company, but the strategic direction and executive control of Air Pacific resided with people holding Fiji passports, including myself. And we had created a safe, modern, high quality and profitable airline for Fiji, carrying more than 50 per cent of the visitors, and around 60 per cent of all freight to Fiji. That seat-of-the- pants, risky, bold Drysdale plan of 1988 had been implemented by Fiji citizens; and it worked.

I've left Fiji now and it is not my place to make comment on what is right, or what is wrong, for Fiji. I grew up in the British Colonial era, saw the country through the adolescence of the post-independence years, the turbulent race-driven elections, and ultimately the coups of 1987. And I feel honoured to have been part of the

Sketches of Fiji

rebuilding of the economy post the coups in my role as CEO of the national airline. I will forever be grateful to the country, and its people, that taught me so much, helped shape who and what I am, and gave me such wonderful memories.

Fiji in the late '60s

Let's get back to the Yacht Club days. Sandra A'Costa was a good looking, vivacious, part European girl. She was one of those girls who became the centre of attention wherever she went; not only because she was good looking, but also because of her effusive, bright and outgoing personality. Presumably with a name like that there was a Portuguese sailor somewhere in her ancestry. I met an A'Costa in Manila once and he looked familiar. By late '64 Sandra had become part of our gang. We saw a lot of each other socially and went out together from time to time; but I don't believe one could say she was a girlfriend in the usual sense of that word. Read what you want into that!

Sandra often came water skiing with us to Mosquito Island and it was quite normal for us to spend pretty well all weekend at the Island; regular trips being made to the Yacht Club for petrol and booze of course. On Boxing Day 1965 we were just lying about, getting over the hangovers and occasionally going skiing. It was one of those hot, but clear, Suva days when the water sparkles with the slight offshore breeze that circulates between the two islands in the bay. I was at the southern end of the beach near the mangroves, under the big *Dilo* tree.

Upon looking back towards the coast, I 'espied' as they say in novels, an attractive young lady leaning against one of the trees on the edge of the beach looking across to nearby Admiralty Island. There was something about this girl that I couldn't figure out, and I guess I must have stared for quite a long time. She wasn't one of our group, and she

Sketches of Fiji

was not a tourist, they have a certain look. In due course I learnt that she was a good friend of Sandra's, her name was Elizabeth Gillmore, she had gone to the Grammar school and lived at Lami.

Her father, John Gilmore, had come to Fiji during the war years as a special forces officer in the New Zealand Army. He met and married Madeleine MacIndoe (long time Fiji European family) and stayed on in Fiji; after a while getting a job as the Secretary to the Native Land Trust Board. Those of you who know Fiji will know that this is an extremely difficult and sometimes heart- breaking job. At times he had to give evidence in court on land ownership that would result in families, usually Indian families, being thrown off the land that they had farmed for many years, and in situations where they had nowhere to go. I know how deeply he felt about this as we talked during the long nights of fishing that we shared together. He was a remarkable man, scrawny, athletic, and with a driving passion for boating and fishing. He was, in many ways, a mentor to me.

Often there were dances at the Yacht Club. These were either Island nights with colourful dresses and shirts, or formal dance evenings where the ladies wore evening gowns and the men dressed in white tuxedos. Given the heat and humidity of Suva this was a challenge and we would emerge from the dance floor dripping with perspiration. No problem, the bar was there to solve that difficulty. The band was always live and usually it was The Young Ones headed by a schoolmate and good friend of mine, Joe Chang.

Fiji in the late '60s

Sometimes it was the army or police jazz band, but that was only for special occasions.

New Year's Eve was always the major formal dance of the year and there was never a question of going to bed that night. In the early hours of New Year's Day there would be a swimming race for the men starting at the little jetty near the bar, out around one of the yachts moored about a quarter of a mile off, and back again. This was done in underpants and refreshed one so that we could then take a boat along past the wharf and up Nubukalou creek to get some curry and *dhall* soup for breakfast from one of the Indian lodges. We must have looked strange to say the least walking, if that's the right word, along Cumming Street still in our evening gear and tuxedos in our search of sustenance. Then it was get changed and head off to either Mosquito Island or Nukulau for a day of rest and recovery, aided of course by sufficient fluids to keep one going.

Great days, fond memories! Thinking about this now I'm surprised that nobody ever got hurt. We've just come through the Christmas season here in Australia with a terrible number of fatalities, yet I don't recall anybody even getting bruised during these happy times. My father used to say, 'the devil looks after his own'!

Kismet and other places

Liz Gilmore and I were married by the Anglican Bishop of Polynesia in his private chapel on the hill near the Fiji Arts club on 16th. December 1967. The reception was held on the lawn of the Gilmore's Lami home under a temporary corrugated iron and tarpaulin roof *'vakatunuloa'*. It was a classic Fiji wedding with enormous amounts of food laid out on buffet tables, lots of beer, yagona, and Great Western 'champagne' served in saucer- shaped glasses as we did in those days. There were the usual speeches following the preordained order, the Bishop was there to bless the food, and of course we had the typical Fiji fights once the booze had taken effect. These were the usual scuffles over nothing much, nobody got hurt, and it all ended up with arms around each other either crying or singing very loudly.

At one point a wharfie mate of John's nicknamed 'gorilla' (if you saw him you would know why) took on two or three other guys and they ended up rolling down the steep bank to the sea through Madeline's garden. This kind of sobered them up and they returned full of apologies and demanding forgiveness all round. There was much laughter and the party went on. As is the custom, for months afterwards gorilla would appear at our house with his traditional *sevusevu* of dalo, pineapples and other food to make amends for his behavior. Nothing would make him desist.

Our first home after we married was a rather nice one- bedroom apartment on the top floor of an old building called 'Kismet', set in large grounds and with wonderful views across the harbour. It was on a little hill over the road from the sea at Lami, not all that

Kismet and other places

far from John and Madeline. An old lady lived downstairs who was neighbourly and did not interfere with our lives in any way. As I guess most people do, we painted the place ourselves and furnished it very simply because we had very little money.

We were living in Kismet when I went off to England for my Hawker Siddeley 748 training. After a little more than two years there, Kismet was sold, and we moved further out, but still in Lami, to Solomoni Street and a house owned by an Indian gentleman called Kuku. Known to us obviously as Kuku's, the house was a simple wooden building and the kitchen was very basic; a single bench and sink with one cold tap – that's it. One wall of the living room was gloss blue enamel paint which I hung the Bishop's tapa over.

Our neighbour was Ratu (later Sir) George Cakobau, paramount Chief of Bau, *Vunivalu,* and the direct descendant of Ratu Seru Cakobau who was instrumental in the ceding of Fiji to Queen Victoria. He was to become Fiji's Governor General after Independence. We got to know Ratu George, his lovely and gracious wife Adi Lelea and their children very well. Their young son used to tease me over the back fence 'Andriu, la, la, la' and it became something of a joke between our families.

I was on duty at the airport on the evening Ratu George and the delegation to Fiji's constitutional talks in London left for Nadi. It was very formal with lots of media present, but George saw me, waved frantically and called out in a loud voice 'Andriu, la, la, la' with his wonderful

Sketches of Fiji

laugh. This caused something of a stir amongst his more sombre colleagues, the assembled media and well- wishers. Whenever we saw each other after that he would say it with a laugh; even when sometimes, in my later business life, the situation was formal and tense.

After a while however, Kuku returned from overseas and we had to move again. This time, in September '70, to a flat at the far end of Gorrie Street near Albert Park. It was great in the early days but after a while it came to pale for me. The view out of our bedroom window was a sewer vent, and above us lived a well-known Suva businessman's daughter. This girl was a real party animal and it was not uncommon to see ladies' underwear flutter past our little veranda during the evening. There were drinking parties and sometimes fights. On one occasion she was off running down the road wearing just her panties. I think the real problem for me was a sense of claustrophobia, being hemmed in by other flats and other people. But it was also a place of great joy for the two of us as it was the home of our first born, David.

HS 748, and the training role

We had introduced the Hawker Siddeley 748 turbo-prop aircraft in December of 1967. In late August of '68 I went to England to study the aircraft's operations, maintenance and technology and returned as the engineer on the delivery flight of the second aircraft VQ- FBH in December of that year. The company took delivery of a third in October of '69 and these aircraft began to take over the regional flying from the Herons; although the last Heron didn't leave till '75 as they continued to be used domestically to SavuSavu, Matei and Labasa.

Stepping ahead for a moment, but to finish that story: the Herons were replaced beginning in '74 with Britten Norman 'Trislanders'. This was a weird aircraft grown from the very successful 'Islander', with a third engine on the tail; and a propensity to shed the prop from that engine because of vibration. This was very exciting for passengers and pilot! It happened to one of our flights during the take-off roll on departure from SavuSavu, so the prop was under full power and spiraled forward – thankfully over the top of the fuselage. Understandably, and quickly, Britten Norman and Lycoming introduced a modification to stop it happening.

Not long after my return to Nausori from the HS748 delivery flight I was promoted to hangar foreman. Out of the grey overalls and into white. I was the first of the apprentices to reach this position and was very proud of myself. But shortly after this Grahame Marriott asked me to take on the little training school that Ken Cristofferson had started and to teach both pilots and engineers theory of flight and type courses on Herons and 748s.

Sketches of Fiji

To call it a school is a bit grandiose. It comprised one tiny room that could house eight students and a mock-up of a 748 cockpit made from enlarged photographs stuck on plywood panels. Nevertheless, we made the most of what we had, and I found a real affinity for this work.

There I was in my early 20s, lecturing experienced pilots and engineers on the flight characteristics and operating systems of what was then a state-of-the-art turboprop aircraft. I guess it taught me to be comfortable in front of a class, helped polish my presentation skills, and it certainly taught me a lot about watching and understanding your audience.

The courses had to be approved by the Civil Aviation Authority and so in the early days Ron Cooper would regularly sit in and listen. This was a bit unnerving, but I quickly grew confident in what I was doing and after the first few months, rarely saw him.

As the company expanded, we quickly outgrew this tiny classroom and on occasion used conference rooms in Suva hotels. It was obvious that we needed a proper training school and Ken Cristofferson and I regularly approached senior management for the budget to be allocated. But the company was losing money, partly because of the cost of introducing these new aircraft, and there were no funds for our school. So, full marks to Ken, who convinced the Army engineering unit that it would be a good idea for them to build the school as a training exercise with Fiji Airways providing the materials; and this they did.

HS 748, and the training role

We were very proud of that little two-classroom school when it was opened, but I only taught there for about one month before being transferred back to the hangar as an inspector (a kind of auditor) of the engineering standards. Out of overalls now and into a white smock coat. This also entailed a lot of office work with warranty claims and general behind-the-scenes administration.

As I write these notes it is 50 years since the first moon landing (20 July 1969) and I recall sitting at my very first official desk, in my white coat, listening to those famous words from Neil Armstrong on a scratchy sounding little transistor radio. Many years later I was to meet him a few times and recounted the story. He was gentleman enough to not say 'Oh no – not another one'.

Not long after this Warren Seymour, then the Chief Pilot but originally an engineer and my shift boss, and I were invited by Hawker Siddeley to attend an operator's conference in Manchester. I really did my homework for this and prepared charts and stats, trends and failure rates to be able to contribute to what was to be my very first conference. I've attended many hundreds of conferences over the years but for obvious reasons this one stands out rather strongly in my mind. For three days the design engineers and production team at Hawker Siddeley sat at the head table in front of some 300 airline delegates and went through every single line item on the maintenance and operation of the aircraft. I found myself on my feet speaking far more often than I had expected, and it quickly became obvious that

Sketches of Fiji

very few of the other delegates had really done much homework. But at the same time I learnt a huge amount about the philosophy of aircraft design and how the manufacturer developed modifications to improve where weaknesses lay.

One of the problems, sort of pedestrian really, was that the plastic hand basin in the aircraft toilet deteriorated rapidly in our tropical heat and was expensive to replace. Aircraft parts tend to be expensive, so we had gone to Burns and Ferrell, the stainless-steel urinal makers in Auckland and got them to make us one. The plastic Hawker Siddely version lasted about six months and cost £280; our one, which lasted forever, cost £32. When questioned about the failure of these manufacturer's basins, the design engineers, sitting on high, said they would be prepared to develop a modified version but that the customers would need to pay for the research and development. Drysdale immediately leapt to his feet and told the story of the New Zealand urinal makers, whereupon there was something of a hush in the room. Finally, Sir Geoffrey Hull, then Chairman of Hawker Siddeley, said through gritted teeth 'Mr. Drysdale I'm sure that at morning tea there will be quite a number of people who will want to talk to you'. Still, I don't think I queered my pitch too much with them because I was asked to deliver both the closing speech of the conference and the 'thank you' address to Hawker Siddeley on behalf of the delegates at the final dinner. I was in my mid 20s.

Independence and citizenship

Fiji had been ceded to Queen Victoria on the 10th of October 1874. Independence came on the same date in 1970, just short of 100 years as a British Crown Colony under the direct control of Whitehall and a British appointed Governor.

There had been constitutional talks in London in the lead up, which finally resulted in a Constitution being approved by the various racial groups and HM Government. Most of the delegations to these talks left Suva for Nadi by air so I got to see them off. I've referred to this earlier, but it always struck me as a little strange – there was I in late teens and early 20s wearing my grey engineer's overalls saying goodbye to these leaders of our nation on this important mission. Many I knew well: Ratu Mara, Ratu George Cakobau, John Falvey and Don Aidney in particular come to mind.

These were the years of the United Nations 'Committee of 24 on Decolonisation' which resulted in horrifying turmoil and bloodshed in Africa and other parts of the world. They have a lot to answer for in my mind. That said, because I was so completely involved in my work and with my young family, I didn't take much notice of these independence debates at the time. For that matter, nor did any of my workmates. When I raised the subject of independence the response was usually 'we don't know' or 'that's up to them', referring to the politicians and Chiefs. Still, it was obviously an important step for the country, and I guess we all hoped that Fiji would continue to advance as a peaceful, multi-racial nation.

Sketches of Fiji

The Fijians were extremely loyal to HM the Queen and proud to be part of the British Commonwealth. As a result, their leaders went to great pains to reassure them that the Queen would still be the Queen of Fiji, and we would still be in the Commonwealth.

On the appointed day we duly attended Albert Park to watch the ceremonies and stood in the large crowd. We saw the big car, Prince Charles and the Governor in oversize helmets, with even bigger feathers. We watched the very solemn Fijian ceremonies, heard the speeches and hymns, listened to the bands, were impressed by the precision of the marching and sword waving, saw the new Fiji flag raised (the Union Jack had been ceremonially lowered for the last time the night before), and went home. Looking back, it was good to have been there, but I feel no emotional ties to the event. Reality is many miles away from those ceremonies.

The Constitution required single citizenship. Up to that time I was still an Australian citizen; but post- independence we were given 18 months to either obtain a work permit, thus becoming an expatriate on a temporary visa, or to renounce our existing citizenship and become a Fiji citizen. Note, Fiji citizen, not Fijian. It was very clear in the lead up to independence, and subsequently in the Constitution, that that term would only relate to the indigenous people. Over the intervening years I've heard several local Europeans, and even part Europeans, express surprise that they were not allowed into the inner sanctum of 'Fijianism'. All I can say is that they must be naive. They may express disappointment, concern, anger even, but surprise – no.

Independence and citizenship

The Fijian sense of *'Vanua'* is fundamental to their being. It is their land and they will own it forever. They will support and welcome their guests but can never give away their Vanua. I was content to simply be accepted as one of the races in Fiji and pleased to be allowed to continue to build my life in the country I felt part of, and close to.

The constitution that came into force at Independence gave we 'others' (or 'General Electors' as we were called) a completely disproportionate control in Parliament. The Fijian and Indian races were given an equal number of seats (each more than us) but because the other two were so racial in focus it meant that whoever we supported would have the majority in Parliament and hence, effectively, control. It was probably the best the negotiators in London could achieve at the time, but as history has demonstrated, it was not a formula that could survive.

I formally renounced my Australian citizenship and had the corner cut off my passport. Then took out a bright blue Fiji passport. The pride in now being 'of Fiji' was strong and there were no regrets at relinquishing the Australian link. Over the years there were occasions when a few Fijians reminded me of my status, but it never bothered me very much; still doesn't in fact. I grew up with the Colonials, then the expats, and post- independence it was the Fijians in charge of their country. In my view at the time, that's the way it should be.

I now live in Australia and for that reason I will avoid comment on Fiji's current politics and direction. It is no longer my place to make

Sketches of Fiji

such comments, and I get annoyed when people like me, former Fiji residents, spend hours telling the world what is right or wrong with 'their' country. As far as I'm concerned, we all abrogated that right when we chose to live in another country. I don't even like the endless reminiscing that goes on when former Fiji people get together. That door is shut guys – move on through the other. And, having got all that off my chest, I probably should do so as well.

But let me make one final, and important, point. These notes refer to a time past; they record my thoughts, and the reality of those days in the 1960s, '70s and '80s. I admire the ideals of Prime Minister Bainimarama in creating a holistic nation today and sincerely wish him, his Government, and the people of Fiji great success in achieving that goal.

I'm reminded of a quote from Aristotle drummed into my high school ears by Brother Placid 'the sum is greater than the parts'.

Suva / Levuka Yacht race

Father-in-law John Gillmore had a 24-foot launch called *Sereana* (song of Anna). The word has a beautiful, soft, melodic sound in Fijian. She had originally been built for a British Civil Service doctor at the government shipyard, where years later I was to build two ships. She was powered by a four-cylinder converted Ford car engine. John and I spent hours maintaining that boat; beaching her at Mosquito Island, or on the little strip of sand in front of their Lami home, to scrub and anti-foul the bottom, cut out the inevitable rot, or just paint and titivate. The engine was underpowered for the size of the boat and this resulted in the exhaust valves burning out regularly. I got very good at whipping off the head, grinding the valves, reassembling and getting it operational in time for our next trip. We would go on family picnic days to Nukulau or on fishing trips to Bega island, Tomberua or Naselai passages, and occasionally to the beautiful islet of Leluvia in Bau Waters.

It was on these trips that I again took up spear fishing and John became an ardent follower of the sport with me. On occasion we would shoot a turtle for the pot and John would make one of his famous turtle curries. The feature of his recipe was lots of the bright green turtle fat; yes, it is bright green. For years we had a Hawksbill shell on our wall that was almost four foot long. I remember shooting it at Tomberua. The spear went through the back of the neck and into the body. The turtle died instantly – luckily, as fighting one that big would have been very interesting.

Every year we would compete in the Suva to Levuka launch race. This was not a race as in high speed, but a time-trial rally where one

Sketches of Fiji

declared an average speed and navigated to maintain that speed. For weeks prior, John and I would spend hours at the dining room table poring over maps, plotting positions, and calculating time between way-points. We would also spend hours chugging up and down Suva harbour between the two beacons that marked the measured nautical mile. We would do this in as many weather and tide conditions as possible in order to best understand our boat, and its speed at different engine RPM settings.

The race in those days went from Suva through the Rewa delta, across Bau Waters, and around the North coast of Ovalau island to Fiji's first capital, Levuka. The prize- giving night at the Royal Hotel was festive to say the least. Sunburnt, tired, inebriated and nervously waiting on the results, we would all gather at the hotel, eat an enormous meal of Island food, and yell and scream and thump the tables as each result was announced.

The race was held over the 'Cession Weekend' as it was called then, and the weather was often rough in mid- October. There were many breakdowns and rescues. There were no rescue boats, we simply looked after each other. In 1971 we were en-route from Natovi on the main coast to Ovalau when Bill Cruickshank came roaring past us in a small boat with an enormous outboard engine. At that time Bill headed Millers shipyard and they were manufacturing this little boat for commercial sale. He was trying to beat the speed record for the race.

Suva / Levuka Yacht race

About 200 yards past us he hit a large wave and the entire transom tore away, still with the motor attached roaring at top speed. Rather spectacular. We stopped and picked up Bill and his passenger, secured the boat and eventually handed them over to the *Ai Soukula,* an inter- island vessel that came past. Quite by chance just then, Nitin Lal, one of Fiji's best photographers and a friend, happened to fly past in an Air Fiji Baron aircraft and we featured on the front page of the Fiji Times. The race committee awarded us a special prize that night which, assisted by several others, we managed to drink.

We never won that race, but we were always in the first ten, and several times in second or third position. However, we did win the equivalent Suva/Pacific harbour race on my birthday 10th August 1974. I still have the Omega watch that was the 1st. prize for the navigator. The festivities were a wonder to behold.

After a few years John replaced *Sereana* with the more modern 21-foot plywood *Camelita*. She was powered with a 110-horsepower Chrysler outboard, the most powerful available, and could reach up to 25 knots on a calm sea. This was one of the fastest boats in Fiji at the time. *Camelita* enabled us to go much further from Suva in our spear fishing endeavours and we have several photographs of very successful weekend fishing trips.

John was a strong character who featured prominently in my life and his memory remains very clear. He died in April 1978 and we buried him in

Sketches of Fiji

the MacIndoe family gravesite in the old Suva cemetery overlooking the Yacht Club and his beloved Suva harbour. It was one of those Suva days with thunderstorms all around. The Army had sent a party of soldiers to pay respects, and just as the bugler ended the last post there was a flash of lightning and a clap of thunder. Coincidence – I suppose.

Gypsies and Tamavua home

Then we moved again in 1971, this time back to near Kuku's house in Lami and into a small cottage owned by the Anglican church which we called, naturally, the 'church house'. It was here that our second son James was born.

By this time we had been fortunate to secure a block of land in the new Native Land Trust Board (NLTB) subdivision in the suburb of Tamavua and had commissioned Larsson and Holtom as architects to design a home. This was intended to be an executive subdivision and there were restrictions on the minimum size of the house. It had to be greater than 1100 square feet, but money was very tight, so our design was exactly the minimum. This caused consternation amongst our neighbours who built massive homes around us, but there wasn't a lot they could do.

There were problems during the construction phase. Firstly, the builder went bankrupt, and we had to find someone else to finish it off; and then hurricane Bebe tore one corner of the roof away and this had to be repaired. We simply could not afford to pay the builder and rent at the same time, so we moved in with Madeleine and John. And after a while, to give them a break, we moved to my parents' home.

But eventually our Tamavua home was finished and we could move in. It cost $11,000. I often think of that when we buy the family car for three times that amount these days. In the intervening period we had put a lot of work into the half acre of land that we had. The lawn

Sketches of Fiji

was pretty much established in place of the earlier para grass (a very big project) and we had planted several trees and shrubs. Some of the trees were provided by my brother Peter who was working for the forestry at the time. In particular he gave us some eucalyptus trees. I was in Suva recently and many of them are still standing, now almost 50 years old. They are massive trees, one, a *eucalyptus deglupta*, must be more than six feet in circumference.

By now we had a Doberman dog, as one did in those days, and needed to fence the property. I did it myself – three sides of a half-acre block of land is a very long fence. I dug the holes, set the pine posts in concrete and nailed literally hundreds of four-foot-high, four-inch- wide, treated pine boards to the rails, by hand, with just an ordinary carpenter's hammer. I made, and hung, gates in the same material and made a hand-mixed concrete drain down one long boundary and across the front of the property.

The fence on the fourth side was erected by our neighbour who was a Fijian businessman, and later a government Minister. The fence was imported Australian arc mesh fencing. He told me I didn't need to contribute to the cost as it had been erected by the manufacturer as a 'show fence'.

Trislander delivery

In mid-March of '75 Warren Seymour, George Marlow and I delivered the first of the Air Pacific Trislanders to Tarawa to replace the trusty Heron. It was a very long haul over the Pacific Ocean with basically no sight of land on the way. Suva to Nadi, then to Funafuti in what was then the Ellis Islands, and on to Tarawa. These last two were more than six-hour sectors. We had taken out the seats and filled the cabin with 44-gallon drums of high octane fuel rigged to an electric pump to transfer the fuel from there into the wing tanks through plastic pipes. One small spark and we would, as they say, 'never have been heard of again'. But in those young days we had absolute confidence that our engineering skills would ensure that no spark would happen, and that there would be no leaks.

On arrival at Tarawa we were interviewed, live, by the local radio station. The interview covered the normal stuff; length of flight, why the Trislander was good for Kiribati (as it was called by then) and so on. Right at the end the reporter, a good-looking local girl called Anna Muller said, 'And so Captain (to Seymour) can you tell me why your company is called Air Pathetic?'. Remember this was a live transmission. But Seymour was quick – he replied 'No, you've got that wrong, it's Air Terrific'.

BAC 1-11

In 1972 we introduced the 84 passenger BAC1-11 (British Aircraft Corporation to those of you too young to remember the company that gave the world half of the Concorde) twin-jet aircraft. The model we selected was the 475 because it was fitted with a 'gravel kit' and several of our airstrips were still unpaved. I was sent to England to learn about these aircraft and their engines and again came back to run a series of training courses for both pilots and engineers. I also went to England and Germany in March /April 1978 to carry out the engineering inspection on a third aircraft, this one acquired from Germanair in Munich – and this has a story to it, but I'll come back to that later.

We flew these aircraft throughout the Pacific and they also allowed us to start international flights to Auckland (via Tonga) and Brisbane (via Noumea). This unusual routing was because of the totally biased 'Air Service Agreements' that the Colonial Government had left Fiji with at Independence. It's complex and difficult to cover in a few words so I'll come back to this again a little later. Suffice to say, these are the trade agreements between countries that permit the airline industry to operate. Getting these balanced was one of the biggest battles I had when, many years later, as the CEO of Air Pacific we created a truly international airline for Fiji.

I was engineer on the inaugural flight to Brisbane on 1st. June '73 and there are photos of this young fellow in his uniform sitting talking to the then Minister for Civil Aviation, Ted Beddows. We had a planefull of VIPs and very few paying passengers – ah, the days when one did those things! We also had an awful lot of 'champagne'.

BAC 1-11

Charlie Stinson (Sir Charles, then Minister for Finance) took over the cabin PA and led the singing of popular and Fijian songs. We invited him to return to his seat at top of descent but allowed him one final rendition of the Fiji National Anthem before he did so. On the return we lost one of our VIPs and had to leave him behind. He was found eventually, attending someone else's function in the terminal.

We also conducted two sightseeing flights for Government dignitaries and travel agents down to Coolangatta. I had no idea where that was at the time, but it was low-level and about an hour's flying. I was horrified on return to see how much fuel this low- flying had consumed. At first I thought the gauges were wrong, or that somehow I had incorrectly fueled the aircraft before departure; but reference to the manuals showed this was the correct consumption for that flight. It certainly bought home to me the inefficiencies of a jet engine at low altitude.

For several months afterwards I travelled to Brisbane on the aircraft, overnighted, and returned the next day. But occasionally, after we had approved a Brisbane-based Qantas engineer (Col Cruden, who became a very good friend) I would get off at Tontouta airport in New Caledonia to check things like the fuel depot and safety facilities. I was an inspector of these things by then. As a result, I got to know the restaurateur at the airport very well. He was a giant of a man, larger than life, and very effusive in a French way. We met one day when I ate at his restaurant and ordered tripe off his menu. On being told the order was from the 'Air Pacific man' he emerged from his kitchen like

Sketches of Fiji

a galleon in full sail, exclaimed to all the guests that this was the first time a non-Frenchman had 'ever ordered la tripe' and proceeded to drag me around all the tables to exhibit me to the diners. I explained that my mother would sometimes cook tripe at home, so it wasn't all that unusual – that just set him off all the more.

We became friends and would eat lunch after the aircraft left for Brisbane. His trick was to drink up the wine left by the lunchtime guests; often half a bottle or more per table. He would tell me all about the various wines, but I'm afraid the brain was not retaining a great deal. On one occasion we sampled a bottle of Algerian Shiraz (he was from Algeria – what the French call a 'Pied Noir' – it's not a nice term). The wine's claim to fame being an alcohol strength greater than 14 per cent. I do remember asking him once what he thought of Australian wines. He pulled himself up to his full height and boomed out 'Monsieur, le Cote du Rhone is in France'.

After lunch we would go over the road to his house. Staff at the airport lived in company-provided housing across the road from the airport because Tontouta was 60 miles from Noumea over a rough dirt road, and through the mountains. His house was amazing; almost every inch covered in animal hides. Floors, walls, furnishings, everywhere. Mostly black and white cows it looked to me, but I guess there were others.

He would then pour each of us a glass full of Chivas Regal which he poured from a four-gallon bottle on a hinged stand. As he handed it over, he would say 'if you drink quality you will not get drunk'; believe

BAC 1-11

me, not true. But perhaps he meant you would not suffer as much the next day. He would then produce a huge revolver and would begin blasting away at coke tins in his back yard. Fortunately, this backed onto a sandy cliff, so I guess it was not quite so dangerous. He and I were very drunk by this time. His Kanaka wife would bring food now and then, but generally stayed in the background – probably the safest place to be. The next day, thankful that I had only drunk quality, I would conduct my inspections, board the aircraft on its return from Brisbane and head home.

By the time the 1-11 was introduced I had received several promotions, and by the early '70s was made a foreman. This placed me alongside the expatriate engineers, indeed senior to several of them, and some were unsure how to handle this. It didn't help that they knew I was earning less than one third their salaries and was more qualified than most. For my part, whilst I wasn't particularly happy about this, it didn't bother me all that much. I had grown up in a world where the expats were privileged, and I had come to expect it. However, as I explained earlier, the expats of my early apprenticeship years that I admired so much had gone, and these were a different breed. They were still highly trained and professional in their work, but what annoyed me was the constant complaining and negative attitudes that some of these privileged men displayed. One weekend when I was on duty, using just black electrician's tape, I put up a sign on the wall in the foreman's office that said, 'think positive'. Things were a bit quiet after that between us, but they did tone it down, and the sign stayed there.

Honiara engine change

The BAC 111s were powered by Rolls Royce 'Spey' engines. Not long after we introduced the aircraft there was an engine failure at Honiara in the Solomons, and this was a logistical nightmare. Firstly, the fault was intermittent, and it took hours of testing on the ground, and communication via the Nadi control tower, to Rolls-Royce in East Kilbride using a combination of HF radio and international phone links to determine that we did indeed have a failed engine. I don't recall the detail, but we must have used a special radio frequency for this – not the usual aircraft frequencies.

To get the engineers, relief engine, spares etc. to Honiara we reached an agreement with the New Zealand Air Force to conduct a 'navigation exercise' using one of their Hercules from Christchurch. The aircraft flew first to Fiji to uplift the spare engine, tools, and extra engineers, then to Vila in the New Hebrides; and there the Hercules broke down! They needed an engine RPM indicator, so we got one onto that evening's Air New Zealand flight out of Auckland. Then Tony Wong located an American who was delivering a Cessna aircraft to Australia and was overnighting in Nadi. Tony found him in the bar at the Mocambo hotel, slipped him some cash and he delivered the spare to Vila on route to Australia the next day. In due course the Herc. arrived in Honiara and we began work.

Fortunately, the 1-11 engine lifting gantry can travel in a relief aircraft and is bolted to the aircraft hull when an engine change is needed, so no problem there. The engine change proceeded quickly

Honiara engine change

enough but we encountered another problem when we came to do the new engine's power runs after the change. We were doing this at the height of a tropical storm and the readings we were getting were strange and difficult to relate to the R-R power charts for full wet power. This 'wet' has nothing to do with the rain; it's a mix of water and methanol injected into the engine to increase the power for take-off. So again, it was a matter of talking to the Rolls-Royce engineers via Nadi HF and telephone relay. I can still recall sitting there with the engine roaring away at full wet power calling out the figures we were seeing and waiting for the response from Scotland as they frantically worked on their slide rules in the middle of the night. Anyway, all was well, and we eventually returned the aircraft to service; albeit this whole exercise took ten days.

Speaking of 1-11 engine changes, on one occasion we did one at Nausori overnight and were doing the full power runs around 3.00 a.m. in the morning. Into the hangar came one of the local rice farmers, wearing his loin cloth *dhoti* and wielding a cane knife. It seems we had disturbed his sleep. Anyone who has heard a Rolls-Royce Spey engine at full wet power would understand. Anyway, we calmed him down, gave him some tea and biscuits, a bowl of yagona, and allowed him to sit in the cockpit as we ran the engine - and off he went happy as Larry. I guess it's difficult to imagine something like that happening these days. A member of the public wandering airside and half naked around an airport, in the middle of the night, armed with a cane-knife – somehow not likely.

Snapshot around 1976

Let's pick up the story in '76. By now Fiji Airways had become Air Pacific in a rather convoluted business deal with a new start-up domestic airline which began with the name Air Pacific and ultimately became Air Fiji. We were operating three HS748s, three Trislanders and two BAC 1-11s. The last of the Herons had gone. My life consisted of regular flying throughout the Pacific as the engineer on board these aircraft and duties as a supervisory inspector in the new hangar that we had built at Nausori for the 1-11s. In the early days of these aircraft the only engineers licensed to certify them were Danny Jorgensen, Gill Gillam (both expats) Abdul Khan and me. One of us had to be with the aircraft at all times. Lots of travel; and I smile to myself when, these days, I hear all the moaning about excessive crew dutytime.

In the intervening period the Civil Aviation Authority of Fiji (CAAF) had moved Air Pacific away from the old engineering licences system to the more modern company approval concept. Under this scheme the company was itself approved by CAAF and now issued its own approvals in lieu of licences. I was the first to be awarded one of these and was given a round rubber stamp to sign any paperwork; somewhat like a signet ring. My approval number was AP 001 which, I guess, is a bit special.

We were living in our Tamavua home, and on the 22nd. of January that year our third son Richard was born just up the road in the Medical School which was part of the Leper and TB hospital buildings! We decided on Richard John as his Christian names (I see it's called 'first names' now) so the proud father rushed on down to the office of

Snapshot around 1976

Births, Deaths, and Marriages in the basement of the old government buildings where, after waiting the usual morning or so, registered him as "Ritchard John". Then went to John and Madeline's place proudly bearing the document. Madeline took one look at the certificate and promptly turned me around and sent me straight back to the registry to correct the spelling. I still think it should be spelt with the "T".

We spent every spare moment, and every spare dollar, improving the house and grounds. The first of several additions to the building had been made and I had learnt a great deal about plumbing, mixing cement, and general building works. One day I was standing up to my bare ankles in mud at the back of the kitchen using a crow bar to break up some cement in order to install a new grease trap when the crowbar hit the main power line into the house. I've had a few 'belts' before and since, but this was a beauty. I was thrown about six feet back and flat on my back. It was probably the mud that saved me because the crowbar was stuck deep, and this would have conducted most of the belt away.

If I had one of the very few free weekends I would go with John on *Camelita* for a day's spear fishing; and sometimes we would go as a family. Our friends had changed somewhat and by then we were very much the married couple with kids. The Hellwigs lived over the road and had children about the same age as our boys. David had started school by now at Suva's International Primary school and James was at a 'school of nine'.

Sketches of Fiji

This was basically a kindergarten run by mothers who, by keeping it under 10 pupils, didn't have to register with the Education Department.

One of the things I did was to build an underground oven *'lovo'* in the backyard. I cheated a bit; it was actually half a 44-gallon drum buried in the ground and with a tin lid. But we did everything else the right way. The families would gather mid-morning bringing their traditional *'sevusevu'* of food and booze to add to the pile. Over a few beers the boys would light the fire (after a while I learnt how to keep it hot and burning in the hole– it took a bit of practice) and when the time was right, carefully place the rocks 'just so' in the hole. The rocks were specially selected from the Tamavua river. Get that wrong and they would explode with great force. The ladies would wrap the food in banana leaves and plait these into coconut fronds gathered by the boys between beers.

Then came the really technical stuff; layering the food in the drum over the hot rocks in the correct sequence and with varying levels of banana and breadfruit leaves. The first layer would be the pork which went on top of a few green coconut sticks so that it didn't actually touch the rocks, then followed the dalo, yams if we had any, chicken, then the *palusami* and *rourou*. On top would go layers of breadfruit and banana leaves jammed hard down so no smoke could be seen escaping. Then the tin lid went on and finally wet sacks over the top. Very civilised. Then we got into the real drinking for about three hours – sometimes with a keg of beer. There would also be a bucket of yagona to help out.

Snapshot around 1976

Knowing when to dig it up was pure judgement, and I claim to have become quite good at that. I was even able to get crackling on the pork. We would eat well by mid- afternoon then continue grazing till quite late at night. We experimented a little beyond the traditional pork, chicken and fish. Turtle meat came out okay but a bit tough and dry, lamb was quite good, but turkey did not work in a lovo. The real secret to lovu food (and the hard work) is in the preparation and the ladies did that extremely well.

Industrial problems

Suva was a small place and it was not uncommon for me to be at a party with Stan Quigg who was then the General Manager of Air Pacific, so I got to know him personally as well as through work. Stan was the last of the Qantas General Managers and took the brunt of the militant industrial action of that time. There was a great deal of criticism of Qantas for its handling of the unions during this period and I tend to agree, albeit not as critically as many, even if Qantas did bring it on themselves in the beginning. The unions had an agenda that was political in nature and it didn't really matter who was managing the company, the problems would still be there.

It came as a great challenge to us (by then I was 'management') to keep the airline flying when strikes occurred. Nothing annoyed the unionists more than seeing those flights depart despite all they tried to do. The scores were about even between us in getting the aircraft away - or not. Over time we developed quite sophisticated techniques and skills to handle these industrial problems. Ernie Dutta managed the rescheduling of passengers and keeping up the contact with them, Tony Wong became a past master at scheduling aircraft changes and crew rosters, and I helped him by providing as much flexibility as possible on the maintenance side.

As we moved towards the mid '70s the Airline Union became even more aggressively militant and there were many strikes. The union leaders knew that because the airline was so critical to Fiji's tourism and economy, they had the perfect tool to apply pressure on management and the Government. In my (not so) humble opinion, their leaders also reveled in the personal media coverage they received.

Industrial problems

On one occasion the union initiated an illegal strike and the Minister for Labour ordered them to return to work. They refused, and so Stan Quigg fired the lot, and delivered their notices by registered mail. From this you might get some idea of the intensity of the animosity that prevailed. The union then went to the Minister with a *tabua* (traditional whale's tooth) seeking his forgiveness and support. The Minister agreed, despite it being an illegal strike, and even though Stan had cleared the action with him in advance. They were also acting in defiance of his own Ministerial Order for them to return to work. He then directed the company to reinstate the workers.

At that time the workers were all gathered outside the hangar on a little playing field under a tree, and under a nearby tarpaulin, drinking yagona. The only people inside the hangar were Ken Cristoffersen, Robert Southey, the engineering manager (by now a Qantas guy called Neil Geddes), his secretary and me. There were about 340 union members outside, and we had closed the doors of the hangar to prevent them entering. They got the message about the Minister's decision first, lifted the union executive on to their shoulders and moved towards the hangar shouting loudly about their success. The emotion was very high. Ken and I stood at the entrance to the hangar and refused to let them in. Courageous or plain stupid, I don't know – it just seemed to be the right thing to do.

The union leader, GP Singh (a classmate of mine at MBHS) got down from the shoulders he was on and confronted me, demanding that I let them in. I said 'no' and stood directly between him and the door. In

Sketches of Fiji

hindsight it was possibly a somewhat dangerous moment, but I was not about to give in. Then Robert Southey came up to us – he had been in the manager's office and Geddes had just received a call from Quigg telling him to reinstate the employees. So, we stood aside and let them in, shouting and yelling as they did so. Many years later when I was CEO of the company Atu Waga, one of the union leaders at the time, and a fellow apprentice from the early days, told me that I had earned respect that day. It was certainly a memorable experience – especially standing toe to toe, eyeball to eyeball with my former classmate!

1-11 delivery and a strange request

In late March of 1978 I was asked to travel to the UK and Germany to do the engineering inspections on a third 1-11 that we were to buy from German Air. I did this during the early part of April, clearing the paperwork first at the BAC headquarters at Herne on the south coast of England, near Bournemouth; and then travelling to Munich to physically inspect the aircraft and spares.

Getting to Germany proved a bit exciting. I had been told by the Fiji Embassy in London that I did not need a visa because I would only be there for a few days. That was wrong. To make matters worse, my arrival into Munich coincided with a major break-out from prison of *Baader-Meinhof* terrorists and the place was alive with troops and police. There I was, white skin, blue eyes, Fijian passport - and no visa. I was interrogated in a small windowless airport room for several hours before finally convincing the heavily armed security officers that they should check with German Air. They did so and, somewhat with bad grace, let me go.

We finally completed the acceptance of the aircraft and flew it from there to Bournemouth to prepare for the delivery flight to Fiji. The pilots, Barry Rankin and Alastair McLean, joined me staying at the Roundhouse Hotel.

That delivery flight was a great deal of fun and nowhere near as basic as the 748 delivery I had done previously. We did however have a little difficulty in Bahrain when we were unable to raise the ventral staircase. We were faced with the possibility of several days in Bahrain (remember this was well before its current modernization), so the pilots

Sketches of Fiji

turned to me and said very firmly 'Drysdale, get it fixed'! No problem, ever resourceful I got eight of the biggest porters I could find, and we simply lifted the staircase into place, then thumped it home with a powerful shove. The latches locked into place and we were off. Once we arrived at Nausori the problem was easy to fix; the main hinge shaft had never been lubricated and was corroded and jammed.

There were the traditional Fijian ceremonies of welcome on arrival and then we went home for a day's rest.

I was back in the office early the following morning to help clear paperwork when I received a phone call from Stan Quigg, asking me to come into the head office in Suva to see him on a personal matter. I did so thinking it would be to do with the difficult marriage break up of two of our mutual friends. It was more than a little different to that; he asked me to resign from Air Pacific and to become the General Manager of Blue Lagoon Cruises, a tourist cruise ship company that he and a friend had just taken control of. There I was in my boss's office, being asked to resign, and go to work for a company that he had an interest in. In fairness he assured me that he had discussed this with the Board of Air Pacific and had their sanction to approach me.

There's a story behind this though. During the previous year I had been asked by the then Commercial Manager, Ross Keenan, who was on secondment from Air New Zealand, to apply for the forthcoming vacant position as Commercial Manager - his contract was coming to an end.

1-11 delivery and a strange request

Ross assured me that my track record in management had been carefully considered by the Board and that I stood a very good chance of being successful, even though I did not have commercial experience. I was then receiving quite good local pay because of my licences and approvals, and to take on this commercial role would have meant a reduction in salary of around $3000. This was an awful lot of money in those days, especially for a young couple with children and a very big mortgage. We talked this over and I went back the following day to tell Ross to put my name forward for the commercial position. The reason for this difficult decision was pretty fundamental; I was fully licensed, so there were no more technical qualifications I could get, my boss, Ken Christoffersen, was relatively young, and I had stopped learning anything professionally meaningful. As it happened there was intense political lobbying by one of the other candidates whom I won't name, and I was not successful.

The Board was of course aware of all of this when Stan approached them about the possibility of his offering me a position outside of the company. As I learnt later, the confidential understanding that Stan reached with the Board was that I would manage Blue Lagoon for Stan and his partner David Wilson for two or three years and then, having gained the commercial experience, would return to Air Pacific, perhaps as General Manager. It took a bit longer than that, but of course it did eventually happen.

It was a tough call. It meant moving from our Tamavua home to Lautoka, taking our kids from the International school and putting them

Sketches of Fiji

into a local school there, and generally making the biggest move of our family life. Nevertheless, we decided to accept the offer as I realized from the recent experience with the commercial position that if I was to move on beyond Air Pacific engineering, I had to make a break. Thus began a completely new phase in our lives, and one that put me very firmly back on the learning curve.

One final thing before I move on. DQ-FBQ, the 1-11 that I had inspected and accepted in Germany in April '78 was scrapped in September '81. An X-ray inspection found serious corrosion in the tailplane. She now lies in the grass behind the hangar at Nausori quietly corroding away with the tailplane being used as a bridge over a little creek.

Sketches of Fiji

BELOW:
Dornier Libelle Forrester Lindslay
left self centre at the engine

Sketches of Fiji

ABOVE:
The Hangar after Bebe

LEFT:
DC3 and HS748 at the Nausori Hangar before hurricane Bebe

BELOW LEFT:
Heron maintenance

Sketches of Fiji

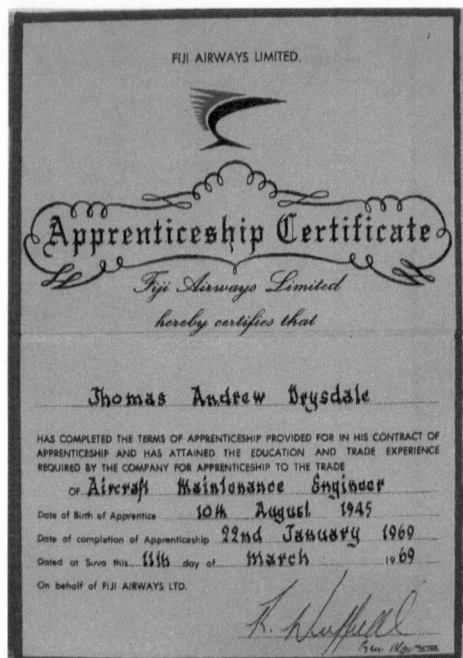

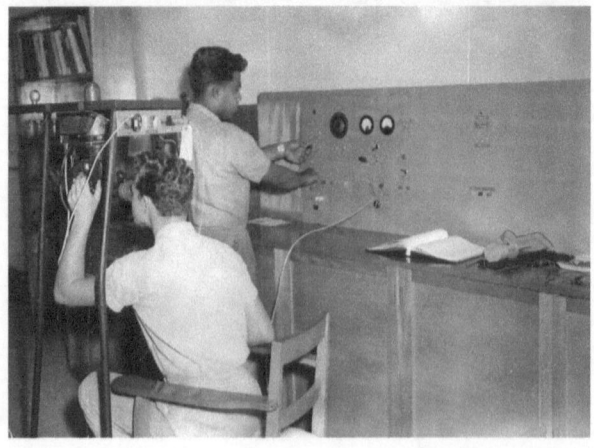

ABOVE:
Apprenticeship completion 'book',

ABOVE RIGHT:
Ken Boehm who got me into aviation,

RIGHT:
Roni Munideo and self calibrating a periscopic sextant

Sketches of Fiji

LEFT:
Apprentice of the year presentation,

BELOW:
HS748 Engine change Funafuti

Sketches of Fiji

ABOVE:
Tamavua Home

RIGHT:
Rolls Royce engine change Honiara

BELOW RIGHT:
Minister for Transport and Civil Aviation Sir Charles Stinson presenting Licence

Sketches of Fiji

LEFT:
Fiji airways aircraft 1967,
HS 748, DH Heron, DC 3

BELOW LEFT:
Air Pacific Crew Honiara

BELOW:
BAC 1-11 Bauerfield Port Vila

Sketches of Fiji

RIGHT:
loading John's speargun.

BELOW:
Suva Levuka launch race
Sereana making up time

Sketches of Fiji

Sketches of Fiji

Blue Lagoon Cruises
1978 - 1986

A new career

Stan Quigg's partner in Blue Lagoon Cruises Ltd. was David Wilson, a New Zealander who had been in Fiji for many years and who was prominent in the tourism business. They had recently purchased controlling interest in Blue Lagoon, the Lautoka-based tourist cruise ship company, from Captain Claude Millar. The company was publicly listed but with many small investors thus giving Claude, and now Stan and David, effective control by way of a large block of shares.

Claude in turn had purchased the company from its founder, another New Zealander, Captain Trevor Withers. The history of Blue Lagoon is in itself a story of pioneering tourism in Fiji, but not one for me to cover here. Suffice to say that Withers was a pilot in the New Zealand Air Force based in Fiji during the War. He was a lawyer, and a colourful, intelligent personality. Like many others, Trevor stayed on after the War, bought a service boat from the Air Force base at Laucala Bay and commenced fishing for sharks. This apparently strange business arose because of a post-war demand for shark liver oil that was considered a valuable tonic. Unfortunately, he couldn't catch enough sharks and the business failed. Interestingly his partner in this was Harold Gatty, the founder of Fiji Airways in its *Katafaga Estate* years, and a man of significant aviation fame.

Trevor was left with the boat and, recognising that he had been catching more game-fish than sharks, decided he would begin taking tourists from Lautoka to the Yasawa Islands on game-fishing trips. He converted his launch *Turaga Levu* to accommodate six to eight passengers, complete with a toilet and shower, and set up in business. A fundamental

Sketches of Fiji

problem was that there were no tourists to speak of! So, Trevor, along with Iris and Harvey Hunt, began promoting Fiji in the US, Australia, and New Zealand. In this they were true pioneers of Fiji's tourism.

After several false starts, Trevor finally got the tourists flowing. In my early Blue Lagoon years I had the pleasure of spending time with Trevor at the Defence Club where he had been living, and he told me many tales of those early years. Fortunately, he wrote a great deal of this down in his log books which I believe his brother still has; and I gathered enough information to write a brief history of the company for our passengers.

Trevor had quite serious ulcers on his legs from coral cuts sustained many years earlier and eventually these became so bad that he had to retire. He sold the company to Claude Miller and in fairness it was Claude who grew the company from a one-vessel fishing operation into the Blue Lagoon Cruises that were so famous in those days. (Sadly, the company is now only a shadow of what it was in the '70s and '80s). By the time Stan and David bought Claude's shares there were four cruise ships and one mixed passenger and cargo ship.

There was also one former World War II *Fairmile* submarine-chasing torpedo boat that Claude had used to build the company post Trevor's *Turaga Levu*. This was now used exclusively for cargo.

I completed the negotiations with Stan and David and found them both fair and responsible in those talks. The reason I make this point is that

A new career

David was a hard- drinking, hard-partying businessman. Many people did not like him because he could be aggressive, particularly with a few drinks on board. He loved to challenge people and was believed by some to be not a nice person. I worked with David very closely for the next eight years and I stand testimony to the fact that behind that brusque, hard-nosed exterior was an intelligent, clever businessman who really did care about his people. He went into a business deal intending to win and to profit. I had no problem with that, and at no time did I ever see David act in an improper manner in his business dealings. To use his own words 'firm but fair'. David was the most brilliant marketing man I ever met. I'll come back to all of this but remember that I went into this job as an aircraft engineer, presumably a good one, but still knowing only aircraft and aircraft engineering. I knew nothing at all about ships, business, finance, marketing or the tourism industry. Boy, was I to learn fast!

I flew to Nadi on the morning of the 15th. of October 1978 and was met by Stan in the company car. Stan had spent the previous night being entertained at the Vatukoula Emperor goldmine by its manager Jeffrey Reid, a renowned drinker, and was very much the worse for the wear. He had kept me waiting for about 15 minutes, which I didn't mind, and his opening remarks when he did get there were 'on the principle of better late than never'. We drove to Lautoka where Stan introduced me to Claude in the Blue Lagoon offices. He spent the day with us and then returned to Air Pacific, leaving me as Blue Lagoon's new Chief Executive. The next day Claude's term with the company finished and, except for collecting his mail, we didn't see him in the offices again.

Sketches of Fiji

On that first day I asked Claude where the records were and he pointed to a small tin box on the floor, similar to a working man's lunchbox. 'They're in there' he said. When I opened it, there were two letters of complaint and an unsigned copy of the contract for the construction of the MV *Marieanda* that had just been delivered from the government shipyard. And that was it; that was my brief.

Claude's executive assistant had been his wife and she left at the same time as he, i.e. the next day. So I latched on to the company's operations manager, Captain Bob Southey, a distant relative of the Robert Southey of my apprenticeship and school days. Bob became a friend and provided wonderful support for me during those early steep learning curve days. He was a big fellow, very straightforward and with a wonderful sense of humour. He was a ship's captain qualified to operate the company vessels and, as I found, the man who really maintained the discipline on the ships. I could not have achieved what we did with Blue Lagoon without Bob's ever-present support.

There were other characters as well, Juanita Williams who headed the commercial side and the reservations department, Claude's niece who managed the finances, and a whole range of really wonderful people. I met all the head office staff personally on that first day and found everyone a little nervous about the new arrangement, it had been very much a family firm, but they showed a great willingness to help.

On day two Bob took me to the workshop down near the wharf. I was

A new career

horrified. I had come from an aircraft engineering background and what I found was Steptoe and Son gone mad. There was junk, broken toilet bowls, bits of engines, smashed up aluminum boats and a kind of carpentry shop that was, at best, a fire risk. Nevertheless, the staff were just as willing to help as those in the head office; down to earth people, who really knew their business, but I suspected were lacking leadership.

And then we went to the ships. If I was horrified at what I found at the workshop, what I saw on the first ship that I walked on board was far worse. Fire extinguishers that were two years out of inspection date, and alarm systems in the engine room that had been disconnected. There were fire boxes with no hoses in them, pipes that had been repaired with Epoxy, and some of those were fuel pipes. I could go on, and on, and on. I went to the Northern Club with Bob that night, the first of many such nights, and we talked for hours over many beers and curry from the canteen.

Claude had always been tight fisted, and I have no problem with that, but in the year leading up to the sale of the company it appeared he had maximised the profits by spending virtually nothing on the ships. His tug-master view of engineering was entirely different to mine. I don't think you could have found two ends of the bookshelf further apart.

Over the rest of that week I took the opportunity whenever a ship was in port to inspect the safety aspects. It seems the marine department surveyors were keener on drinking yagona supplied by us than in checking the ships; albeit they would occasionally emerge, complain about something

Sketches of Fiji

and disappear again. Like any good aircraft engineer I compiled a schedule of safety deficiencies and, having reviewed these with Bob, rang David Wilson and told him I was tying up three of the five ships because they were unsafe. He was naturally very concerned, so I faxed him my lists, and from that moment on he was completely supportive.

We focused on the really serious defects first such as the firefighting gear, and with some smart rescheduling didn't disrupt the passengers very much at all. At the end of that first week I satisfied myself that all the items on my safety deficiency list had been properly remedied and gave permission for the ships to return to normal schedules. In hindsight my aviation ideals were probably a bit over the top for coastal shipping needs but, apart from satisfying myself as to the safety of the ships, I had to set a standard. What pleased me the most was the way all the staff responded so positively to this message.

Blue Lagoon week two and on

At the beginning of the second week I drove into the workshop yard to find a European man loading cases of alcohol into the boot of his car from our stores. Still being a little cautious as to how this company worked I discreetly asked George Ravai, the chief storeman, who he was. It was one of Claude's sons, and George told me that it was normal for the Miller family to help themselves when they needed alcohol, or indeed any supplies. Even though Blue Lagoon was a publicly listed company it was clear that it was still run as if it was a family affair.

I politely introduced myself and invited him to the office for a chat. He did so and, in turn, introduced himself as the Operations Manager for the company. I was a little taken aback but thought, okay, let's see how this goes. I explained to him that the days of staff taking company supplies had to come to an end and that we would run the company from here on as a responsible, publicly listed, organisation. The expression is 'he hit the roof'. He yelled at me that he would do what he damn well liked, and that if I didn't like it I could talk to his father. I told him I had no intention of doing so as Claude no longer had anything to do with the company. He stormed out of the office yelling that I would hear from his father. I thought it sensible to brief Stan and David and I'm pleased that I did, because within half an hour Claude was on the phone to both complaining bitterly about my arrogant attitude etc. etc. etc. They supported my position and suggested that Claude should talk to me.

That happened later in the day and, after a little chat, I found Claude sensible and understanding of the situation.

Sketches of Fiji

That night at the Club the son was very drunk and not happy; I really thought I was going to get thumped. It's possible that this did not happen because Bob Southey was sitting with me as we continued our discussions about the company – and Robert is a very big lad. We dismissed the son the next day.

In week three I decided to clean up the workshop and stores area. I asked all the staff working in that area to come on duty for the weekend and turned up myself in jeans and tee shirt to physically help. We took away truckloads of rubbish, and scrubbed, and cleaned, and tidied, and labelled all through that weekend. I kept them supplied with yagona during the day and we had a few (few?) beers and a Chinese takeaway meal sitting amongst the workshop gear on the Saturday night. This continued during the Sunday despite it being the Sabbath '*Sigatabu*'. By Monday morning we were all very tired, but they were pleased with the results of their efforts. I then called them all together and said that that was round one, next weekend we were going to get serious. Interestingly they continued to work during the week, partly in their own time, and on the Friday invited me to inspect the shop. It was still a marine workshop but by comparison, unbelievably clean and tidy.

There were many tales like this as I dug into the history and operations of the company, but the important thing was that I sent repeated strong messages that things were going to be different. I'm pleased that the staff of Blue Lagoon responded tremendously well to this message.

Blue Lagoon week two and on

While all this was going on I was also trying to come to grips with the finances and commercial aspects of the company. I was an aircraft engineer and my knowledge of business was so bad that I had to ask my wife the difference between an invoice and a statement. Boy did I learn fast. And in this I am tremendously indebted to the Lautoka partner of Coopers Lybrand, Jerry Jeraj.

Coopers, and their senior partner Adam Dixon, had been very close to Claude over many years and Jerry had continued this relationship when Adam moved to Suva. Jerry spent hours with me going over the budgets, the accounts, the capital expenditure; and teaching this new kid as much of his financial trade as he could. We would sit late at night in the office over a bottle of scotch, wandering down the road for a curry and then back to the office. Other nights we sat on the veranda at the club talking and talking and talking. He did not charge Blue Lagoon or me one cent for this work.

And on the commercial side Juanita Williams played the same role. She walked me through the intricacies of the reservation system, which was simply a large, hard-covered notebook, and how the tourism industry worked. She introduced me to the Society of Fiji Travel Agencies (SOFTA) and to the Pacific Asia Travel Association (PATA). This was a completely new world to me of long lunches and dinner parties and what the engineer in me found strange. But that was the way the industry ran in those days. David Wilson was also a tower of strength. He left me to run the company as I saw fit, but

Sketches of Fiji

worked with me, imparting his enormous knowledge of marketing, sales and distribution, and encouraging me to take an active role in the social community of the tourism industry. In particular, he encouraged me to use the marketing power of PATA.

It turned out that Claude was the Chairman of the Western division of the Fiji PATA chapter and I inherited that position. I went to my first meeting in that first week with Juanita by my side because I didn't know what PATA was, or what it did. I met some wonderful people who were universally supportive and provided tremendous encouragement. I found myself not only Chairing the meeting but having responsibility for organizing a promotional roadshow by the Fiji tourism industry throughout the US scheduled to depart in four weeks time. This came as something of a shock as I didn't know what a promotional roadshow was!

Four people stand out: Radike Qereqeretabua, Gray Hanson, Allan Woolly and Lorraine Evans. These four took me under their wing and coached me on the niceties of what lay ahead. Gray died a while back and I wrote to her son Peter to express again my deep-felt thanks for the way she 'mothered' me in those early tourism days. She was also one of those wonderful Yacht Club people who shaped our lives.

And so, the commercial learning curve began.

The magic of Blue Lagoon

Blue Lagoon carried tourists from Lautoka to the Yasawa islands in steel-hulled 135-foot cruise vessels of 20 cabins each. The newest, *Marieanda*, was 22 cabins. The ships had been designed by Claude, based on the hull design of the Hong Kong ferries, and built in the government yards in Suva. They were simple vessels, twin Detroit diesels and twin Yamaha generators. The cabins were air conditioned using a chilled water system, sewerage simply drained into a holding tank and was pumped out whilst cruising - hopefully. There were two passenger cabin decks; cabins for the master, mate and engineer immediately aft of the wheelhouse, and crew's quarters in the bow.

On the top deck was a galley attached to which was a bar, and a large, open, partly covered deck that served as the passengers' entertainment and dining area. The wheelhouse was also simple with Furuno radar and VHF/HF radio, barometer, compass and depth finder – that was it. The crew consisted of the three officers, two cooks, two barmen, one greaser, and several deck hands, some of whom doubled as stewards and waiters. It was an all-male crew. Claude had tried stewardesses once but got fed up with both crew and passengers trying to get into their pants.

There was a magic about a Blue Lagoon cruise that people remembered. Indeed, if you flip through the old visitor's books on board the ships you will see that word appear time and time again. But what was it? It was many things. Let me see if I can describe at least some of them.

Sketches of Fiji

Firstly, it was the Yasawas: 20 or so islands, running Northwest from Nadi, in-part sheltered by the Great Sea Reef that runs across the North of Viti Levu. And 22 traditional Fijian villages. People speak of the pristine waters, white beaches, calm bays, tiny coconut-covered islets and dramatic cliffs of the Pacific; that's the Yasawas. The sand on the furthermost beach on the last island of Yasawa- i- ra is so fine that the Fijians call it *'bogi walu'*, meaning that if you get it into your hair it will take eight nights of washing before you get it out. The water in this bay is so clear that I have seen the anchor hit the bottom, and the swirl of sand - in 60 feet. On one occasion I told the passengers that that was the depth and they simply would not believe me until I took them to the wheelhouse to show them on the depth finder.

Then there was the camaraderie of the ships. Twenty cabins and about 40 passengers crammed together on a ship 130 feet long. They shared the public areas and the magic of being at sea in an idyllic environment. The passengers came together as strangers, bonded, and left knowing they would probably never meet each other again. As a result, there were no airs and graces, no one cared much about your background or how much money you had, or who your great aunt was.

And then there was the crew. I don't need to tell you how wonderful the Fijians are as hosts. There is a joyous larrikin in the Fijian make-up that causes enormous delight for the visitors to Fiji. On board those ships, they showed that larrikinism, their humour, and sense of fun; and they were in their element as Fijians at sea. One example will do:

The magic of Blue Lagoon

we arrived and anchored one day at the island of Nanuya lai lai; the passengers were milling about on the main deck ready to go ashore. Suddenly the cook emerged from the kitchen nearby with a big knife in his hand and ran, yelling at the top of his voice, through the passengers, leapt off the back deck into the sea with a loud scream, and disappeared. The passengers were shocked, probably a little frightened, until they looked over the side, and there was the cook bobbing in the lagoon, laughing his head off and waving to the passengers – with the knife still in his hand. It's a sense of humour that is difficult to describe, but it is incredibly captivating.

I said it didn't matter who you were, and we had lords and ladies and plumbers and undertakers all sharing a common bond of the islands, the ships, passengers and the crew. On one occasion one of our passengers was a lawyer from Los Angeles who regularly featured in the gossip columns as defending film stars, rock stars and sundry politicians when they had been sniffing or taking the wrong stuff; and generally behaving as some of these people do. He boarded wearing Gucci sneakers, tailored linen slacks, silk shirt and with his taxi driver carrying his large YSL bags up the gangway. I saw some of our crew watching this and talking amongst themselves and knew that this guy was in for an experience.

When the ship returned, he disembarked wearing just an old faded sulu and carrying his own bags. He had a smile a mile wide and was very difficult to recognise as the man who boarded just three days earlier. I learnt that after the ship had sailed the crew got him into the crew's quarters,

Sketches of Fiji

stripped him to his underpants, gave him one of their T shirts and a sulu, and commanded that he wore nothing else whilst on board. That they were able to carry this off is indicative of the wonderful personality of the Fijian people. He became a regular passenger with us and would stop off en-route between the US and Australia to take the cruise and unwind from his high- pressure job. We never saw the Gucci shoes again.

And then there were the elderly couple, the Robjohns from Bluff in New Zealand. Bill had managed the oyster processing plant there and had written a book on the subject. By the time I left Blue Lagoon they had done ten cruises and were vowing to continue for as long as their health held out. I visited them in their home at one time and they are what we describe as 'salt of the earth'.

There was another element that we debated time and time again, and that was the length of the cruise. Three days and two nights seem to be the perfect length. It was enough for people to break down the barriers, bond, enjoy the islands, the crew and the environment, and then leave. They left wanting more. Again, reading the visitors books, the most common comment was that 'it should be longer'. My view was that it was better to leave it like that than to have the magic begin to fade. I believed that after three days they would begin to see the cockroaches, the rust, and some may perhaps even tire of the boyish humour of the crew.

We did have a longer seven-day cruise to Labasa but it never really worked. Dan Costello also tried a longer cruise, but it failed. In recent

The magic of Blue Lagoon

years the two competitor cruise companies Blue Lagoon and Captain Cook Cruises, have started an occasional longer voyage to Lau and that seems to be working; but then it's marketed as a special one-off cultural cruise, and Lau is today what the Yasawas were 40 years ago. Also these are now much bigger ships.

And then there was the fact that we took away from the passengers the need to make any decisions at all. The ship sailed at a certain time, anchored at a certain time, and took the route that the captain decided without any input from the passengers. They were delivered their meals, usually a buffet, when we said they would, and had their morning and afternoon tea given to them on the beach - when we said. When the ship moored in a bay the boats were lowered and the crew would yell 'all ashore for a swim', and that they would do. In the evenings they would sit on the back deck and be entertained by the crew whether they liked it or not; and usually they did, their only decision being what it was they wanted to drink. We used tokens rather than cash for the drinks, so they didn't even have to think about money. We took them completely out of their normal environment, even a holiday environment, and let them experience something completely unique. And they loved it.

Yasawa Fijians and business

One of the more interesting parts of the Blue Lagoon job was tiptoeing through the delicacy of business with the villagers in the islands. Trevor had lived amongst the Yasawa Fijians in the village of Yalobi at the Southern end of Waya Island. He had a close relationship with them, and he was there in the very early days of tourism development. Claude had a very pragmatic view, was tough in his business dealings, but respected as a result. I fully expected that my arrival would give rise to a significant amount of 'testing the water' and I was not wrong. Almost from day one there was a stream of people through the office seeking this favour or that. Usually the request was for a free passage to the islands or for the carriage of food or freight. I was very conscious of our responsibility to the community environment we were operating in, but also that we had to run a public company under the principles of good governance.

Bob Southey was of enormous help in providing guidance in those early days and had an innate ability to see through the stories and seek out the truth. The fact that he spoke the Yasawa dialect fluently was a great help. Nevertheless, it became clear that we had to establish rules that everybody understood and would be guided by. This was particularly so for our captains who would often be prevailed upon when in the islands, and it was sometimes difficult under Fijian tradition for them to refuse. We said that we would support needy children, education and health – nothing else, except in exceptional circumstances.

The pilfering of food such as legs of lamb and pork became a particular problem just prior to Christmas, or when a senior chief died. Linen

Yasawa Fijians and business

seemed to disappear, and outboard fuel just seemed to vaporise. I had to continuously remind myself that as most of our crew were from these villages they were under very considerable pressure to give their 'share' to the communal life. Where I did draw the line was when I found that the passengers were complaining of not having enough to eat. Then all hell would break loose and things would be under control for a few more weeks. In the end, whilst we kept strict control on shore, once the ship sailed there was little we could do; so we budgeted this as a cost of doing business in a traditional communal environment.

Another problem was that passengers would become emotionally involved with the villagers during the cruise and on return to their homes would send us large parcels of goods for delivery to the islands. There were several problems with this. Firstly, Fiji Customs would levy duty on the goods, and as they were addressed to us, we were obliged to pay. As these were unsolicited by us, and even by the villagers themselves, we were disinclined to do so. The other was the naivety of the people sending the goods. What does one do with a woolen overcoat in the northern Yasawas? Or a French mathematics textbook? But the one that really got me was a container of religious books produced by one of the more obscure Californian religions who expected us to pay the duty, warehouse and distribute the books on their behalf. In the early days I would write to people explaining the problem and asking them to transfer the funds to cover the duty; which not one of them ever did. After a little while we simply left the items in customs and I have no idea what happened to them. We briefed the captains to respond

Sketches of Fiji

to well- meaning questions from our passengers that the best way they could help would be to send money to either the Fiji Red Cross or the Lautoka Rotary. Some may have done so, I wouldn't know.

What we did do was to pay the villages for the '*meke*' (dance) they performed for the passengers on one night of the cruise. We tried to move these opportunities around to as many villages as possible. Some would get themselves organised and do a really good job, and others simply didn't care. Rather than a fixed fee we paid an amount per passenger. The rationale being, the better the quality of meke and hence the experience given to the passengers, the more the cruise's reputation would be enhanced, and the more we would both benefit. In addition to this we gave preference in recruiting to people from the Yasawas so the wages went into that community; and we purchased fish and vegetables from the islands whenever we could. We also made one-off payments from time to time in special circumstances, particularly following hurricanes, and on one occasion to celebrate our 30th. anniversary. Given that there was very little alternative income for the islands other than selling their produce in the markets, this did represent a considerable source of per capita cash.

The ladies of the villages would sell their handicraft to the tourists and that helped as well. One thing that did bother me though was the arrival of large volumes of imported Filipino tourism junk that some of the villagers began to sell as being their own handiwork. After repeated warnings we simply stopped going into the villages that were selling the stuff. It was the passengers themselves who alerted me

Yasawa Fijians and business

to this problem through the passenger comment cards, letters, even phone calls after their return. We wanted to encourage the development of indigenous Fijian arts and crafts, not the retail of poor-quality imported junk. I know that this was probably being patronising but offer no apology for that decision. After a few months the message got through, and thankfully we again saw the fine mats, fans and handicrafts for which the Yasawas were renowned.

I'll talk about the anniversary in a moment, but for now just comment that the anniversary payment we gave to the villages was calculated based on one dollar per person and amounted to around $22,000. (This included those Yasawa people living on the mainland.) To put this in perspective, remember this was the '70s and the fare at that time for the three days all-inclusive cruise, except for booze, was $110 per passenger.

To arrive at the correct number of people in each village we cross-related the information from the last census and the Fijian equivalent of the doomsday book called the *Vola Ni Kawa Bula*. It was important that we did so, and that everybody knew that this was the case, to avoid controversy. The payment was made village by village, in cash, by me and Rob Southey. We travelled, sometimes as passengers on one of the cruises, but at other times used the MV *Colvile*, the last of the old WWII Fairmiles in our fleet.

In each case the villagers greeted us with formal Fijian ceremonies of welcome. We then showed the headcount calculation to the village elders

Sketches of Fiji

and, after they confirmed the numbers, proceeded to count the money out note by note – in one, five, and ten, dollar bills. All of this was naturally accompanied by many rounds of yagona. We were given in return food, mats, and tabua. Except for the tabua this was then distributed amongst the crew and shore staff of Blue Lagoon. The tabua went into a box of these which we kept for when it was our turn to make a presentation. In all it took us just over ten days to complete these payments.

We took note of what the villagers did with the money. In some cases it was wasted on drinking parties, but in others the money was used for maintenance of the church and meeting hall (these are same thing in some of the villages) or children's schoolbooks, uniforms and maintenance of the school. My observation would be that where there was a strong leader, as was Ratu Tevita from Yasawa-i-ra, the money was well spent. Sometimes though, sadly, it was wasted.

Living in Lautoka

For the first few weeks after my arrival at Blue Lagoon in 1978 I lived in the Cathay Hotel. Three star would be a compliment, but I was too busy to care. In due course it was time for the family to join me and I moved with them to the Saweni Beach Hotel (motel really). We were reasonably comfortable there while we waited for Claude and his wife Lilly to leave the company house at Redhill at the back of the new Lautoka hospital. This was not the hospital that my mother had worked in during the war, but a gift from the British government to Fiji at the time of independence and built next to the original. Jumping ahead a little, it was here that our daughter Jackie was later born.

Now, for the first time in my life I was the proud driver of a company car. It had been used by Claude and therefore was second-hand, nevertheless it was a Datsun Laurel and it had *air conditioning*. My goodness, the hours we spent driving around in that car just to cool off and to experience this new technology like some country bumkins. I think we might have overdosed a bit because on a trip to Suva not long after that the air conditioning compressor failed and had to be replaced.

Social life in Lautoka centred on the Northern Club, or if you were Indian, the Farmers Club. There was a lot less entertaining of guests at home than in Suva, and even a family barbecue would often be held at the Club. In our early Lautoka days we went to the Club quite regularly, but gradually our interest waned, and we began to spend less time there than was the norm. By now I was heavily involved in the tourism industry and regularly attended cocktail parties and social functions in Nadi, often at

Sketches of Fiji

Denarau – a drive of an hour or more each way. That drive to and from was precarious; especially the from bit. I also found myself for the first time on the Fiji version of the 'person to invite' list. This never was, and still isn't, my scene but it went with the job and generally I played my part.

Christmas time was almost unbelievable with a continuous round of cocktail parties. It was not uncommon to attend two or even three functions in one evening and to meet basically the same people on the same circuit. Colonel Paul Manueli, who was then the head of British Petroleum in Fiji, and I had a standing joke that we would start a conversation at one cocktail party, continue it at another, and finish it at a third. Joke it may have been, but it was regularly possible to do this.

Blue Lagoon Cruises and its Operations

At that time in the late '70s Blue lagoon had a very strong brand name throughout the tourism industry and for many visitors it was considered a 'must do' on a Fiji holiday. There is little doubt that the experience was a powerful one for the passengers and with very, very few exceptions they went away enthused about their cruise experience. The very few complaints we received usually related to the weather, or to things that had happened when the weather was rough or wet. The reality however was that the powerful emotional experience of the cruise hid a rather ordinary quality of ships, technical maintenance, and cleanliness. Once we had addressed the fundamental safety issues, we then turned our attention to the overall standards. This meant a major refit and upgrade of the technical and customer aspects of ships over the next 12 months. This in turn was followed over the next two years by an even more in-depth strip down, repaint, and refurbish of all cabins and public areas. I certainly learnt a great deal about ships and their maintenance during this period. But I also began to understand some of the niceties of cabins, the fit-out, décor, and amenities.

But we got some of it wrong of course. The dining tables on the main deck had been finished in that brown 'wood grain' Formica that I'm sure you will remember. Perhaps this was okay when the ships were new, but by the time I arrived the Formica had been rubbed to the point where the surface was simply a brown smudge. One weekend I told Paul Fong and the boys in the engineering department to strip the Formica off the tables on our oldest ship the *Lycianda* and replace it with something brighter. I should have known better and should have told them what

Sketches of Fiji

to use. I was away for the weekend and on the following Monday morning found the ship outfitted with each table a different, and brilliant, colour of Formica. I think Paul had just gone to Morris Hedstroms and got one sheet each of the very brightest colours he could find. Given the tight schedule it was some weeks before we returned the area to something that did not look like a crazy columbine.

The toilet paper in the cabins was that interleaved, glossy, single-sheet-at-a-time, packet held in a rectangular stainless-steel container against the wall. It made the toilet look like a public convenience. Again, I gave instructions to Paul to take these off and replace them with good quality toilet roll holders. This was done, and we were all very pleased with the outcome - until the first cruise took place! By the end of the first day the captain reported by radio that several of the toilets had clogged and there was raw sewage flooding along the floors of the lower deck. And so I learnt the problems of shipboard plumbing, the very shallow 'fall' that exists, and the need to ensure that any bits of paper that go into these toilets are as small as possible. We put the original fittings back again very quickly.

On this rather unsavoury subject, the ship's sewage system was nothing more than a series of holding tanks that were pumped out while the ship was cruising at sea. Except of course when the engineer forgot to do so! There were several occasions when they pumped ship while at anchor in some glorious secluded bay in the Yasawas and that usually caused a couple of letters of complaint. As far as I know they never did it while the

Blue Lagoon Cruises and its Operations

passengers were swimming. One enterprising engineer decided to save himself the trouble of having to remember and fitted fluid level switches in the tank to automatically start the pumps once a certain level was reached - regardless of where the ship was. The letters of complaint alerted me to this little trick and the modification was quickly disconnected.

The villages on the islands were served by a small fleet of 30 to 40-foot cutters which acted as both passenger and cargo ships. These are simple fore-and-aft rigged, single masted sailing vessels. Some had very basic diesel auxiliary engines. They were often poorly maintained, and we would regularly need to tow one of them back to port. This we did with good grace and it added an element of excitement for our passengers. I can imagine the postcards home talking about the wonderful exploits of saving the poor souls adrift at sea. Not long after I arrived however, we noticed a rapid increase in the number of occasions that this occurred. It became very clear that some of the cutters were simply using us for a tow to save fuel or to speed up the journey. This was quite a dilemma; how do you tell a legitimate breakdown from a fake, and how do you exercise judgment on such a basic law of the sea.

It got so bad that our captains asked me to do something about this as it was beginning to seriously affect their cruise schedule and operations. What we did was to run a diary for a few weeks to see if there was a pattern emerging, and sure enough there was. We found the same few cutters being towed on regular occasions; and even if it was a different cutter it was often the same Master. We compiled this into a report and

Sketches of Fiji

gave it to the Marine Department who thankfully acted forcibly; on one occasion by suspending a Master's ticket for a few weeks. The message was clear, and the problem was fixed. Thereafter we only towed three or four cutters to port in a year.

Speaking of the air-conditioning system, there was one event that caused bafflement for some time. Let me start by explaining that one of the biggest problems in designing and building ships is to get enough 'fall' in the water drain pipes. There usually isn't enough fall between the decks. We had one ship, *Salamanda* (Claude named all his ships ending with an 'anda'), that was both a cargo and passenger ship and was used on the six-day cruise to Labasa. On one trip the engineer reported by radio that a cabin on the upper deck had tea leaves coming out of the air conditioner and all over the passengers while they slept at night. This was a bit tough to believe and the captain was summoned to the radio. 'Yes boss,' he confirmed, 'I seen it myself'. Nobody had an answer, so the passengers were moved to another cabin – bet they had a story to tell as well!

Sure enough, when the ship got back to Lautoka there were the tea leaves all over the cabin. Much scratching of the head and rounds of yagona. It was little Paul Fong from the workshop who found the problem while working on another fault. The cook had been complaining of sluggish galley drains for several trips, so Paul blew them through with compressed air, resulting in a cloud of tea leaves emerging in that same cabin. What happened was that the tea leaves backed up in the blocked drain pipes during the day, from there they floated into the air conditioning conden-

Blue Lagoon Cruises and its Operations

sate pipes, backing up there to flow onto the condensate tray under the fan-coil unit in that cabin, which was closest to the galley. Then overnight the drains would drain, the tea leaves would dry, and voila – misty clouds of tea leaves gently wafting all over our sleeping guests. Shangri – la.

That six-day cruise to Labasa was a problem. Claude had designed the ship as part-passenger and part-cargo, so neither the one, nor the other. The trip around the North coast of Viti Levu from Lautoka to RakiRaki was pleasant but with not a lot to see; the crossing to the Southern end of Vanua Levu was often very rough as the ship was beam-on to the big swells coming through the Koro sea. Not pleasant for the customers. Once there though, the cruise up the Bua coast was spectacular.

Beautiful clear water, lovely islands, brilliant reefs and an incredible mountain range behind the coastline. But if it was anything lower than half tide when we got to the mouth of the Labasa river we had to wait till the tide rose in order to cross the sandbar. Boring. The passengers found the trip up the river through the winding, narrow, mangrove-covered banks interesting; but then Labasa was boring again while they waited for us to unload the cargo and take on the Southbound load. We tried many different ideas to fill in the time, but none really worked.

Then the river silted up even more and we had to find some other way to deliver the cargo. What we did was to position our World War II Fairmile *Colville* at the island of Galoa near the Southwest corner of Vanua Levu and transship the cargo to her from the *Salamanda*.

Sketches of Fiji

Colville would take the cargo to Labasa and return the next day with the Southbound load. All well and good, but what to do with the passengers while all this was going on. There is a truly beautiful little uninhabited island near Galoa called Naniqaniqa, and we paid the Galoa villagers to build us a traditional *bure* there.

The schedule called for us to be there on a Sunday so the Galoa people would come over and celebrate '*Lotu*' with our passengers in the bure. Whether they were religious or not, the passengers were 'blown away' as they say these days by the solemn ceremony, prayer and beauty of the Fijian choral singing, in a thatched bure, on a beach, in a most remote part of Fiji. I was there the first time we did this, and I freely admit it brought goosebumps to my skin as well.

The villagers were building a new church at the time and one of our passengers became so emotionally involved with this that she paid for a large stained-glass window to be made and shipped to the island. We were asked to take it from Lautoka to Galoa and I readily agreed to do so. In the end though the six-day cruise just didn't work commercially, and we converted *Salamanda* to an all-passenger ship to join our others on the three-day cruises to the Yasawas.

Crew discipline

We had three strict rules of discipline for the crew – no alcohol, no sex with the passengers (regardless of who initiated the contact; and there were several instances where a passenger, of either sex, did so) and no love-bites showing when on duty. Bob Southey enforced these rules rigidly; the captains and ships officers looked after the more mundane rules and regulations. I first came across these 'Southey' rules one morning shortly after my arrival. Bob and I were seeing one of the ships off when a crew member walked past us on the wharf. Bob grabbed him by the scruff of the uniformed neck, lifted him bodily off the ground and yelled in a loud voice 'love-bites – you're fired', then dropped him to the ground; all in full view and hearing of the passengers, and a very surprised new CEO. Still, I learnt.

Our crew were divided into two parts: the technical crew under the command of the bosun, and the passenger services crew under the command of the first officer who was the senior of the two; both of course reporting to the captain. The ships officers were required to have licences, and the seamen had certificates of competency issued by the marine department. This was not normally a problem as the Fijians are wonderful seaman, born to the water, and the theory part of the exam was not intense. By and large our crew were professional, if at times mischievous. Some were extremely reliable, and others would come to work for a few weeks, make some money, and disappear; only to appear standing at the wharf one day, bags in hand, looking for a job when the money ran out. Bob Southey and George Ravai managed the hiring and firing of the staff and personally knew the large pool that was available in the Lautoka area. It was not uncommon

Sketches of Fiji

to see Bob or George leap into their cars and drive off into the back blocks of Lautoka to almost press-gang somebody into taking up a missing seaman's slot for that day's sailing. They were invariably successful in doing so, albeit sometimes the recruit would be looking a little worse for the wear, on more occasions than one having just been released from an overnight stay in the Lautoka police headquarters.

As I found later in Air Pacific as well, there is a keen balance between ensuring discipline, technical competence, and high standards of safety on the one hand, and the need to allow that gregarious humour and sense of fun amongst the Fijians that is so loved by the visitors. I think we managed it quite well, and the success in doing this went a long way to making a Blue Lagoon Cruise the marvelous experience that they undoubtedly were.

But it wasn't all plain sailing so to speak. We had our fair share of crooks and villains who had to be dealt with by the ship's officers or Bob Southey. Sometimes the justice got a little rough, but never in my judgment unfair. On one occasion we had a series of thefts of cash from the cabins on the six-day cruise MV *Salamanda*. Always just a few dollars, never big enough to warrant major investigation and, as we found later, often of such small amounts that the passengers didn't even notice.

Rather clever actually; $5 to $20 from each cabin on each trip adds up to a lot of money for a Fijian seaman. But we began to get rumours and eventually the thief got greedier then greedier. We tried everything; interviewing the staff individually and collectively, calling in

Crew discipline

the local security company to conduct the interviews more professionally, and calling in the police who were powerless because there had been no actual complaint. On one occasion we even resorted to laying traps where we deliberately left five dollar notes that had been dusted with a special forensic dust invisible except under black light.

Nothing worked, and the thefts continued. So in desperation at the end of one trip, where a number of passengers had reported the possibility of theft to the captain, I lined up the entire crew on the aft of the ship and said to them 'Guys there's only thirteen of you, you all live together on board, have been doing so for months, and you must know who the thief is. So, you are all under suspicion, and unless we find out who is doing this, we will be forced to suspend every one of you. I'll make that decision at the end of the next trip.' During the course of the next cruise the captain radioed back to base to say that one crew member had had an unfortunate accident when he fell down the access ladder to the crew's quarters and sustained a number of injuries to his face and body; as a result, he had been discharged at Labasa and would not be re-joining the ship. I asked no further questions, and the thefts stopped.

Bob Southey was a master at sizing up new recruits and the interview process usually lasted less than a minute. His word was law, and nobody ever disputed their success or otherwise in getting a job. When I spoke to him about this on one occasion he just laughed and said he'd learnt from the super-master Claude Miller. His story was that Claude would look the prospective recruit up and down, check that he had a

Sketches of Fiji

certificate of competency, and ask whether he could either sing or play a guitar. If the answer was in the affirmative, he got the job. True or not, somehow it has a ring of truth in my Blue Lagoon experience.

Sadly, Bob died in Lautoka hospital of a stroke on 11th. April 2018 – just as I was reviewing these notes *and* at this point in the notes. He is missed. He was a good friend and mentor.

Blue Lagoon's 30th Anniversary

Not long after I began work at Blue Lagoon, some simple calculations showed that we were about to celebrate our 30th. anniversary and it was decided to make this a big event. So in June of 1980 we set aside one cruise on our newest ship the *Marieanda*, and invited a whole swathe of dignitaries, including the Governor General, Ratu Sir George Cakobau and his charming wife Adi Lela. About half of the guests were the chiefs from the Yasawas and the relationship between them and Ratu George as the *Vunivalu* of Bau, and hence one of the paramount chiefs of Fiji, was extremely interesting to observe. This was more so because Ratu George had spent many years as a young District Officer serving in the Yasawas. We were fortunate that Trevor was still well enough to travel and became the chief guest for the cruise along with Ratu George.

At every stop there were Fijian ceremonies of welcome, and with Ratu George on board these were lengthy and formal. Over the three days we drank enormous amounts of yagona, several kegs of beer, many bottles of Johnnie Walker Black Label, and cases of 'bubbly' and red wine.

We had the official party on the second night and there were lengthy speeches both in Fijian and English by a range of chiefs, David Wilson and Trevor. Then we bought out a huge cake that had been baked for us by the chefs at the Regent Hotel at the request of our cabin services manager, Alfred Powell. It was about four-foot square and the top had been iced with a very fine and detailed picture of a Blue Lagoon ship at anchor in a bay in the Yasawas. Eventually it came time to cut the cake. By this time Trevor was more than a little emotional,

Sketches of Fiji

understandably I guess, and aided by his friend from the Yasawas he stepped forward to cut the cake through the icing. But oh dear, such embarrassment, he wasn't able to do so. His friend held his hand to help, but even he couldn't pierce the icing. It was then we discovered that the icing had been done on a sheet of plywood which in turn had been laid over the cake. Laughs all round, the icing was lifted gently off the cake and Trevor proceeded to do the honours. On the return to Lautoka he proudly carted away his iced sheet of ply.

All of this sounds like great fun, and it was, but behind the scenes the logistics were extraordinarily complex as we dealt with both Fijian and Western protocol, even to details such as the respective sizes of the tabua to be used at the different villages. I was on edge throughout the cruise watching every detail and particularly anxious that we did not offend by inadvertently breaching protocol related to the *Vunivalu*. The fact that everything went smoothly, Trevor's icing notwithstanding, was a great tribute to all the people of Blue Lagoon and in particular Bob Southey, Alfred Powell who managed the catering, George Ravai in the stores and Juanita Williams.

Drysdale the salesman

Now, it's one thing to grow up enjoying things mechanical, go on to complete a five-year apprenticeship, another ten years of fixing aircraft, and then get into the business of managing the technical and engineering operations of a cruise ship company; but it's a whole new world to transition to a tourism wallah and a salesman selling the product.

However, that's what the job required. In the early Blue Lagoon days David Wilson was extremely supportive of my playing this role and he became something of a guru to me as I learnt the ropes. I've said before, David was without a doubt *the* best marketing man I have ever met. I was indeed fortunate to serve my marketing and commercial apprenticeship under a man as accomplished as this. Like me he had no formal training in sales and marketing but truly understood his customer and what it was that turned people on; what 'pic' would catch a potential customer's eye in a brochure, and what sales pitch would work. He was a past master of the glossy brochure blurb and after a while let me have a crack at it - and was gracious enough not to make too many changes.

The other thing I learned about was 'public relations', or PR as it's known these days. Blue Lagoon was a public company and very high profile in Fiji's tourism industry so it was necessary to ensure our reputation was viewed positively within the community. This meant press releases and interviews to tell the public what we were doing, and to present our views to the media. Stories on new ships, the impact of hurricanes, any upgrade of the fleet, the anniversary cruise, all

Sketches of Fiji

played a part in presenting this publicly listed company in good light. It was, yet again, a whole new world to this engineer.

I was fortunate to have a friend, George Rubine, who was in that business and who became my PR mentor. He was an outgoing, colourful character, and a former American Peace Corp volunteer who had stayed on in Fiji after his posting was over. George's ready advice was invaluable as I made the transition to be a commercial wallah. That apprenticeship also served me well in later years with Air Pacific when we, and I, were so constantly in the news.

Being thrown in at the deep end of the tourism pond was a memorable experience. I mentioned earlier that in the first week at Blue Lagoon I found myself not only Chairman of the Western Division of the local PATA chapter, but that I was about to lead a Fiji Tourism group on a roadshow throughout the West Coast of the USA. Given that I didn't even know what a roadshow was, I talked this through with David who just laughed and said go and do it. With the wonderful help of my new tourism colleagues I did so. They probably raised the odd eyebrow at the level of minutiae and documentation that I drew up to cover the detail of the itinerary and contingency plans, not something the tourism guys normally do, but they were good hearted and probably carried me along a lot more than was obvious at the time.

We toured all the main West Coast cities using the PATA local chapter's monthly meetings as our venues for promotional sales pitches. These

Drysdale the salesman

roadshows are a high-intensity, fast-moving series of breakfasts, lunches, cocktail parties and dinners. Air and ground travel are kept as tight as possible and there really wasn't much time for sleep. I loved every minute of it. David was travelling with us representing his company Tapa Tours and it was rather strange for me, knowing almost nothing about what was going on, to be leading a group that included my brand-new boss who was a master at this stuff. Nevertheless, it worked, and the team was complimentary in the de-brief at the end of the trip. I suspect that David was watching my sales performance as well, and I must have done okay because thereafter he was perfectly happy for me to do the PR work for the company.

I also learnt about negotiating rates with the wholesalers, arguing with them over the Blue Lagoon page in their brochure, selecting, and at time taking, the 'pics' to be used in the 'glossies'. And gradually (thinking about that - probably not so gradually) I learnt the commercial side of the travel and tourism industry.

A great deal of this work entailed public speaking at breakfasts, lunches, cocktail parties and dinners, in halls and in conference rooms. I guess my Marist Brothers debating sessions, time in front of a blackboard, and at trade union rallies proved a good training ground because I have always been comfortable in front of an audience, albeit always just a little tense inside. Indeed, I've said many times, and now I tell my students, that unless you go into a speech with a few butterflies fluttering around, you will be flat in your presentation. It's probable also that my trade union experience gave me an inherent

Sketches of Fiji

understanding of negotiations and this became valuable in reaching commercial agreements with the various suppliers.

Thinking about all of this, I've just realized that at no time did I have any formal training in commercial matters or negotiations. The reality of it is that you learn very fast when you are thrust into a position of having to make decisions, and judgements, and arguing your case. In any case it all seemed to work, and we were able to push Blue Lagoon's product, image (and the rates we charged) higher every year. Indeed, profits trebled in three years.

In addition to being the Chairman of the local PATA chapter I also found myself on the committee of a thing called the Society of Fiji Travel Agencies (SOFTA) and this was extremely valuable in quickly teaching me the intricacies of the travel agency world. Again, the SOFTA committee members were outstanding in their support and advice and guidance. Because I was coming from the outside, I would sometimes put forward views that differed from the norm or questioned 'how we've always done it', and that sometimes got me into controversy. What was interesting though was that over the months SOFTA gradually moved from a focus on internal debate to taking a stronger leadership role in Fiji's tourism industry. Now I don't for one-minute claim to be the reason for this, but I do believe that throwing open the discussions to new ideas did help. In hindsight, those years in the commercial arena, and working through organisations such as PATA and SOFTA, gave me a good insight into the travel and tourism industry that served me well in the later Air Pacific and IATA times.

Of ships and hurricanes

I spoke earlier of our experiences during hurricanes and obviously this was a major problem for us running a tourist cruise ship company, particularly on the Northwestern side of the main island. Hurricanes generally spawned Northwest of Fiji and typically swept Southeast. This put the Yasawas and the Northwestern side of Viti Levu at most risk. Our procedure once a hurricane seemed imminent was, as far as possible, to bring the ships home and to put them up the Drasa river. This was the same principle we applied at the Suva Yacht Club.

The ships were tied with multiple ropes to the mangroves and anchors put out, although the very soft mangrove river mud made anchors of limited use. The ships would be manned by a small 'sea watch' who volunteered for the duty. The rest of the crew would go home.

Like the Vesari river in Suva there was a sandbar at the mouth of the Drasa river and the timing to get the ships back to Lautoka and across the sand bar at high tide was critical. Once the tide was below three quarters it was not possible to shelter the ships in the river and we had to anchor them as best we could around Lautoka harbour. After the blow was over it was usually just a matter of waiting for the next high tide before returning the ship to the wharf for the inevitable scrubbing and cleaning to remove the leaves and rubbish that accumulates.

I mentioned leaving a sea watch on board. We never had any difficulty in getting volunteers for this purpose. Indeed, I was extremely impressed on the first occasion I saw this and made comment to Bob

Sketches of Fiji

Southey. He just laughed and said, 'they're after the *Kukas*'. Now nature is a wonderful thing; immediately after a hurricane has passed, the mangrove swamps in that part of Fiji come alive with millions upon millions of small, very tasty, crabs. These are difficult to find otherwise, and one could argue that it is nature's way of providing food to people following the devastation of a hurricane. Whatever the case, the main excitement for our crew was gathering bucket-loads of these crabs as the blow subsided; laughing and yelling as they leapt into the mud of the river to do so. Ah, that Fijian sense of humour.

The final decision on returning to Lautoka or remaining at a secure anchorage in the Yasawas lay with the captains. They took their decision based on their location in the Yasawas, and the forecast position, speed and direction of the hurricane. Whilst it didn't happen often, sometimes their considered and professional decision was to ride the hurricane out in a sheltered bay in the islands. They were a remarkable set of men. Sometimes we had difficulties with them in the administration of their ships, and with the paperwork, but when it came to seamanship they were outstanding. They were all well-seasoned to hurricanes and I would listen to Bob Southey talking to them on the radio as they considered their position and took their decisions. This was always calm, methodical and sensible. It's important to remember that in addition to their ships and crew, they were responsible for up to 40 foreign tourists, many of whom would be terrified at the thought of being on board a small ship surrounded by reefs in an isolated part of Fiji during a hurricane. Not to mention their families and friends overseas! Yet nev-

Of ships and hurricanes

er at any time did I receive a complaint from passengers who had been forced to ride out a storm in the Yasawas. Quite the reverse, there were letters, phone calls and even people visiting the office to compliment and congratulate these captains and the crew afterwards.

There were of course, all the preparations onshore as well. Securing our buildings, getting standby power available to protect the freezers in the event of power failure, and generally battening down. Once all was in readiness, we would leave a sea watch on board the ships and in the workshops and the rest of us then turned our attention to securing our homes. This was always a joint effort with staff from the company helping each of our employees as best we could given the, by now, short time that was left. The loyalty of our staff in preparing the company's ships and buildings before their own homes was remarkable.

Over the years the damage to our ships was minimal and being able to say this pays an extraordinary compliment to the professionalism, skill, and dedication of our captains, crew and staff. But there was one occasion when we were badly caught out. There was no formal Marine Board inquiry after the event, but I believe that in the lead up to hurricane Oscar we were given very bad advice by the Meteorological office. I say this having personally conducted our own internal inquiry afterwards. So, what happened?

In March of 1983 a very powerful hurricane named Oscar moved Southeast towards Fiji. The Yasawas were in its direct path however,

Sketches of Fiji

as is typical, its track was erratic and its speed variable. Nevertheless, our captains took the appropriate precautions and returned to Lautoka to discharge their passengers. Unfortunately, their arrival coincided with low tide. This had been considered and, based on the Met. forecasts, the captains and Bob Southey believed there was time for the tide to rise and for the ships to be taken to safety in the river before the hurricane arrived. As it turned out this was not the case. The hurricane was 'on us' much earlier than the forecast time.

A decision was made to secure three of the ships at the wharf. Our newest ship, *Marieanda* was secured to the more sheltered Eastern face with large tractor tyres acting as shock absorbers, adding to the existing wharf fenders. *Salamanda* was moored to the North face and *Oleanda* on the exposed Western face. *Lycianda* had been on a maintenance day and was already up the river, and *Taleanda* was given extra anchors to ride out the storm in the lee of Bekana Island in Lautoka harbour.

I believe Bob and his team took the right decision at the time based on the information available to them and their professional knowledge of both seamanship and the effects of hurricanes in the area. Nevertheless, Oscar proved to be a more powerful hurricane than was expected and the results were devastating, not only for Blue Lagoon, but for Fiji in general.

The net effect when it was over was that we had both *Marieanda* and *Salamanda* badly damaged, and *Oleanda* sunk at the wharf. The wharf itself had also sustained significant damage. *Taleanda* had ridden the storm out

Of ships and hurricanes

well, albeit through a frightening day of being dragged across the harbour in several directions. *Lycianda* needed cleaning but was fine to operate. Thus, out of a fleet of five ships we had only two operational. Thank goodness no-one was hurt. We were not alone with these problems; Fiji's tourism infrastructure had been devastated. Virtually all the offshore Island resorts were seriously damaged as were many of the coastal resorts.

It was somewhat ironic that the owners and CEOs of many of those properties were with me on a promotional tour of New Zealand at the time. Air Pacific scheduled a special flight to bring us, and emergency relief supplies, back to Fiji immediately Nadi Airport was open. Warren Seymour was the captain and flew us very low over the Yasawas, Mamanucas and the Southwestern coast of Viti Levu to enable us to view the damage from the air before landing. I have seen many hurricanes and the damage that they cause, but I have never seen anything as bad as this. Dan Costello looked down on his famous Beachcomber Island resort to see that it had become mostly just a sandbar, I looked down on the damaged ships and the shadow of the *Oleanda* lying sunk at the wharf. It was an extraordinary emotional moment, with many on board near to tears. But emotion doesn't fix the problems. Max Stork who was the CEO of United Touring Company had arranged cars for us to be taken quickly to our respective headquarters. Then the rebuilding began.

Raising Oleanda

George Ravai and Juanita Williams took charge of getting the cruises operating again using the two ships we had. Remarkably we sailed the next day with very nearly a full contingent of passengers. One of the things you learn about hurricanes is that they are usually followed by a period of clear skies and calm weather and this was the case post Oscar. Bob Southey and I concentrated on the damaged ships and the sunken *Oleanda*. I learnt a great deal about the insurance industry in those next few days and learned how valuable it was to have a competent broker to assist. We were required to act as if we were uninsured and we certainly did everything we could to fulfil that caveat.

First, we carried out temporary repairs to *Marieanda* and *Salamanda* and sent them quickly to Industrial and Marine Engineers (IMEL) shipyard in Suva. The government yard was out of the question as they were fully engaged repairing the Marine Dept. fleet. IMEL worked around the clock, pulling in resources and skills from wherever they could, and we supported this by scheduling our own engineers and crews to assist wherever possible. Remarkably *Marieanda* was back in service within a week and *Salamanda* shortly thereafter. Indeed, we even took the opportunity to do a little modification here and there that we had been planning in any case.

Oleanda of course was another story. First, we had to move her from where she was alongside the wharf, but at the same time we wanted to minimize any additional damage in the hope that she could be repaired and returned to service. Together with our Insurance company and bro-

Raising Oleanda

ker I negotiated a deal with Ian Hoskisson's salvage company, Marine Pacific, on the basis that they would be paid nothing if they could not raise her, and a substantial bonus if they did raise her without causing additional damage. In particular she had to be raised vertically in order to prevent the hull twisting. If that had happened, she was finished.

Fortunately, if you can use that word in these circumstances, she had sunk straight to the bottom in the vertical position and not on her side. One of the problems we faced was that the bottom of Lautoka harbour was a thick muck of soft 'mill mud', the effluent from the nearby sugar mill. We knew that raising her vertically meant that somehow, we would have to break the suction of this mud to the hull. The salvage was led by Ian, but most of the work was done by Charles Saint-Julian. Charles had been an apprentice at Fiji Airways, and a spearfishing companion, but had left to take up professional diving. I knew him well and respected his highly professional attention to detail.

Charles and his team explored every inch of the *Oleanda*, taking photographs and measurements before they began any real work. They imported what can best be described as miniature parachutes which were attached to brackets which in turn were secured to the hull with bolts. Each bracket had four 3/16th bolts; so all along the hull at roughly four-foot intervals Charles and his team drilled and tapped the holes to take these bolts. I never worked out how many they did, but for a ship of 132 feet in length that's an awful lot of holes to be tapped; and under water in a constant cloud of thick silt, it was not a nice place to be.

Sketches of Fiji

Nevertheless, eventually it was completed, and they began to pump air into the underside of these parachutes. This was done extremely carefully and slowly until there was an equal lifting momentum on either side of the ship. Then in turn they would apply a little more air, firstly on the port and then the starboard sets of parachutes. This caused the ship to rock almost imperceptibly at first but gradually this movement increased. Then they began to blast compressed air into the ship's fuel, sullage, and water tanks; again, carefully building a lifting pressure. If this was done too quickly, or without their highly specialist skill, the danger was that she would pop to the surface and turn turtle once the suction to the mud was broken. And it would be very dangerous for the divers. But she didn't, and Charles and his team finally got her to ease away from the bottom and to rise slowly. Even so, once the momentum had started there was a sudden and nerve-wracking moment when she broke through the surface of the water.

We didn't know, and couldn't hope to tell, what would happen next. I'm looking now at the photograph I took on the evening of Friday, the 8th. of April 1983 shortly after she settled. It's a terrible photograph with the light in the wrong place (remember she was on the Western face and this was just at sunset) but you only get one moment for such a photograph.

Once she had settled, Charles and his team began the work to stabilise her. They worked overnight and finally left her in the care of a watchman just before dawn to get a few hours of sleep. About 7.00am the watchman called me and said, 'Boss you better come down, there's a

Raising Oleanda

problem with the crew on *Oleanda*'. Crew? What crew? I pulled on some clothes and drove quickly to the wharf. There were crewmembers rummaging around the ship to collect their personal effects from under the mud in the crew's quarters. And to collect the crabs that had moved in while she was on the bottom! I didn't know whether to laugh or scream at them to get off. In the end I laughed and yelled at them and they came off laughing with me. Ah – that sense of humour again!

Marine Pacific cleaned her up as best they could, removed the parachutes and towed her to Suva where she went into the IMEL yard. This was a complete strip to the bare hull and rebuild from scratch. The result was that Blue Lagoon had essentially a new ship for its fleet. That's easy to say, but it was a long and arduous task, not the least of which was filling in the multitude of 3/16th. holes in her hull. When last I saw her in 2004 she still looked good and was doing sterling service for the company.

Back to Suva

We had been in Lautoka just over two years and began to worry about the kid's education. It was fine in those earlier years, but we could see that it would become more difficult as they grew older. At the same time David Wilson had been experiencing problems trying to find a suitable manager to run his tour wholesaling company, Tapa Tours, from the Suva office. A couple of expat managers had failed rather badly, and he was keen to move to Australia and to expand the company. The upshot was that we recruited Bob Dodds to take my place in Lautoka. I became General Manager of David's restructured company now named The Travel Company and we moved back to Suva.

Bob was a local whose family went back to the very early days of European settlement in Fiji. He had spent his life in the Civil Service rising to the position of Permanent Secretary for Transport and Civil Aviation. I remained on the Board of Blue Lagoon and oversaw the operations through a management contract. It was a little complex, but Bob and I worked well together, and the arrangement continued successfully for several years.

The Travel Company included Tapa Tours which brought groups of tourists to Fiji, represented American Express and Pan Am (remember them), owned a travel agency, ran a tourism ground transportation company and, for a short while, a butcher shop. Yes, that's right – a butcher shop. We were paying very large sums of money for meat for Blue Lagoon and an opportunity came up to buy a Suva company that catered primarily to the expat community and to the hotels. We did so; these days it

Back to Suva

would be called vertical integration. It didn't last long as we couldn't stop the thieving, so we sold it to the manager whom we suspected of being the main culprit, and he went bankrupt in a few months.

The family moved back to our Tamavua home with great relief. Then it was back into the rounds of Suva's cocktail parties and friends, by now though very rarely at the Yacht Club. We were married with a mortgage and children, and that changes one's perspective on the world. Socialising, when it wasn't for business, was usually at our home, or the homes of our friends.

Nevertheless, the social whirl of the business, government, embassies and aid agencies cocktail parties and dinners was intense. It also became yet another period of learning for Drysdale. This time I learnt about travel agencies, tour wholesalers, airline representation, ground transportation and the organisation lying behind the tourism and travel industries. Again, David Wilson was my mentor; some of the lessons were tough, but then it was a tough, competitive business.

The kids went to school at Suva's International School. I had been involved on the edges of the organisation of this school before we went to Lautoka and David was Chairman of the Board of Governors. I soon found myself appointed to the BOG, as it was strangely named, and in due course to the exalted position of Chairman.

This was one of the most difficult and frustrating roles I have ever had to play. It was difficult for me as a businessman to understand the teachers

Sketches of Fiji

and their work ethic. I became angry at the undeclared public holidays which they euphemistically called 'teacher only' days, their complaints of long hours when I was working till 7.00 p.m. or later most nights, and the continual negative carping. Having said that, there were some extraordinarily dedicated and competent teachers. Gillian Pattie who started the school and was first headmistress, and Wayne O'Conner who eventually headed the primary school, were exceptional people. Overall the quality of education at the school was good. Indeed, when our kids eventually moved to Australian schools they did well.

The other side of the coin was the continual complaints by parents. Everyone seemed to believe that their Johnny or Mary was the brightest student in the world and when the exam results did not demonstrate this they inevitably blamed, firstly the teachers, and secondly the school itself. Over the years that I was Chairman I gradually came to grips with the academic side of the school, but not the parents. Sometimes I found myself becoming quite terse. On one occasion the French Ambassador wrote to me to complain, on Embassy letterhead, about the quality of the French lessons at the school. 'Your French teacher can't even speak French,' he cried. Admittedly the lady who was providing this service was not particularly skilled; she was however the best available to us in the small Suva community. My reply to the Ambassador was a rather short letter which simply said, 'We are using the best resources available to us, however if the Embassy could provide either a French teacher, or funds for us to recruit the aforesaid from overseas, then that would be most appreciated'. Never heard anything more.

Back to Suva

Hopefully my time on the Board of the school did some good. At least we left the legacy of a brand new two- story high school block, and the acquisition of adjacent land for a future sports field for the school. I also donated a trophy to be used for the annual 'Dux of the school' prize.

So, on the one hand life went on with me working as General Manager of The Travel Company, keeping a watch over Blue Lagoon Cruises, doing the marketing for Blue Lagoon on overseas promotional tours, and our family growing up around us. Eventually Jackie joined the boys at the International School and formed friendships with some of the girls in her class that have lasted into her adult years.

The other thing that happened was that I built three ships for Blue Lagoon Cruises; and that warrants another tale.

Of building ships

During my Sea Scouts days I had repaired our 18-foot, clinker-built, whaling boat the *Sea Eagle*. Then during the Yacht Club years I'd mucked around in boats in any spare time that could be squeezed from a very busy life. Blue Lagoon had taught me about ships maintenance, repair and operations, but I had absolutely no idea about how one actually built a ship. The Blue Lagoon fleet at the time comprised five ships built by Claude Millar in the government's Suva shipyards. He built them cheaply and from inferior grade steel. There was little internal protection of the steel, and the welding contained high levels of impurities; so rust, both superficial and structural was a problem.

The oldest ship was MV *Lycianda* and at eleven years of age was already showing serious structural corrosion in the water and sullage tanks. Access to these was almost impossible and so her days were numbered. One day in 1981 Bob Southey and I were standing at the wharf in Lautoka when she came in a little fast and hard against the wharf. As we watched she actually twisted quite significantly before settling back against the wharf. 'That's it, she's buggered,' declared Southey. So David and I sat with Adam Dixon and Jerry Jeraj to draw up a financial strategy to begin replacing the vessels.

We also started looking for a second-hand ship because the need was becoming quite urgent. The job of doing this fell, for the most part, to me. Initially I reviewed shipyards around the world that specialized in ships of the 130 to 150-foot size. Then I travelled to

Of building ships

the US and Holland talking to shipyards and looking at vessels that might be possible as second-hand acquisitions. These ranged from a yard just south of Amsterdam that built multimillion-dollar private yachts for people like Malcolm Forbes (a little out of our field) to a second- hand ship cruising in Glacier Bay in Alaska. This latter came quite close but was designed for an entirely different climate and would have been too expensive to convert. Call it serendipitous, but in 2017 I went on a cruise from Juneau to Glacier bay – yup, by absolute chance it was on that same ship.

Gradually we came to realise that the best opportunity lay in building our ships in the government yards in Suva, or in Industrial, Mechanical and Electrical Ltd. (IMEL) as the old Millers shipyard was now called.

Late one night in David's office with Adam Dixon and a bottle of Black Label scotch, David said to me:

'Andrew do you think you can build them?'

And the scotch replied, 'Of course I can'. And the learning curve started again.

A fellow I had met at the Yacht Club, and from time to time at the various parties, Colin Dunlop, was a naval architect working for Millers shipyard. When the yard was sold and became IMEL he decided to leave and set up his own company to do naval design work in Fiji.

Sketches of Fiji

This was a rather bold decision at the time, but one that turned out fortuitous for me, and for Colin. He was an interesting fellow; a Scot who had served with the Gurkhas, then worked as a cowboy in Alberta, Canada, then in the outback of Australia, then for a shipyard in Sydney where he obtained his naval architect's degree; then he moved to Fiji. He was a real character who lived on his yacht (later houseboat) in the bay opposite the Tradewinds Hotel and near Mosquito Island. He had long scraggy hair and often wore what can best be described as Columbine pantaloons. He also liked the not-so-occasional drink and playing the bagpipes. All well and good, except when he did this latter on his yacht moored close to the Lami homes at 2.00 a.m.

Colin agreed to become our naval architect and set himself up in the offices of Architects Pacific. This was a local architectural firm owned by another friend of ours, Stu Huggett, who was highly thought of throughout the Pacific and who designed several extensions to our house in Suva; and in later years our home at Dreketi near Nadi.

Another member of the team was Brian La Budde, a New Zealand marine engineer I had recruited to look after the Blue Lagoon ships. Brian was a highly competent engineer, good at his business and I knew that I could work with him. As an aside, during my trip to New Zealand to interview candidates for the Blue Lagoon job I went through the usual Q&A with them; and then I would ask 'looking round this room what maintenance problems do you see?'. Most were

Of building ships

hopeless. Brian however got up, walked round the room and reeled off everything that I had found before we started. He got my vote.

David played his part by looking at the overall concept of the ship, cabin layout, fabrics and colours, and what might be called the passenger side of things. Everything else he left to me and my team. One of the very early debates was whether we should build a ship bigger than the current fleet, but we opted to stick with the known formula of 130 feet and 22 passenger cabins. We also debated the name but decided to stick with Claude's *Lycianda*, adding II after the name.

Colin drew up the general arrangement drawings of the ship and I commenced negotiations with both the government yard and IMEL. Pricing negotiations were detailed and complex and I am very grateful for the understanding and support that I received from both Colin and Brian. Fortunately, I could at least read a set of plans, and understood the basics of engineering; but the terminology was very different and the learning curve very steep. We finally opted for IMEL.

We decided that we would import all the materials ourselves and provide them to the yard rather than have the yard mark up the cost of materials. We rented a warehouse over the road from the Carlton United Brewery in Walu Bay and I recruited a local part-European engineer to be our store manager. This turned out to be a good decision as he performed his role brilliantly. I apologise to him – his name simply won't come.

Sketches of Fiji

The project was very, very, hands on; to the extent that the management of the yard expressed surprise on many occasions as to the lengths our team would go in ensuring that everything was right. On one occasion IMEL reported that they had finished work up to the 'double bottoms' that formed the fuel, water and sullage tanks – basically the hull of the ship to the lower deck level. It was Friday night, and I spent all the next day inside those tanks inspecting every weld, surface paint condition, and the measurements between the frames; marking all the errors with chalk. These tanks were very constricted and, probably foolishly, I did not have anyone else with me. In hindsight, had I got caught, or passed out with the heat and lack of air, it would have been extremely dangerous. But I was young, enthusiastic, and very committed, so none of this occurred to me at the time.

On Monday morning I invited the General Manager of the yard, a fellow called Howard Pugh, to get into one of the tanks to have a look. He stuck his head into the first hole, shone the torch around, then asked me to join him in his office. Then followed a rather a stormy session during which I told him his shipyard standards were unacceptable (the actual adjectives were a bit different) and that he needed to get the errors fixed – quickly. In fairness he eventually accepted what I was saying, and thereafter we had no further problems with the quality of work.

Finally, she was ready to launch. If there was one part of building those ships (eventually three) that I found most fascinating it was the calculations and organisation underpinning a launching. Too lengthy and complex to go into here, but essentially a series of hardwood blocks

Of building ships

about 18 inches square by 15 foot long are set between the slipway timbers and the hull, with grease inserted between the two timbers. These are called the 'Standing Ways' and the 'Sliding Ways' in the trade. Then large wooden wedges are driven into the gap between the sliding ways and the hull to lift the ship off the keel blocks used during construction, thus taking the weight on the 'ways'. The 'sliding ways' are held in place by a trigger mechanism.

In addition to all the technology, I also arranged the social events to accompany the launch. David Wilson's wife, Pam, was to launch this first ship and there were to be many dignitaries, and lots of 'champers' and food.

The appointed time is actually set by the tide. One needs to launch at the highest possible tide to ensure the ship does not stick her keel into the mud at the bottom of the slipway. The appointed time arrived, drinks all round, speeches ad infinitum, and then Pam pulled the trigger. Great big nothing! There she sat.

IMEL had provided two tugs, but even they were not able to get my ship moving. The crowd went on drinking and eating and finally rolled home. Colin, Brian, the shipyard manager, and I spent a sleepless night trying to work out what went wrong. We finally realised the mistake. The grease had been placed between the ways the previous morning and the wedges driven in, thus the whole weight of the ship had been carried on those blocks for more than 24 hours. The grease

Sketches of Fiji

had simply been forced out over that time by the pressure, and it was wood jammed against wood. In the quiet of the weekend we separated the timbers, inserted new grease, pulled the trigger and away she went! Ah, how we learn!

It took us just on a year to build *Lycianda II* and I'm still very proud to say that she was finished on time, and on budget. We were all very pleased with her. Colin in particular, was quietly pleased that the first ship he had ever designed actually cruised at the specified speed, with the right fuel burn, floated along the waterline he had calculated, and when we did the stability trials, she passed with flying colours. We sailed her to Lautoka in atrocious weather and she performed perfectly. Then a short cruise through the Yasawas to settle her down, and she entered service.

Lycianda, Columbia Pictures, drilling for oil

It was with a great deal of relief that we withdrew the original *Lycianda* from service. In the preceding months we wondered what to do with the ship and had considered sinking her to be a dive wreck. This proved an expensive and extraordinarily complex thing to do. She had to be completely stripped, fuel tanks steam cleaned, taken to her final resting site, and have the bottom blown out by naval divers who were qualified to do this work. At the same time a spearfishing mate of mine, Tiko Eastgate, who had a restaurant in Suva, developed the idea of building a floating restaurant to moor along the Suva waterfront. Two and two make four. I sold him the ship for what it would have cost us to sink her ($8000) and he converted her into Tiko's restaurant. More than 30 years later she is still afloat, albeit those rusty tanks are now full of lightweight concrete and oil. As an aside Tiko's is where our son David got his first job.

But before we handed her over to Tiko she did two rather special charters for us.

Columbia pictures had decided to make a re-run of the 1927 Jean Simmons film *The Blue Lagoon*, this time with Brooke Shields and Christopher Atkins as the hero couple. Two Fiji entrepreneurs, Dennis McIlwraith and Richard Evenson had convinced them to do this in the Yasawa Islands where the original had been filmed.

Richard was an American who had purchased an island, *Nanuya Levu*, in the Yasawas from the Doughty family. This was immediately

Sketches of Fiji

adjacent to *Nanuya Lailai* which I had earlier purchased from Burns Philip for Blue Lagoon.

Even though the original had been filmed near the famous Sawa-i-Lau limestone caves in the Northern Yasawas (more on this in a little while) the deal was that this time it would be on Richard's island. As they would be there for six months, he was to build accommodation for the stars, the Director, and other senior people on the island. But Columbia needed more accommodation for the crew – step forward Drysdale with an offer to charter *Lycianda* and moor her in the bay opposite the film site. We would also act as providores for them from our Lautoka stores operation.

I was in Los Angeles at the time of the film's release and was invited to attend. Yup, there I was at the big Hollywood event with all the names. In one scene there is a dramatic moment where a native cannibal tribe captures and murders a victim by whacking him over the head with a club. It's at night with wild native dancing around flares, drums, an evil looking God in the background covered in blood and very loud, scary music. Except that the evil native chief who does the 'whacking' is dear old Tevita from Yalobi village – the nicest gentleman you could ever meet. I burst out laughing and was told to sshhhh.

After Columbia left, Richard Evenson converted the accommodation he had built to house the stars and executives into a very upmarket tourist hotel. He used the name 'Blue Lagoon Lodge' in order to gain marketing leverage off the film. Fair enough; but then he began to

Lycianda, Columbia Pictures, drilling for oil

market the resort as three-day, two-night, packages (as per our cruises) and charged very nearly the same as we did. This began to cause confusion in the travel industry, so we sued, and I quickly found how hard it is under English law to win cases like this.

Amongst other evidence we produced mail addressed to him that had been delivered to us, and vice versa, to demonstrate 'there was evidence that the general public was confused' about the similarities between the two company names.

The proceedings dragged on, and as time passed it seemed Richard would win the case because he claimed that the bay in front of his island was called 'Blue Lagoon' and he was therefore entitled to use the name. That argument was gaining traction. On the evening prior to the last scheduled day in court I was sitting on the stern of one of our ships drinking yagona with the captain and told him the story. He replied, 'Oh no boss – Blue Lagoon bay is further North at Sawa-i-Lau; the Fijian name is *Buasali*. It's where they made the first film.' I questioned him closely and he confirmed that to the masters of ships in Fiji 'Blue Lagoon' was the Northern bay; and that the bay opposite Richard's island was '*Nacula*'. The next morning, we presented our captain as expert witness and won the case.

Richard changed the name of his resort to Turtle Island Lodge. His resort went on to become a model for the exclusive island resorts that are now a feature of Fiji's tourism scene.

Sketches of Fiji

As that charter drew to a close I was approached by a company that held a licence to conduct exploratory oil drilling in Bau Waters, my old spearfishing ground. They wanted to anchor the ship next to the drilling rig to accommodate their staff and to move her as they moved the rig. We negotiated a deal and positioned *Lycianda* for them. Based on my Columbia pictures experience I played hard-ball with them in the negotiations. Lucky that I did because the drilling crew were a rough bunch and did a great deal of damage to the ship. On one occasion they broke several of the hand-basins off the wall in the bathrooms and threw them over the side.

Fortunately, the contract required the drilling company to make good any damage and our mark-up on that was large. They also had completely different meal requirements to our normal tourist passengers. Bacon and eggs (lots of them) and big steaks and roasts, but our cooks adapted quickly.

David and I purchased a high-speed 21-foot boat *Victoria* so that I could get out to the ship to check on how things were going, and to calm any difficulties between the crew and the riggers. And of course, David and I got to use her from time to time for picnics and fishing trips. On one occasion my three boys were with me when I took her from Lautoka to Suva – only we didn't get there. Crossing Viti Levu bay the bottom opened up and she began to sink. The boys were wonderful, they just quietly put on their lifejackets and waited calmly for me to get her ashore. At one point I fired off a flare, but it was faulty, and part of the flaming debris entered the cabin where the boys were. Even then there was no panic – I was very proud of them. As she began to sink the Vol-

Lycianda, Columbia Pictures, drilling for oil

vo engine took on water and stopped, so I started the 10 HP Mercury outboard that was used whenever we were maneuvering slowly or spearfishing, and that little engine pushed us forward even after the water was above the floorboards - enough to get us to shore. An exciting day!

At the end of four months the contract ended, and we sailed a somewhat worse-for-the-wear *Lycianda* to Suva and handed her over to Tiko. This was done with a Fijian ceremony where, after a Yagona ceremony, the ship's captain made a speech handing her over, and Tiko responded with a speech of acceptance and thanks to the captain and crew. Then we had a party! She had served us well.

Yasawa Princess

Now while all this was going on we realized that the next ship, *Taleianda*, was also getting a little shaky, so it was decided that we would build a second replacement. We were also becoming rather confident in our abilities as the *Lycianda* project was going very well. Largely driven by David's vision, and a belief that we had positioned the company such that a bigger ship would now work, we decided to build a sleeker, modern looking, ship and to make her significantly larger (170 feet and 64 passengers) than the earlier fleet. Colin started on the design and I started work on the contract.

At this time the IMEL yard was still building *Lycianda* and had only one slipway, so that was out. We turned to the government yard and in late 1982 proposed a rather novel idea to the Marine Department and the Ministry of Transport. We were confident that the yard had the skills and the machinery to build the ship, but were equally confident that it would be difficult for their executives to manage the construction of a ship this big. In fairness, up to that time their management team had primarily been building government inter-island ships and landing barges. The other complicating factor was that we had decided to build her to the exacting standards of the American Bureau of Shipping (ABS).

Our proposal was in effect a labour contract. We would design the ship, import and supply all the materials, project manage the entire construction; and call on them to supply the skilled manpower, tooling and slipway under our supervision. The negotiations around this were extraordinarily complex and delicate, but in the end agreement was reached.

Yasawa Princess

One of the first things we did was to build a site office on top of the shipyard winch house overlooking the slipway. From here we could see everything that was going on below us. Then we started building *Yasawa Princess*. She took us nearly two years but was finished in less time than planned and right on budget. I'll only tell a few stories of the hundreds that spin around in my head when thinking of those days.

As you may know, ships are built on keel blocks that angle upwards about three to five degrees from the water. The 'standing ways' lie under the chine area and act to stabilise the ship vertically during construction. They come into play for the actual launching. Given the angle, there is a particular skill to installing fittings so that they will be level once the ship is afloat. When it came time to install the mirrors in the cabins we discussed the details of this with the Indian man who was the yard's mirror installer. It was a Friday night and we all went home leaving him to do the work on the weekend without the burly welders bumping into him as he carried the mirrors around the ship. This was one of the few weekends that I didn't spend at the yard. On Monday morning he proudly showed us his work and, indeed, every mirror was perfectly true in accordance with the ship's hull angle, except that the mirror installer was five foot two inches and every mirror was set at a height to suit his height! Great for navel gazing.

And now to the big launch day. This time she was to be christened by Adi Lady Lala Mara, wife of the Prime Minister. *Yasawa Princess* was by far the largest ship the yard had ever built and for the first time I

Sketches of Fiji

saw Colin truly anxious. The launching bothered him for many reasons, not the least of which was that the harbour behind the slipway had silted up. We needed every inch of a King tide to ensure that, with the momentum of the launch, she didn't hit the bottom and break her back. Remembering our problems with the previous launch, we carefully timed the moment when the grease was put between the standing and sliding ways and the wedges driven in.

At IMEL the driving of the wedges was a fairly simple affair; at the government yard it became a major Fijian ceremony. It started on the morning of the launch with more than a hundred big Fijian men seated cross-legged on the floor in the huge welding shed, wearing traditional dress, and with bodies oiled with coconut oil. First was the ritual of a formal yagona ceremony. When this was finished the shipyard manager delivered a long speech in Fijian to them, after which the men, led by their foremen, began to chant. They stood, formed two lines, and moved forward, each one picking up a large sledgehammer as he passed the store, all the time continuing to chant. The sledge hammers were coloured either red or green as in port and starboard. They then peeled off to their respective port or starboard sides of the ship taking up positions, each next to a wedge. Then the chanting picked up a pace and changed into a rhythmic beat interspersed with a loud yell. At each yell the sledgehammers struck their respective wedge. Thus, yell by yell, each wedge was struck at exactly the same time causing the ship's weight to be transferred slowly, and smoothly, onto the ways. It was an amazing sight.

Yasawa Princess

Then when all was ready, we dispersed to change in time to greet our guests. As before, 'champers' and food were dispensed, speeches made, and then Adi Lala pulled the trigger. Then nothing happened! Again, the tugs were bought into play, and again she remained firmly stuck on the slipway. Again, the guests finished the food and booze and went home. Again Dunlop, Drysdale and La Budde agonised over what had happened.

This time though it was a lot more serious than with *Lycianda*. We had planned to launch at King tide and if we didn't get her off within the next 24 hours she would be stuck there for at least three months until the next King tide. We decided on brute force and hired not two, but five tugs (actually every tug in Suva at the time) whose cables we attached to various points on the hull. Then at the following high tide, with Colin in charge, we applied every force we possibly could. And away she went!

But what a sight – the friction between the standing and sliding ways was so great that these huge pieces of timber caught fire. There was smoke and sparks and flames going in all directions and this enormous ship, now completely out of our control, slid at ever increasing speed backwards into the sea.

In the end, all was well, and she floated beautifully and without damage. I can't say the same about the slipway though. Colin turned to me and said in a quiet voice 'You know at that point she was in complete control of her own destiny; there was absolutely nothing we could

Sketches of Fiji

have done once she began to move'. The moment is burnt deeply into my memory. It was Christmas Eve 1984.

So, what happened? Quite simple really, we had used the wrong specification of grease! It was too thin, and the weight of the ship simply forced it out from between the ways. Ah, the lessons we learn.

We finished *Yasawa Princess* on time and under budget by early April 1985 and decided to take her on a proving cruise to Kadavu over the Easter weekend of April 25th. Invitations were duly sent out to dignitaries and friends; she was loaded with fuel, water, food and booze and we set off. Notable on the booze front were several cases of Beaujolais supplied by Bill Apted's shop, which became a great favourite, and none survived the trip.

The crossing was a bit rough as it usually is at that time of the year but Colin, Robert Southey, the captain and I soon became more than a little concerned as she seemed to toss more violently than we expected. We soon found the problem. As it was just a short cruise the engineer had not completely filled the fuel and water tanks, so she had 'slack tanks' as they say. It was this fluid sloshing round that was causing the problem. Quickly fixed; we consolidated the loads in the tanks, got the centre of gravity right and all was well. Albeit, one of the ladies spent the entire cruise wearing her lifejacket!

The rest of the trip went off very well with lots of conviviality and beautiful weather. Even so Colin, Brian LaBudde, Southey and I were very

Yasawa Princess

much on edge watching for problems. On the second night at around 1.00am the engine room alarms went off. I don't even remember leaving my bed but seemed to arrive instantaneously in the engine room wearing just a sulu. Behind me quite literally dropping down the access way came Dunlop, La Budde and Southey, also in their night attire. And here we found the ships engineer looking very startled at these apparitions. He was simply checking the alarms to ensure they were working and to pass the long night on watch. Once the adrenalin faded a bit we began to laugh – what a sight we must have looked. So, it was off to the bar to do away with another bottle of Beaujolais.

With *Yasawa Princess* off the slipway blocks we decided to build a third ship. And the process began again. Colin drew up the plans for a ship midsize between *Lycianda* and *Yasawa Princess*, we cut the deal with the government shipyard as before and began importing the materials. *Nayuya Princess* was at main deck level when I accepted an offer to begin a new and challenging career. I'll speak of that in a moment.

Fiji Tourism Convention

I also found myself serving on the organizing committee for Fiji's annual Tourism Convention. The Convention was a big deal in those days and was usually opened by the Minister for Tourism, occasionally the Prime Minister or the Governor General, and with up to 800 delegates in attendance. Travel industry leaders came from all over the world to attend this four to five-day annual event. There were serious discussions during the day with speeches and opportunities for contract negotiations. In the evenings though it was party time and, boy, the tourism industry in those days really knew how to party.

Behind the serious events and the fun lay an extraordinarily detailed and professional planning process. Fortunately, by the time I got involved this had been honed into a very slick operation each year. The convention was held under the auspices of the Fiji Visitors Bureau and the Chief Executive of the FVB would be on the committee. However, the Chairmanship of the planning committee was always given to one of Fiji's tourism leaders. In 1986 it became my turn and I approached the event with some trepidation. It was the Convention's silver jubilee and the expectation was high that it would be the 'best ever'.

At the time the General Manager of the Hyatt Regency on the Coral Coast was a friend of mine called John Wallis and the suggestion was that the Convention be held in his hotel. John and I had lunch at the Red Lion restaurant in Suva and talked this through. Aided by 'a little red' we shook hands and agreed to do it. I won't go into all the details, but we met the expectations. The final night was amazing; in the space of just a

Fiji Tourism Convention

few hours John's team and the local villagers turned the enormous lobby area of the hotel into a complete jungle. I have no idea now how many truckloads of leaves and branches and small trees were carted in and set up throughout the lobby. Everyone dressed for the part and there were more Tarzans and Janes per square foot than you could ever imagine – and some apes! Even more extraordinary, by breakfast the next morning it had gone. There was not a trace of what had been there the night before. Certainly, something remembered long after the event.

There are many other memorable Tourism Conventions and one that comes to mind was the year it was held at the Regent Hotel in Nadi when Robin Stork was Chairman of the planning committee. At the time he was the boss of both 'Tip Top' ice cream company and a large commercial chicken farm. His then link to the tourism industry was as a provider of supplies, but the family had been part of Fiji's tourism industry for many years; indeed they were among the pioneers of the industry. His parents ran the *Oolooloo* and *Oolala* 'glass bottom' reef viewing boats in Suva harbor. His brother Max is still a leader of the industry in Fiji.

Robin's idea for the final night was an outdoor cowboy evening complete with a corral. We all dressed up as cowboys and cowgirls and much fun was had by all. But then, late in the evening Robin let loose around 50 table- size chickens to run amongst the revelers. The reaction was extraordinary. Several well-known tourism industry leaders were seen heading off with chickens tucked under their arms (the ho-

Sketches of Fiji

tel complained the next day of the mess in the bathrooms) and there were women in tears trying to save the chickens from the mad stampede. Indeed, a memorable night.

As an aside, it was this Convention that led to my becoming Chairman of PATA, I was the Chairman and moderator of the Convention (Robin was Chairman of the organising committee) and in the audience was Ian Kennedy, at that time the Pacific head of PATA. It seems that Ian thought I did a reasonable job and recommended me to the PATA Executive Committee as a future Board member. I'll come back to all of this later.

Air Pacific – getting to yes

While all this shipbuilding was going on I was also continuing my role as CEO of The Travel Company, of its various offshoots, and as Chairman of the International School. We were back in our Tamavua home and often sat on the little veranda at the front of our home in the evening looking Southeast to Laucala Bay and Nukulau, wondering what was going to happen next in our lives. The kids were doing well at the International School, but we were becoming concerned about their futures. What would happen to them in their teenage years, and the need for them to go to University. No different to any parents I guess, but one day early in 1986 something happened that set my mind on a new course. David and I were having one of our 'Black Label' meetings in his office after work, debating future strategies for the various companies when he said to me out of the blue 'You know you will never be able to afford to send your kids to school in Australia'. I was on local wages, albeit towards the top level, but the comment shocked me. David must have seen the look on my face and changed the subject, but we both knew that after eight years the end was in sight for our time together.

Not long after that I received a call from Sir Ian Thompson's office asking for a time when he could meet me in my office. Sir Ian Thompson, former District Commissioner, Governor of British Virgin Islands, now Chairman of both the Sugar Commission of Fiji, and of Air Pacific, wanting to see me, and in my office, not his? I said 'of course' and set a date for the following Tuesday.

Tuesday arrived and Sir Ian came in; David was in his office next door. Sir Ian came straight to the point. 'We would like to offer you the position of

Sketches of Fiji

Managing Director and CEO of Air Pacific,' he said. 'You'll need to discuss it with your family I know, but could you come to see me and let me know your answer on Thursday?' The deal was 18 months living with my family in Australia to study Airline management systems with Qantas, attendance at the three-month residential Advanced Management Program at Harvard Business School, and a five-year contract as MD/CEO of Air Pacific. The salary was F$37,000 per year. On the Thursday I accepted.

Fiji is a small place, so I needed to tell David quickly. He was in Nadi flying out to Sydney, so I drove to Nadi to meet him at the airport. It was 7th. June 1986. He looked me straight in the eye for a moment as he used to do when he was thinking, stuck a cigarette into the holder he used, and simply said 'Well old mate, we'll need to find an answer and move on'. To this day I don't know if he and Sir Ian had spoken, but I'm pretty sure they had. A week later it had become public, and on 22nd. June '86 the Silver Anniversary Tourism Convention at the Hyatt took place. I was the Chairman of the planning committee and tell the story elsewhere about how successful it was, but the rest is a blur until we arrived in Sydney.

For the record, I accepted the job formally on 9th. June 1986 started the sabbatical on 1st. September that year and took up the role on 1st. April 1988. I was 40 when we took that decision.

When I wrote to the then Engineering Manager Ken Christoffersen with my formal resignation, his reply started 'Thank you for your letter of resignation...'. I'm sure he meant well.

Sketches of Fiji

ABOVE:
Typical Ship design team meeting Huggett Dunlop self

ABOVE RIGHT:
Vunivalu's Mata ni Vanua acknowledging the Tabua on behalf of Ratu George Yalombi village Yasawa islands

RIGHT:
Vunivalu and Governor General Ratu Sir George Cakobau receiving the Tabua Yasawa Islands

Sketches of Fiji

RIGHT:
Laundry day
Yasawa I Ra
Northern Yasawa
Islands 1981

BELOW:
Yasawa princess
sketch by Hayes

CREDIT: ZERBIN

Sketches of Fiji

Air Pacific
1986 - 1998

Air Pacific – the interim years 1978/86

A lot had happened at 'the old firm' while I was with Blue Lagoon and in order to link the Fiji Airways and subsequent Air Pacific stories I'll tell it briefly as I saw it.

First, we need to go back a little in time. Qantas had provided management for Fiji Airways/Air Pacific (the name changed in July '71) since buying the company from Harold Gatty's estate in 1957. They nominated the Chairman, several Board representatives, and provided management staff on secondment. Some of the managers who served during that time were promoted to senior positions in Qantas on their return to Sydney. Two, John Schaap and John Campbell, returned in later years as Managing Director/CEO of Air Pacific. I'll talk about that in a while.

From the late '60s Fiji's union movement had focused on the airline and the sugar industries as their most disruptive weapons. Years of farmer discontent coupled with ongoing and bitter industrial disputes in the sugar industry had resulted in the 'Denning report' and consequently Australia's 'Colonial Sugar Refining company' (CSR) pulling out of Fiji. The union movement then turned its attention to Fiji Airways, and to the Nadi airport ground handling operation – both managed by Qantas. Regardless of the union's methods, their single-minded focus to get rid of Qantas eventually struck a chord in the community, including at the highest levels of Government. In May 1974, with the airline in severe financial difficulty, the Fiji Government injected $7m into

Sketches of Fiji

the company and became the major shareholder. Qantas remained as a minority shareholder, and still provided management. The financial and industrial problems continued.

The unions continued to gain political strength by decrying Qantas as the root cause of the airline's problems, and the cause of ongoing-disruptions at Nadi airport. The fact that these disruptions were entirely of their own making and were part of a deliberate strategy to get Qantas out of Fiji, was buried in the hubris. They played the nationalist card and did it very well. It got to the point where even Ratu Mara as Prime Minister began to agree, and the mood in Fiji became one of 'kick Qantas out, we locals can do this better'.

My observation as a local would be that, good though they undoubtedly were as airline managers, the Qantas team failed to comprehend the societal changes that were taking place around them. Or, if they did, then they failed to understand how to manage those changes.

Many of the Qantas managers were liked as individuals, and some were also respected, but as a group they represented a form of 'Raj' to the locals. One story may help set that scene. One evening a member of the Fiji Airways Workers Association (FAWA) went into the bar at the Suva Travelodge hotel for a drink. From there he could see into the restaurant where a party was taking place. The Qantas managers and their wives were having dinner together and,

Air Pacific – the interim years 1978/86

as he put it, they were 'full shot' (drunk). The booze was flowing freely. No locals were at the table. A few days later one of the 'accounts boys' confirmed that the company had paid for the meal and the alcohol. Even if there were good reasons for the party (and for the company to pay) this gave the union a powerful public relations weapon, and they worked that to the hilt.

By the time I went to Blue Lagoon in 1978 the Air Pacific General Manager was Stan Quigg and the company still had a large contingent of Qantas expats in the senior positions. Some locals such as Kit Naidu, Ernie Dutta, and Tony Wong were moving up in the ranks, as I was in engineering, but the top jobs still went to Qantas expats; and the post-independence resentment was growing.

The upshot of this pressure was that in late 1978 Stan returned to Sydney, thus ending almost 21 years of Qantas management. Then in 1981 Qantas sold the Nadi airport ground handling operation to a newly formed company, Air Terminal Services ltd. (ATS). With Prime Minister Mara's support, the shareholders of ATS were the Fiji Government (via the Civil Aviation Authority) and the workers represented by their union. Central to the union involvement and representation was Dhinsukh (Danny) Morarji. After a period of controversy, and after one expat and one local CEO had come and gone, Danny became CEO. In fairness to him, he did pull together an operationally efficient, and profitable (albeit a monopoly) operation.

Sketches of Fiji

Credit where credit is due – the unions had won their battle and Qantas had gone; but as we shall see, only temporarily.

Stan was replaced as General Manager by an English fellow, Capt. Alan Bodger who came via Gulf Air, one of the world's leading airlines of the day. The trickledown effect of the Qantas departure meant that several of my former colleagues were promoted to senior positions within the company. Many of these had played key roles in the early days of the Fiji Airways Employees Association. That is not to decry them, on the contrary, they were already proving themselves to be effective leaders. Changes were also made at Board level; highly respected local accountant Don Aidney became Chairman (Don had been awarded a DFC as a bomber pilot during World War II) and more local Directors were appointed.

In due course, Bodger finished his contract and was replaced by the first local CEO, Aquila Savu. Aquila was an intelligent, long-serving bureaucrat who had been the Government's Director of Economic Planning. Don Aidney was in turn replaced as Chairman by John Hill whose company 'JS Hill and associates' was one of Fiji's largest construction firms. But by now both the CEO, and the Board, lacked aviation experience; and the nationalistic cries for a bigger and better Air Pacific were intensifying.

Amongst other things this resulted in the company leasing a DC 10 and commencing services to Hawaii – 'Project America'. The story is

Air Pacific – the interim years 1978/86

complex, but it was a financial disaster and in just 16 months drove the company to a massive 'negative shareholder worth' and the largest accumulated loss in Fiji's corporate history. The company was able to continue to operate because of loans secured from Westpac that were guaranteed by the Fiji Government. Without that, Air Pacific would have collapsed. But even with those guarantees, the company was rapidly coming to the end of the road.

As the end neared, they began to run out of cash and so introduced a scheme whereby people could pre-purchase blocks of tickets at discounted prices. I recall my former Fiji Airways colleague Victor Sharan calling on me in the Blue Lagoon office to flog this scheme. After he finished his spiel my reply was 'Victor, what you are actually telling me is that the company is in deep financial trouble and may collapse any day. So, no I won't buy your tickets.' I'm sure he remembers.

In December 1984 'Project America' was terminated.

As these problems became public Prime Minister Ratu Mara took direct control as Minister for Transport and Civil Aviation and set out to find a 'white knight' savior. Air New Zealand and Singapore Airlines dropped out of the race early, leaving Sir Peter Abeles' Ansett and Qantas as the bidders. Mara was close to Abeles, liked him as a man and as an entrepreneur, and favoured that bid. Central to Abeles' plan was to turn Nadi into a major international airfreight hub; and in his role as Prime Minister Mara could see the national economic

Sketches of Fiji

value in that. Also, Mara had a long memory - he had not forgotten the last time Qantas managed both the airline and the operations at Nadi airport. But the Board decided on Qantas. Convincing Mara would have been a very difficult conversation.

The deal came into effect in January 1985 and Fiji's Sir Ian Thompson was appointed Chairman in March. This arrangement resulted in an injection of cash, shareholding changes, Qantas on the Board, and again a team of Qantas managers to run the company. They were led by John Schaap who had previously been seconded to the company in the Fiji Airways years; I'll speak more of these men later. Importantly John understood the local mood better than many; and he knew how to communicate, both politically, and with his staff. In this he was supported by his Chairman, Sir Ian Thompson. These two, together with the handpicked mangers John brought with him, quickly began the financial turnaround.

There was a clause in the deal that required Qantas to identify a Fiji local to be appointed as Managing Director/CEO by the end of the three-year contract - enter Drysdale - so let's get on with that story.

The management sabbatical

My contract began with an 18 month management 'sabbatical' while I studied airline management with the assistance of Qantas. The official title was 'Managing Director/CEO designate' but that's a mouthful, so I'll just use CEO from here on.

There's a point I'd like to make. At no time was I employed by Qantas. Several in Fiji, and even within Qantas, drew that incorrect assumption. Indeed, there were times in later years when the rumour machine claimed that the difficult, risky, decisions we were taking was because I had been told to do so by Qantas. That was completely fallacious. I respected some of the Qantas people, but they were not my masters, and I have never taken the Qantas coin.

Qantas was very supportive. I moved around the various divisions interviewing their executives and learning how they ran that company. I also spent time in Kuala Lumpur looking at Malaysian Airlines. From time to time I would return to Fiji to attend the Air Pacific Board meetings and to network with company and government people. It was a wonderful learning experience, but I grew bored and longed to get my hands on the job. I also began to realise that whilst the Qantas systems were excellent, they were 'big airline' systems and we would need to develop our own versions if Air Pacific was to survive in the long term.

In late 1986 I went to Harvard Business School to attend the 13-week Advanced Management Program (AMP). We were AMP 99. This was a program started by Harvard at the end of World War II

Sketches of Fiji

to make business executives out of de-mobbed military officers. As a result, it had about 30 to 40 per cent military guys in each intake. The rest were mostly senior executives about to start a new, more senior role. The 13-week duration was because the WWII officer training programs were 90 days long; the '90-day wonders'. We were the last of these as the big corporations told Harvard it was too long. They dropped it to nine weeks after us.

The program was interesting, and no doubt provided me a wider perspective on the world of big business; but I quickly formed the view that it didn't fit the realities of Fiji, and frankly I was 'over it' as my kids would say today. I just wanted to get back to Fiji and get on with the job.

We were housed in 'Baker' school in groups of ten sharing a common living area (known as 'cans' from the military term – you work it out). Each of us had a small but well- furnished private en-suite room. Mine overlooked the Charles river and I was very pleased about that. Meals were served in a common room. They were good, but three meals a day, every day, in the same room, with the same people, became daunting. Sometimes some of us played hooky just to see a different scene over a meal, and in my case to get away from the same group of people.

There was no letup to the pressure of reading and debating the multitude of Harvard case studies. We started early, continued during breakfast, over lunch and late into the night, often till after midnight. Weekends were simply a time to read more. I did get out a few times

The management sabbatical

to Boston and found it a very interesting city, especially 'round what Boston calls the 'freedom trail' – freedom from the British that is. But it was the environs of Harvard that held the greatest interest.

We were encouraged to go to the gym as a group several days a week on the HBS mantra that 'when the mind is tired, exercise the body'. Rather than go to the gym I learnt to row their one-man Wherries and spent many a beautiful, but cool, evening rowing on the Charles river – then back to those bloody case studies till midnight or after.

One weekend I took a day trip to Nantucket Island where many of Fiji's early whalers came from (and nearby Salem). There is a whaling museum there which was very interesting. Quite a lot of Fiji stuff. They have an old molar on display which they claim had been extracted from King Cakobau by one of their ship's surgeons in the mid 1860s. I'll let you be the judge of that – not sure whalers carried surgeons! What was interesting though was to talk to the curator (old guy with a long beard of course) who certainly did know a lot about the Fiji whaling period. In my Blue Lagoon days I had a part-European secretary with the unusual surname of Coffin who told me that the European *'kai vulagi'* side of her family came from Nantucket. When I asked the bearded one he said, 'Oh yes, they live just 'round the corner'. So 'round I went, and sure enough, there was a small, neat, and obviously old, wooden home with the name 'Coffin' on the door post. I took a photo for Ms Coffin.

Many stories to tell, but let's get back to the real world.

Air Pacific – and then the work started

In February of 1988 we put David, James and Richard into boarding school and returned to Fiji with Jackie. Given Rabuka's recent coups, the flights were understandably light in passengers going to Fiji; but outbound was doing very well! Several people said to me that they thought we would not return, which puzzled me as it had never crossed my mind that I might not do so. I had a job to do and I was going to do it.

By now Sir Ian Thompson had retired to Scotland and Gerald Barrack was the Chairman. In this I was extremely fortunate. Gerald was from an old Fiji planter family and, like Sir Ian before him, was also the Chairman of the Sugar Commission of Fiji. He could 'smell' a political problem almost before it emerged and knew instinctively how to deal with it. He was close to Prime Minister Mara and was respected by all communities in Fiji. We got on very well and spoke to each other on an almost daily basis.

John Schaap was the now outgoing Air Pacific CEO and he was a great support and mentor during the transition. We still see each other from time to time, together with John Campbell who was CEO after me, to share stories and jokes about those days. 'Sharpie' and the other Qantas expats did a very good job in introducing the management systems needed to ensure the company could survive. I am indebted to them for all that they did. They stopped the financial bleeding and set a culture of disciplined management in place.

My job was to build the company from there, and quite frankly I had no idea how I was going to do that.

Air Pacific – and then the work started

Especially as Rabuka had just carried out his second coup, the country was under military rule, soldiers wearing balaclavas and carrying automatic weapons were on the streets, curfews were in place, check points and road blocks were on all major roads, and razor wire was the new landscape. The economy was in free-fall, there had been two major devaluations of the Fiji dollar, and tourism was holding on by the thinnest of threads, propped by heavy discounting.

John and Jeanette Schaap moved out of the company house in Ratu Sukuna Road and we moved in. More than anything else, this was the point when it fully struck home that I was the CEO of the airline. From my very first contact with Fiji Airways all those years ago, this was the house of the 'boss' – and now I was in that seat, and in that house.

I'm not going to write about the coups, plenty of others have done that. Just one story: not long after we returned to Fiji I was at a long, and well-lubricated lunch at the Nausori home of Kuar Battan Singh. 'KB' was a shadowy figure in Fiji's politics but so influential that people would always attend his lunches when invited. He was very close to Ratu Mara. That day Mara was there along with several high commissioners and ambassadors. At one point the British High Commissioner asked Mara something about Rabuka. Mara pulled himself up to his full six foot seven inch height, pointed a huge forefinger straight into the Commissioner's face and said in a loud voice 'Don't you ever talk to me about that man. He has destroyed the rule of law

Sketches of Fiji

in this country and it will take at least two generations to get it back'. The High Commissioner slunk off and left the lunch not long after. I'm told they later patched up their relationship.

The first thing was a courtesy call with my Chairman Gerald Barrack on Jo Kamikamica, the Minister for Transport and Civil Aviation at the time, who was also the acting Prime Minister. By this time Rabuka had conducted his first coup (14th. May 1987), then the second in September when he disagreed with the 'Deuba Accord' brokered by the Governor General and the then 'ousted' Prime Minister Bavadra. He had installed Ratu Mara as Prime Minister and, in theory at least, had returned to the barracks. Mara was touring the world drumming up support for the new Interim Government and for Fiji. Jo Kamikamica was really the man in charge. I spoke earlier of the impression that Ratu Edward made on me; Jo was in like form. Quietly spoken, a gentle smile and unassuming in posture; but deeply intelligent and with an enormous understanding of people and what makes them tick. Despite the unassuming front he was very firm in his commitment once he had been given the details and had made his judgement. (His son later joined Air Pacific as one of our graduate managers, rose to a senior position and was headhunted by one of the banks.) Jo was central to the two key decisions we took that changed the future of AirPacific.

The next was to Nausori to meet the staff; or in my case, my old mates. There was a very moving yagona ceremony with the people I had shared hard biscuit and tinned beef with all those years ago now

Air Pacific – and then the work started

making speeches of welcome to me as the new 'boss'. Even during the height of our subsequent industrial problems these men never forgot where I had come from, and nor did I. When I pause to think about that, it was probably this bond that gave me the credibility and trust I needed when the hard decisions had to be taken. At the end of the ceremony there was storytelling and many funny, happy reminiscences of the old days together.

Strange emotions flowed, especially when, with very big smiles, they asked me to sit behind my old desk in the foreman's office.

One story will suffice: Jone Sowata was one of Fiji Airways first local employees and still worked for us as a technician. He was a huge man from Buretu village in the nearby Rewa delta and had that wonderful sense of humour the Fijians have (and which can be off- putting if you don't understand it):

'Boss,' he said, 'good to see you back because you can stop all the thieving that's going on.'

'Oh?' replied I.

'Yes,' said he with a little chuckle, 'because you used to do it, and you know how it's done.' Time to move on!

People and skills

A key problem was migration of skills. Post the coups many of Fiji's people particularly, but not only, the Indians left to go to Australia, New Zealand and the US/Canada.

By 1988 we had lost more than 20% of our workforce and more were to follow. The first wave were those who already had their visas and were simply waiting an appropriate time; Rabuka gave them that. But it was the second coup in September that really hurt and caused many people, some of whom had not previously applied for visas, to make the decision to emigrate if they could. As always it was those with professional skills who had, or who managed to get, the visas; that's what the receiving country wanted. Seems strange to say this now, but it actually created a staff reduction program without the normal attendant union fuss - and the company was overstaffed. But it certainly didn't seem like a bonus at the time.

We still had three Qantas people on secondment, and they stayed on for a while to assist. I am very grateful to them, it must have been a difficult decision given what was going on. They had returned to Sydney by the end of the second year and we were on our own. I'll refer to them again in a moment. The executive team and I conducted an audit of what skills we had locally and what might be out there in the community. Then by dint of internal promotion and external headhunting we were able to maintain an effective management group.

What we also did was to start a management trainee program. I contacted the University and the technical college where I had studied so

Air Pacific – and then the work started

long ago (by now called the Fiji Institute of Technology) looking for their brightest. I didn't care what they were studying, I just wanted intelligent, disciplined minds. We also held several management sessions where we would suggest names of those working in management positions in other companies to see if we could get them to join us in this trainee scheme. Fiji was a small place and between us we managed to identify several excellent candidates who were keen to join.

We arranged a program for the trainees where they spent a few months in each department to at least get a feel for what went on in an airline; and then we assigned them to the division that we thought best suited their talents. They didn't always agree with us and, somewhat like my time in Qantas, some became bored and anxious to get their teeth into real work. Some left, and others understood what we were doing and stayed. Much later in 2006 when I visited Fiji on my farewell tour from IATA I sat with the then Air Pacific executive team in the boardroom I had built, and at the Board table I had designed – every one of the executives except the CEO (John Campbell) was local, and several were former trainees from that time. I felt very proud.

We also needed to build morale. John Schaap and his Qantas team had done a great job in stopping the financial bleeding, but morale was still very low, particularly post the coups. I began what was to become a signature of my management style. Every three months I would address the staff in great detail and tell them what we were doing.

Sketches of Fiji

Otherwise they read it in the papers, not necessarily correctly reported; or heard it with even more distortion from the unions. I also believed, and still do, that they had a right to know what their management and Board were doing, what our strategies were and how we were tracking as a business. Obviously, I couldn't tell them everything, but I made sure I erred on the side of giving too much rather than too little.

The union reaction was very strong as they saw this as a threat to their control on the opinions and the emotions of our people. They issued a directive to the staff to not attend the meeting and stationed watch keepers outside the building to note those who did attend. They also filed a dispute with the Ministry for Labour over the matter claiming I was trying to destroy the union – perish the thought. We had about 50 staff at that first meeting but within nine months it was full house, including some of the union reps.

I held these meetings in Suva, Nadi, Nausori and all the outstations including Los Angeles and Tokyo, albeit for them it was more six-monthly because of the logistics. When I left the company, these meetings had become deeply ingrained into the culture and I continued the concept in later roles with Hazelton Airlines and IATA. I think, in part, the reason I believe so strongly about this was that during my early Fiji Airways years the Qantas management failed completely to communicate with their employees – possibly because they didn't know how. As a result, the staff did not feel part of the company. You know the old story about employees being mushrooms, kept in the dark and fed on bullshit. The story has merit and I was determined it would not happen on my watch.

The Air Pacific strategy and the move to Nadi

I hope that one day someone with better writing skills than mine will record the many difficult and nerve-wracking decisions we took, and the result of those decisions. Let me at least give you a flavour of the time.

There are basically four things a CEO does beyond that overworked word 'lead': they foster a culture in the company, manage the day to day fires, manage the politics both up and down, and work out a strategy for the future. Taking the last first; I spent many hours thinking about where to take the company, what the longer-term issues were, and what we needed to do to grow the airline. It was obvious that if we did not grow, Air Pacific would likely fail because Fiji's Interim Government simply did not have the financial or governance capacity to bail it out.

Two people were very important to me at that uncertain time - my Chairman Gerald Barrack who understood politics better than any politician and who was a master in the art of keeping the pollies off my back; and Jo Kamikamica who would quietly nod and say just a few words that would at times get my head spinning. He was able, in just a sentence and with his little laugh, to sum up the issue and get his advice across in a way that didn't even sound like advice. To these two I give credit as my mentors in the strategic decisions that eventually built a new and financially strong Air Pacific.

The first twelve to eighteen months from March 1998 were spent in building on the base that John Schaap and his team had left, instilling commercial discipline, controlling costs, battling the unions and building

Sketches of Fiji

confidence and morale in our staff. But it was obvious (at least to me) that we were 'spinning wheels'. The more I thought about the future, the more convinced I became that we needed to move the company to Nadi, the heart of the tourism industry and location of the international airport, and to build an airline that would become the mainstay of Fiji's tourism. It's hard to imagine the magnitude of that decision now; no one had ever done anything like it before, it was political dynamite, and it was emotionally frightening for our people, myself included. It was also very, very high risk. But I was convinced it had to be done for two reasons; Nadi was where the future lay for us in our tourism role and I needed to send a massive shock into the company, its people, government and the community to make them understand that things were going to be different. I needed a cataclysmic change if I was to build a new Air Pacific.

Boy, did that announcement of the move to Nadi do it! The plan, 'vision' if you're more poetic, was:

Move the entire company from Suva to Nadi, get rid of the ATR42 turboprops, get out of loss-making domestic operations (except Suva/Nadi), build a new multi-million-dollar hangar and headquarters at Nadi, and to introduce a new, all-jet, fleet to enable us to increase services to Australia, New Zealand and the Pacific islands.

And *start services to Japan and Los Angeles. And for us to carry at least 50 per cent of Fiji's tourists and 60 per cent of the freight within three years. And remain profitable throughout.*

The Air Pacific strategy and the move to Nadi

It was an interesting concept given that the company was in 'negative shareholder worth', had very large accumulated losses, and was being propped financially by Westpac loans that had been guaranteed by a government that had now been overthrown by the Army. What is more the Governor of the Reserve Bank, Savenaca Siwatibau, had written to Westpac, and to the Board of Air Pacific, to say there would be no capital injection to save the airline, and no increase in the guarantees – the Government was itself in severe financial straits. *We were on our own*. The Army was still on the streets, the Fiji economy was still in free-fall; but hey, no problem! *Sa rauta* brother!

I told my Chairman Gerald Barrack of this grand plan over a cup of coffee in his Suva office in Mid 1989. There were no presentations, no speeches, no papers; just an idea that would be politically, emotionally, and commercially of the highest risk. Gerald paused for a moment, then simply said, 'Andrew, we have to handle the Board and government very carefully, but if you think it's the right thing to do, then let's go'. To his great credit Gerald never once doubted the concept, or our ability to get it done operationally. He saw his role as ensuring the Board and government signed off on the strategy; and he did that.

Fiji's a small place and we knew word would get out the minute the Board paper was written, so we decided to first get government approval, and then go to the Board. I know that's unusual, but the key lay in government approval. The Army had officially returned to the

Sketches of Fiji

barracks and an interim government was in place; but there had been no elections since the coups, and no one was under any misapprehension that stability had returned. There were still highly visible armed soldiers on the streets manning checkpoints and roadblocks.

Gerald picked up the phone and called the Acting PM Jo Kamikamica on his direct line (Gerald could do those things) to set up a meeting. Jo said to come straight away; he knew Gerald would not make that request, on that line, unless it was urgent and important. A little bit shocked at the speed of developments I drove with Gerald to the government buildings where Jo was waiting in the lobby for us. We went directly to his office where I sketched out the grand plan. Jo's reaction was to smile his little smile, walk to the window, and looking down said:

'Andrew can you see the soldiers outside?' 'Yes sir,' says me.

'And even with that you think you can do it?' says he. 'Yes sir,' says me.

'Okay, I'll tell Cabinet; you just let me know when you're ready to announce it,' says he.

And that was it!

Looking back on that moment; it was simple and quiet at the time, Jo was like that, but it marked a turning point in the history of Fiji's National airline – and there would be no going back.

The Air Pacific strategy and the move to Nadi

I just re-read those comments and it suddenly occurred to me that it was lucky no-one asked to see a financial impact study for the move – there wasn't one. As McGreal puts it in his book 'Fiji's aviation history' the move to Nadi 'had resulted from Andrew Drysdale's conviction that it was the best for the airline'!

Then a mad scramble to develop the detailed plan and call a special meeting of my Board who grilled me on the detail. But my executive team had done their work well and we were ready. Interestingly there was no debate on the strategy – only the detail and logistics. The Board agreed and it was 'game on'.

I knew we had to get to our people quickly before the unions and the press blurted out their perspectives and set them, and the community, against the move. So I called one of my staff briefings for the following morning. In calling the meeting I said it was to be a very important briefing that would affect them personally. It was to be held in the Fiji National Provident Fund conference room over the road from our Raiwaga offices as this could accommodate up to 300 people, and I knew we would have a full house.

On the Tuesday morning Ramen Narayan, our Human Resources manager, held a parallel meeting with the unions to tell them. For me, standing in a room completely full of loyal staff, telling them they were going to have to uproot from Suva and move to the other side of the island was a bit adrenalin pumping. I walked them through the logic and the vision and, as far as I could at that stage, the logistics, timing and compensation being proposed.

Sketches of Fiji

Then quickly to Nausori with Tony Wong, Director of Operations, to hold the same briefing there. I knew we had to get this on the table in my words – the unions and the media would distort it to hell and back – my people had to hear it from me. The next day, not surprisingly, we were on all the front pages and the radio news headlines. I'm pleased to say that generally they followed the case we had made in a press release to them and the commentary was complimentary and supportive. Not so from the unions. We had just handed them a wonderful opportunity to regain the ground they had lost with our staff. They went in to overdrive with emotive outbursts – particularly the Air Pacific Employees Association (APEA). After a few days of this one of the newspapers swung behind them with pictures of 'distressed' families, crying babies, children who would be 'torn from their schools and friends'. The other paper, and Radio Fiji were more balanced (there was no TV!).

We had to keep our staff briefed to counter the emotive drama, speculation and frankly the B.S. being spewed forth by the unions. Tony Wong and I spent hours and hours just walking around talking to our people. We drank gallons of yagona at Nausori where the biggest impact would be felt, and where the union base was strongest. Support came from an interesting source. The businessmen and city Councils of Nadi and Lautoka were enthused at the thought of some 500 families adding to their communities, particularly with a stagnant economy post the coups. They spoke out strongly to support the move (naturally I suppose) and gradually the PR pendulum swung in our favour.

The Air Pacific executive

There's a very important point that needs to be said loud and clear.

To make corporate strategies actually happen a CEO needs to build his team. This is from a document I wrote at the time for my Board and the Minister: *'the Chief Executive will be required to build a team of Executives in whom absolute confidence can be entrusted and who, in turn, will give the Chief Executive and the Board their complete, unwavering, support.'*

I am proud to be able to say that the executive team who worked with me throughout those very difficult and exhilarating years was the finest I have ever had the pleasure to know and to work alongside. I don't make that statement lightly – it is made after having worked as the CEO of four companies, two of which were publicly listed, and across a span of more than 30 years. And it is made after having served for almost seven years as the Regional Director, Asia/Pacific for the International Air Transport Association (IATA). In that role I dealt directly with the CEOs and senior executives of the region's airlines, airports and air traffic control providers.

The Air Pacific team's achievement in building a strong, financially viable international airline for Fiji stands testimony to their dedication, hard work, and remarkable skill. If only there were some way I could thank, and recognise, them properly.

When I returned to Air Pacific as CEO I was very pleased to find that almost all of our pilots and engineers were local. It had taken a concerted effort starting in 1964 when I had joined as the first apprentice to get to

Sketches of Fiji

this point. A number of Qantas people stayed on for a while, amongst whom were John Vincent in engineering (I've had the pleasure of working with John again recently on the Council of the Australian Division of the Royal Aeronautical Society) "Scotty" Fairbairn in flight operations and Alan Moore in Finance. Alan had a very smart young man, Narendra Kumar, working with him and ready to step into that Director of Finance role. These Qantas men fitted in well with our team and played a major part in the early years of the Drysdale regime. They left progressively over the next twelve to eighteen months, and we were on our own.

We appointed other expatriates from time to time including Barry Geddes in Engineering, and Geoff Bowmaker in Strategic Planning; Stephen Brown was Chief Operating Officer for a period, and Nick Panza from the USA worked alongside, and then for, Ernie Dutta in the role of Director of Marketing. The point I want to make here is that in every case where we appointed someone from overseas there was a clearly designated local being 'upskilled', as they say these days; and a timeline for that change over to take place. What is more, I reported regularly to my Board on progress in this succession planning.

When Narendra Kumar migrated to Australia in early 1996 the Director of Finance position was taken by his deputy, Josephine Yee Joy Bland. Josephine guided the company's finances with incredible professionalism and skill during my time, and for many years after. Narendra went on the become CEO of Qantas' regional airline Qantaslink and is now the acting CEO of Qantas International.

The Air Pacific executive

I smile to think of a Fiji citizen becoming an expatriate and working at very senior executive levels in Qantas – the wheel turns! I also smile to remember that in his role as CEO of Qantaslink Naren was my competitor. I was, at that time, CEO of Australia's other big regional, Hazelton Airlines. Friendly indeed but, competitors, nevertheless. In one of those strange quirks of fate, Naren's family owned the Flagstaff laundry in Suva and was a competitor to my family's laundry business.

I was deeply saddened when, after I had left, this extraordinary team was disbanded. A team that had taken decades of hard work and commitment to build; a team that had proven their worth time and again.

Let me caveat that statement. It is not my place to pontificate on the Fiji Airways of today. It is for the current Board, CEO and the people of Fiji Airways to determine how they wish to manage their company. My purpose in writing these notes, indeed the central purpose of this book, is to place on record the extraordinary achievement of a remarkable group of Fiji citizens in the aftermath of the 1987 coups. They took a company that had accumulated the largest financial loss in Fiji's history, turned it around, and created a safe, strong, and profitable National airline for their country. That they did so during the political, social and economic turmoil post those coups stands testimony to their tenacity, resilience and skill. To the naysayers I say, look at the financial charts at the end of this section – those are the audited facts.

Air Pacific and the media

Airlines are feeding ground for the media. That becomes more so when they are a Government-controlled national airline. Now add a political coup (two actually) in a small developing nation where the economy is based primarily on tourism, and you can multiply that focus exponentially. From the day my appointment was announced I became 'newsworthy'. Given I knew most of the reporters personally that added an interesting aspect to my life.

Press releases, media interviews and speeches became a very regular part of my life. I learned to not overreact, even to the most spurious of media reports and rumours; and to consistently present a balanced, honest and precise statement of fact. I also learnt that the public wanted to hear it from 'the boss'. In that small community a statement from 'a company spokesman' would not suffice.

It was particularly important to use the media to get our messages out when industrial issues emerged and after the move to Nadi was announced. The unions were masters of media manipulation and had no compulsion in presenting a one-sided perspective. Media feeds on drama and the Air Pacific Employees Association (APEA) in particular understood the power of that medium. There is an argument that in our responding to their distorted messages we may have actually given them opportunity to extend the debate; and there is a public relations principle that a better strategy is to 'deny them the oxygen'. That may be the case in a bigger and more sophisticated environment, but Fiji is a small place, rumour is ever-present, and the destabilised political

Air Pacific and the media

environment meant public and government opinion could easily be swayed. For us, swiftly countering distorted perspectives was critical.

In the early days I decided that I needed professional help and turned to a local public relations firm Wilson/Addison. Matt Wilson and Ross Addison were friends and provided tremendous help and advice. I very much appreciated their guidance, but as time went on I became more confident of my ability to handle the media myself. In particular I preferred to write my own speeches – and have written literally hundreds since then.

My Chairman, Gerald Barrack was also a great help in this public relations work. He understood the triggers of politics better than any man I have ever met. If the issue had a political connotation, and most did, he and I would talk it through before I 'went public'. He had an innate ability to see both the issue, and our response, in the way it would be received within government circles. His advice was always measured and sensible.

One problem reporter for a time was a friend of mine, Robert 'Bing' Keith-Reid. Bing was the son of a long-time Colonial Government wallah. In his own words he was 'the last Colonial'; an emblem he wore with pride. In addition to day-to-day reporting, he wrote a column called 'Beachcomber' which was the 'tittle, tattle' reading in the Fiji Times. His mainstream reporting was, however, always balanced and professional. Bing could usually be found 'round the clubs and bars of Suva with a wry look on his face and a particular view on things. He was very intelligent, but the ultimate cynic.

Sketches of Fiji

There were three local Europeans locked up and treated roughly during Rabuka's coups: Grahame Southwick, Peter Thompson and Bing. He told the story of being released from the Army cells and taken to the officer's mess for a beer with Rabuka – all good mates.

Bing took particular interest in Air Pacific and would report even a 15-minute delay. It wasn't that he had it in for us, but rather that the national airline was always going to be rich pickings for a 'Beachcomber' column. There was nothing to do but roll with those punches and keep focused on the facts. Then, when the well-known business magazine *Pacific Islands Monthly* collapsed, he began his own publication called *Islands Business*. As we were advertisers, and as his audience was different, the pressure from that source dried up (there were plenty of others!).

Sadly, Bing died a few years ago whilst reporting on a Pacific Island leader's meeting in Port Moresby. He is missed as a friend, an observant reporter, and as someone who really did know what made the politics in the Pacific tick. As it happened Ross Addison also established his own company and took on the production of our in-flight magazine.

There is a simple test I used when considering press releases, speeches and advertisements – in fact any form of communication; ask the question 'What's the audience, what's the message?'. There are many times the thrust of what we were saying changed when faced with that litmus test.

The Fleet and ATRs

In the years that I had been with Blue Lagoon, Air Pacific had transitioned from the Trislander, HS748 and BAC 111 days to a fleet of new French turboprops and Boeing jets. I inherited a fleet of an old B747-200 leased from Qantas, a B737-200 and two ATR42 turboprops. With that fleet we flew to Sydney and Auckland, and in 1989 to Melbourne (747s) Brisbane, Honiara, Vila and some Auckland services (737s) Tonga and Samoa (ATR42s). The ATRs also flew the domestic Suva/Nadi and Suva/Labasa services. We worked them hard, but the schedules were very inefficient in the use of crews and in the maintenance programs.

Our engineers carried out all the routine work on the 737 but heavy work went to Air New Zealand in Christchurch. We did some 747 work as they transited Nadi, but basically it went to Qantas. The ATRs were all ours, but being new, the work was not extensive. The B737 and ATR work was done in the hangar at Nausori originally built to house the BAC 1-11s.

We made money on the Australian and New Zealand routes, covered our costs on the regional routes and lost (shall I say our wallets?) on the domestic – particularly Labasa which incurred very heavy losses. That, plus the dramas of flying turboprops over long ocean sectors to the outer edges of their operating envelopes meant the ATRs had to go. So, by 1991, even though it formed part of the 'grand plan' it was back to the then Minister for Transport and Civil Aviation, David Pickering, and the Board to present the detail of the fleet renewal. Again, we had their support despite the political and financial risk.

Sketches of Fiji

ATR however were not happy and lobbied government very heavily. Despite the background grumbling, in 1992 we concluded lease negotiations for a B737-500 with Guinness Peat Aviation (GPA) and as part of the deal sold the ATRs to them. There are many stories I could tell about that change- over; flying to Ireland with Gerald and Narendra Kumar to begin the negotiations with GPA Chairman Paddy Ryan in his castle in Southern Ireland. Of him arranging a helicopter ride over the cliffs of Moher, and of his huge stud bull called DC8. Then the second round of negotiations in the conference room of a high-rise hotel on the banks of the Ala Wai canal in Honolulu - locked up for three days and watching the surfers below when we needed to turn our back on the negotiations to draw breath.

The decision to exit the ATR 42 turboprop fleet directly affected Vanua Levu and at one point a large group of men from the village near Labasa airport donned their warrior gear and face marking and, armed with sticks, axes and cane knives, staged a protest right on the runway. I thought at the time it was a rather strange way to encourage us to return. But in the end, we did what we had decided we must do.

There is often-time a debate that a National carrier has a duty and role to 'act in the National interest' and that argument was rolled out extensively in the period after we announced our withdrawal from domestic operations. I have some sympathy for this, but there must be a balance. It must not be allowed as a crutch for bad management – as Air Pacific had found before my time. Also, if this National duty role is to be ap-

The Fleet and ATRs

plied, then there needs to be a very clear process to identify the cost of doing so. And it needs a businesslike decision-making process to ensure that emotion and politics do not overwhelm the financial reality.

There was a document, agreed between Sir Ian Thompson and Ratu Mara called 'the objectives of Air Pacific'. This had a clause stating clearly that all routes had to contribute to the operating profitability of the company, 'or alternative arrangements made'(i.e. subsidy). It was framed and mounted on the wall in the Boardroom. The only time I had to bring the Board's attention to this was in the debate over the withdrawal from Labasa. The government's representative on the Board had advised of their disquiet about this decision, and I could see there was some momentum in support. I pointed to the 'Objectives' and said that unless government were to change that requirement, we had no alternative but to stop the Labasa services. The Board confirmed we would proceed with our decision. I knew that my action was a direct challenge to the government, but they didn't change the policy.

As far as I was concerned our duty was to get rid of those ATRs, get ourselves to Nadi, introduce the new jet fleet, and to do what we believed we needed to do. And we did it.

Japan and a new Strategy

By the late '80s, driven by their extraordinary economy of the day, Japan was breaking all records in tourism growth across the globe. Fiji was not in that game, so the plan was to fly to Tokyo. This was supported strongly by the Government and the Fiji tourism industry; however it meant a new fleet of jet aircraft. Easy to say, but it was a huge step in terms of financial liabilities and of capacity in both crew and administrative resources. Risky would be an understatement! But hey, we were on a roll.

Starting services to Tokyo however was a problem because every man and his dog wanted a landing slot at Narita airport, and there were none left. It became a major hurdle, and after months of negotiations I decided to bring in the big guns. I arranged, through the Japanese Embassy, for the Prime Minister Ratu Sir Kamasese Mara to accompany Gerald and me on a visit to Tokyo.

We met first over dinner at the top of the Prince Hotel overlooking the Emperor's palace with a Mr. Goto who was chairman and major shareholder of the huge Tokyu group; and owner of the hotel we were in. Tokyu was one of the 'big five' in Japan. Mr. Goto also owned an island in Fiji's Lau group and was close to Ratu Mara who was *Tui Lau* – amongst other things. I explained the problem over a USD 600 bottle of red wine. Mr. Goto ordered a second (I was paying), we had one glass out of that before he invited us to his office in the room next door. It is true I looked back at that three-quarter full bottle as we left the room.

In his palatial office he poured a very nice brandy for us all, called in a secretary and dictated something in Japanese to him; then we simply

Japan and a new Strategy

told stories for an hour or so. The next day we visited the Minister of Transport, and after the usual pleasantries, but even before I explained the purpose of our visit, he said that he 'understood ...etc'. And that our problem would be attended to. We got our slots.

The first flight to Japan took place on 30 October 1988. It became a very profitable and successful operation for many years.

At this time I was coming under political pressure to change the name of the company back to Fiji Airways. How things change. A few years prior no politician wanted to go anywhere near Air Pacific – now it was all national pride and everyone wanting to have a say. I could understand the emotion, but here we were, an unknown airline coming from a small developing nation in the middle of the Pacific, starting services to conservative, safety-conscious, Japan. My belly told me that 'Air Pacific' carried a stronger brand image than 'Fiji Airways'. A straw poll of the all-powerful Japanese tour wholesalers confirmed this, so I told the pollies 'No, we're not doing that'.

What I did do though was to remove the ridiculous marlin from the tail and replace it with the name 'Fiji'. Everyone was happy. The marlin had been dreamed up back in the DC3 days by Neil Stephenson who was the then head of the electrical shop. I never liked it, and at last I could get rid of it. We did however keep the rainbow colour scheme that had been introduced at the time of the BAC1-11s. More recently in 2015 the then American expatriate CEO did change the name to

Sketches of Fiji

'Fiji Airways' and I think the timing was right to do so. But he also introduced a traditional *Masi* logo that was emotively strong to those in Fiji; and meant very little to his market in the tourism source countries. Without intending any disrespect to the traditional aspects of this, I think it's boring – but then that's just me.

In mid 1989 I got the executive group into a huddle for four days at the Hyatt Hotel on the Coral Coast to work out a longer-term plan for the company. By now all the executives were local except for Stephen Brown, Nick Panza who supported Ernie Dutta in the marketing field, and the indefatigable Geoff Bowmaker seconded, at my request, from Qantas to act as Strategic Planning Manager. I'd met Geoff during my stint at Qantas and was impressed by his calm logic. Up to that point the strategic planning had frankly been just the 'seat-of-Drysdale's-pants'. We needed to get more professional.

Geoff did the preliminary work and we had several meetings before heading off to the Hyatt; so that by the time we met there we were ready to take a long hard look at where we were going. And to take another round of hard, and risky, decisions.

That was: *Increase flights to Tokyo, fly to Osaka, fly to Los Angeles and Honolulu and lease a new B767 into the fleet. Easy – no problem. Oh, and by the way replace the two B737s with three of the new NG series 737s that Boeing had not yet even started to deliver.*

No problem! So, we did it.

Politics and fish

All airlines attract political, media and public attention, but the national carrier of a small developing nation becomes central to the rumour machine, especially in times of political troubles. We were that, and what we were doing was very risky and very controversial. We had to constantly manage the shadowy world of rumour and speculation.

By the early '90s the post-coup politics were slowly becoming more stabilised and, like all those who stayed, I was buoyed by optimism about the future; you had to be - or go. But no one could be absolutely sure. My role as the head of the national carrier placed me in the forefront of rumour, sometimes controversy, and always jealously for the supposed high salary and perks ('supposed' being a very operative word here). The cold, hard, fact was that my position was always exposed to challenge no matter what magic we might work in the turnaround of Air Pacific. A contract would not be barrier enough if those forces looking for my job gained a hold, and there were several I knew of who were trying to find a weakness to exploit in order to get me fired.

Shortly after we started the second Tokyo service in April 1991 one of these 'white ant' exercises started to take hold. Grahame Southwick had returned to Fiji in the mid '80s to work in Fiji's tuna fishing industry. In due course he had started his own company Fiji Fish Ltd. and begun exporting high grade chilled fish on our services to Japan. This is a very competitive industry and freight rates are a major cost component. I began to hear snippets of a rumour that my lifelong friendship with Grahame had resulted in him being given

Sketches of Fiji

preferential rates over his competitors. This was absolutely not true, but the stories began to gain traction. I'm reminded of the old maxim 'why bother with the facts when a good conspiracy rumour will do'.

I asked my freight manager Watson Seeto if he had heard the stories as well, and when he said he had, I decided this needed to be to be tackled head-on in a 'knockdown, drag out' session.

I asked Watson to call a meeting of all the players; the Ministries of Fishing/Agriculture, my own Ministry of Transport, Grahame, and his main competitor whom I believed was in cahoots with certain government officials. The meeting opened with a bang. I told them I had heard the rumours, that they were scurrilous and defamatory, and hoped there was no-one in the room who was party to that nonsense. I then said that Grahame and I had gone to school together and were close friends, but that at no time had I ever discussed freight rates for fish with him, nor even with Watson Seeto.

There was silence for a moment, then Grahame also stated very clearly that we had never talked about rates. I turned to Watson and he confirmed the same. Then, turning to the government representatives and to Grahame's competitor, I asked them to say if they had any evidence to the contrary. There was silence. I then authorised Watson to negotiate freight rates for fish without referring that to me, provided he remained within the Board-approved budget and consulted our Commercial Manager Ernie Dutta. I then left the meeting. To this day I don't know what eventuated after that, but the rumours died.

The move to Nadi

We had to build a hangar and company headquarters at Nadi, and that's a whole story I'll leave to someone else to tell. Suffice to say that every time I land at Nadi and taxi past 'my' hangar I feel that it was all worth it. That building is visible testimony to all my team, to all the risks we took, and to the dedication, loyalty and hard work of a remarkable group of people.

Tony Wong supervised the day to day work; and at his suggestion Jone Sowata, who was one of Fiji Airways' first local tradesmen, placed the last bolt in the roof structure on 20th. May 1992. He also autographed the steel frame next to the bolt. Fittingly Jone was from the Rewa delta near Nausori airport and the event was conducted with full traditional Fijian ceremonies. The hangar was finished on time and officially opened on 30th. April 1993. It cost $18 million and was the largest 'space frame' open-span building ever constructed in Fiji. Thanks to Tony Wong's tight control it was also completed under budget.

Tony and the operations team moved first, and then over the next twelve months the rest made the move. We had the inevitable front-page emotional stories, complete with photos of mothers with crying school kids by their sides.

I admit that at the height of the protests, with government beginning to vacillate (not my minister David Pickering I must say), and with vocal, emotively strong, union and media negativity, I began to wonder if they might have a point. It was a very brief interlude! Those

Sketches of Fiji

doubts were cast aside when I paid a visit to Samoa and returned late at night in one of the ATRs in a tropical thunderstorm. Almost four hours of being tossed around the sky at night in a turboprop brought home to me very clearly that these aircraft were not right for our operations and we had to move on. The vision was safe. If anything, I was even more determined to press on.

We had a ten-day strike and I got very angry at the unreasonable and obstructive attitude of the unions. On day eight of the strike I printed the names of all the strikers, full page, in both the newspapers – an unusual industrial relations action methinks!

Despite the intensive efforts of the union to ground our flights, with a few loyal crews, and the extraordinary skill and hard work of Tony Wong and his team, we kept most of the services operating. We broke the strike. Long story but we did it, and the company has never looked back.

In the middle of all this drama, in February 1993 the Board renewed my contract for a further five years and the President of the Royal Aeronautical Society invited me to become a Fellow of that 150 year old learned Society.

B767

We needed to add a B767 aircraft to the fleet – a third B747 would be too big a step in capacity. This aircraft was state-of-the-art at the time, and expensive. After reviewing the various leasing offers in 1994 we settled on the Los Angeles based International Lease Finance Company (ILFC) as the most likely. Negotiations for a brand new B767, and an interim second-hand aircraft, started in their offices on the 57th. floor of their headquarters on the Avenue of the Stars. I was joined in these discussions by our very canny Director of Finance Narendra Kumar, and our Los Angeles Attorney, Rod Margo from the law firm Condon and Forsyth.

ILFC at that time was the second largest aircraft leasing firm in the world. The President was Steve Udvar-Hazey and his deputy was John Pfluger; these two individuals were *the* names in that business, and that's who we were negotiating directly with, based on *their* pro-forma leasing contract, and in their offices. Do the words stress, or pressure, come to mind?

On the last afternoon I looked up from the papers on the desk across at Narendra who was facing the window behind me. He was looking shocked and wiping his glasses very rapidly, so I turned around, and saw the building opposite us sway to one side, and then back again. Then it did it again, and I realised it was an earthquake. We all of us turned to watch for a minute or so as the buildings continued to sway in opposite directions. Then, because it settled a bit, and because we had a flight to catch, we carried on with the negotiations. It turned out to be a big earthquake centered near San Francisco. We cut the deal before we left.

Sketches of Fiji

Later, when I checked quietly with the Qantas fleet purchasing guys, they agreed we had done alright for a single aircraft being leased to a small airline from a rock in the middle of the Pacific. A few weeks later Gerald joined me for the formal contract signing in Los Angeles and afterwards Hazey and Pfluger hosted us to dinner at Hollywood's famous Brown Derby restaurant. I became quite friendly with Hazey and we caught up each year at the IATA Annual General Meetings. He came to Fiji often and on one occasion took his son on a Blue Lagoon cruise and loved it.

For reasons I don't recall, ILFC wanted to make a big show of the acceptance of the new aircraft from Boeing at the Seattle factory, so in early September 1994 I flew there for the occasion. Back home plans were put in place to welcome the aircraft with all the dignitaries and the Fijian welcoming ceremony of '*Cere*'. We also planned to use the occasion to introduce our new crew uniforms to the public – so big deal it was to be. The chief guest was the Prime Minister and there were many other Ministers, our Board, and the leaders of Fiji's tourism industry and commerce. Yup – big deal – except that Seattle was fog-bound that morning and our departure was delayed by several hours.

The Air Pacific team again proved their worth. While we poured on all speed to get to Fiji, they reversed the program and introduced the uniforms first, taking quite a while to do this of course. Then the party started, so that by the time we finally did arrive everyone was very happy to see us; emotional might be a better word.

Tales of Tonga

I'll tell some tales of Tonga.

As you will of course know, the Kingdom of Tonga lies very close to the Southeastern Fijian group of Lau islands. It is the last of the Polynesian monarchies. The two countries have had a long and sometimes very close (as in raiding, wars and intermarriage) relationship. Indeed, the chiefly families of Lau are related to those of Tonga; Ratu Mara in particular.

Fiji Airways had pioneered flights between the two countries with Herons way back in the late 1950s and we were by now flying daily services to Nuku'alofa with a mix of ATR42 and B737 aircraft. Some of the B737 services went on to Auckland. Tonga was one of the island nations who bought shares in Air Pacific when it morphed from Fiji Airways in 1970 and I had a Tongan Government representative, Dr. Langi Kavaliku, on my Board. I got on well with Langi, he was a bit like Jo Kamakamica and didn't say a lot, but when he did it was worth taking close note.

On 1st. July '88, not long after I took over the company, the King celebrated his 70th. birthday and I was invited. We flew to Tonga in a special service ATR42 with Ratu Mara and other invited Fiji guests, including several Lauan chiefs. Then it was off to four days of long (very long) church services and feasting. I had an audience with the King and presented him with a rather nice, and suitably inscribed, mantlepiece clock. He thanked me politely, then the *'TalaTala'* prayed for the King, me, our respective families, the company etc. etc. etc. for

Sketches of Fiji

what seemed like an eternity. At one point I noted that His Majesty seemed to be asleep; I'm sure of course that he was just praying!

On Friday came the Royal feast. More than 1000 guests sat on the lawn in front of the palace. Each person had a long wooden tray in front of them with a whole suckling pig, a fish, a chicken and a mound of green and root crops. After the guests had eaten, the Army came in and took the leftovers for distribution to the people. As Ratu Mara said on the way home 'that was probably the last ever true Polynesian feast'.

Over the years the Tongans had tried to form their own international airline and had failed in a very expensive way each time. However, by 1994 Royal Tongan, as the latest iteration was called, had recruited my former head of strategy, Geoff Bowmaker to the CEO position. Geoff had returned to Qantas after his secondment to Air Pacific, but the call of the Islands was strong, and he decided to accept the Royal Tongan position offered to him by my Board Director Lagi Kavaliku. I knew we could work with Geoff and a key to doing business in the Pacific is trust. Without that, the going will be almost impossible.

We were operating one B737 and I needed about 1700 to 2000 more hours per year on these aircraft but could not justify the quantum jump in hours that a second aircraft would give us. To achieve full utilisation of a B737 in our neck of the woods it had to operate around 3000 hours per year. The remaining 1000 hours or so was exactly what Royal Tongan needed to operate services to Auckland.

The move to Nadi

I cut a deal with Geoff in January 1994 to jointly lease a B737 from an Ansett group aircraft leasing company (AWAS). Royal Tongan would have the aircraft for approximately 1100 hours per annum and we would have it for the rest. Air Pacific would be the operators of the aircraft and provide crew, maintenance and insurance (known in the trade as ACMI). We agreed a completely open-book arrangement where Royal Tongan could at any time inspect the operating costs of that aircraft and challenge us if they felt we were overcharging. Whilst they did from time to time ask questions (Geoff was a good CEO) there was never any disagreement.

The concept was easy to say, but a joint lease like this had never been done before, and ultimately resulted in yet more long hours in a room in Los Angeles – this time also with Boeing and a raft of very expensive lawyers. Still, eventually we got the deal done.

One of the rather strange things we did was to paint one side of the aircraft in Royal Tongan colours, the other in Air Pacific's livery. Again, sounds simple but the big debate was which side was which. We both wanted our colours on the port side where the passenger door was. I won that debate, but the deal was that we would ensure we parked the aircraft with the Tongan side facing the terminal at Nuku'alofa, assuming of course that the prevailing wind would allow that. The B737 needs to be parked head-on to the wind if it is over a certain strength.

On the big day of the inaugural flight to Tonga the King and his retinue were seated in a specially constructed stand at the airport, the

Sketches of Fiji

feast and prayers were ready, the Army was lined up in polished uniforms, the brass band was playing, and our pilots had been briefed to ensure we parked the right way around. You guessed it, fate and weather intervened. The wind was from the wrong direction and we had to park with the Air Pacific side facing his majesty!

To end that story, after I left Air Pacific the then Tongan crown prince cut a deal in Kuala Lumpur with the brother of the Sultan of Brunei to lease a B757; and then terminated the Air Pacific deal. Royal Tongan had been making money on the B737 lease with us, the B757 deal rapidly incurred very large losses and the airline collapsed. The financial impact so scarred the nation that even now, some 20 years later, no one is game to propose a National Tongan airline again. The Crown Prince went on to become King on the death of his father.

Treaties and politics

One of the biggest obstacles to our growth were the restrictions imposed on us by the International Air Services Agreements (AsAs as they are known) between Fiji, Australia and New Zealand. AsAs are one of aviation's most misunderstood, misrepresented, and misreported principles. They have more armchair 'experts' than the weekend football – often with the added complexity of vested interest.

These are complex international trade treaties between States that govern the rights of the international aviation industry to operate. Rights created under these trade agreements are then 'designated' by each country to an airline whose 'substantial ownership and effective control' resides in that country. They are based on the concept of Sovereignty that countries claim over the airspace above their territory, agreed to in Paris way back in 1919; and on the principle of the States having the right to then regulate air traffic within that airspace.

It is important to understand that, although we often hear of liberalisation and 'open skies', these AsAs are in fact a collection of *restrictions*. They restrict, in varying degrees, the ports to be used, the number of seats to be operated, the number of flights, the type of aircraft, where the flight can operate, in some cases the airfares, who can do the ground handling, whether an airline can set up its own offices in the country, the export of currency and in some cases access to airport slots. Even though they are styled 'freedoms of the air' these trade agreements, and the so called 'freedoms', are no more than a release from part, note *part,* of these restrictions.

Sketches of Fiji

What is more, it's important to understand that these negotiations take place between the States; the airlines are not at the table. Whilst one would hope that the government negotiators would take their National airline's views into account, I know from personal, and bitter, experience that that is not always the case.

During the Colonial era the Foreign Office in London had given Australia and New Zealand what amounted to unrestricted rights to, and beyond, Fiji with *no equivalent reciprocal rights for a Fiji airline*. One could argue that this was because no-one ever envisaged a day when Fiji would have its own international airline. Fair enough for those days I suppose, but it was a major obstacle to our growth; especially in the case of New Zealand.

With the advent of the BAC1-11 jet aircraft in the early '70s Fiji Airways/Air Pacific had morphed from being a domestic and regional carrier into an international airline. The problem was that this occurred post-independence; the Australian and New Zealand governments pointed to the Colonial era Agreements and reminded Fiji that they had no air rights treaties other than those created by the former Colonial government. The first round of negotiations granted the Fiji carrier access to Brisbane and Auckland *but only via an intermediate port*! As a result, in those early 1-11 days we had to fly via Noumea or Honiara to Brisbane; and via Tonga to Auckland. It would sound like a 'Yes Minister' joke, except that it was real, and it was serious.

Treaties and politics

Those early 1970's negotiations dragged on and were at times bitter, especially with New Zealand which took the view that they had pioneered the routes and therefore they had exclusive 'grandfathered' rights. At one point Fiji became so frustrated that they threatened to give notice to cancel the treaty altogether. This is a big deal in international relationships and the Kiwis backed off a little. Gradually, gradually, Fiji was able to bring about a number of changes, but the problem was still serious when I became CEO in 1988.

As our strategies began to develop it became obvious that the 'grand plan' to build an international airline for Fiji was heavily dependent on those shackles being removed. Australia understood this and, although progress was slow, we got there. New Zealand was a very different case; they fought tooth and nail to retain the historically biased air services rights for their airline.

In particular, under the then existing AsAs we were prohibited from carrying passengers from the US to New Zealand unless they stopped over in Fiji for at least a day. Yet Air New Zealand had no such constraints; indeed they had almost unfettered rights to fly passengers to and from the USA, both over and through Nadi, and with or without stopovers. It was the same for Japan to New Zealand via Fiji. The simple fact was that if we could not fully access those markets, the entire strategy to build a successful international airline for Fiji would be in jeopardy.

Sketches of Fiji

The debate intensified in early 1994 with our increased Japan services and planned commencement of Los Angeles flights. The Kiwi's played hardball. Through their contacts within the tourism industry they (more correctly Air New Zealand) caused the hotel industry and some individual hoteliers to publicly argue their case. Unfortunately, many of these ill-informed and vested interest opinions were aired in the media. 'Armchair experts' had a field day.

Then, at one point during a very tense period of negotiations, Air New Zealand invited Fiji's chief negotiator to travel to Auckland as their guest to watch a Fiji versus All Blacks rugby game. Not surprisingly, on his return his views had changed somewhat. We were told he even visited Prime Minister Rabuka, who was in hospital, to convey his newfound perspectives.

In September 1994 my then head of strategy, Ramen Narayan, and I decided to fight fire with fire and asked the Minister for Transport and Civil Aviation for the right to address Cabinet. Ramen was my expert on these matters and together we made a presentation to the full Cabinet. We played it at two levels; first pragmatic passenger numbers, seats and tourists, then switched to the more nationalistic and emotive 'they can't do this to us, we need your help' message.

At the end of the presentation there was a deathly silence, but I'd been reading my audience and knew we had them on side. Rabuka looked around the room, then thumped his fist on the table, and said in a very

Treaties and politics

loud, commanding voice 'It's time for Fiji to grow up'. He then turned to the Minister and said, 'you make sure Andrew gets what he needs – cancel the Agreement if you have to'.

If Jo Kamikamica's agreement to 'the Drysdale plan' and the move to Nadi marked a turning point in the National carrier's history, this was another. That moment is seared into my memory.

I knew how volatile politics could be and that we needed to cement this decision in place. So it was off to the media where we made the same presentation; and then to the tourism industry where I told them their support for the Kiwis was damaging the national carrier of Fiji, impacting Fiji jobs and the Fiji economy. I also reminded them that Air Pacific was locally controlled and managed, paid dividends to the Fiji Government, and paid local taxes into the economy.

Then I turned the guns on them, reminding them that the major hotels were owned by offshore interests, managed by offshore companies, that their executives were all expatriates and that they repatriated their profits overseas. The press came out in support of Air Pacific, the hoteliers muttered about having been misunderstood and that they were supportive of Air Pacific. It took a long time but gradually the bias was removed.

Boeing versus Airbus

Part of the strategic plan called for us to replace the two B737–300s and to build a fleet of initially three, then to five, narrow-body aircraft. In 1996 we sent out detailed specifications to both Boeing and Airbus. I also developed a very clear set of governance procedures and required all involved in the selection process to sign a document stating they would abide by those procedures. We set up a formal program to keep the Board and the Ministry briefed on progress. This hadn't been as necessary for the B767 because at that time Airbus had only just started to produce the A330. I had several on my executive team, and some of my Board, who I suspect thought this was a bit of overkill – but they were subsequently proved wrong.

Then the fun began with both companies sending in to the fray, first their sales teams, then their technical guys, then the contract teams. One thing we did was to ensure that if one company asked for certain extra information, both were given the same reply. Also, all documentation was held in one room open only to those who had signed the 'Drysdale declaration' on governance. The pricing information went only to Gerald as Chairman, Josephine as CFO and me.

It took months to evaluate the offers and it's too long a story to tell here – the upshot was that we chose the 'Next Generation' Boeing 737–500 series and ordered three of them in August 1996. The aircraft was still under development at the time and was an update of the B737 aircraft we had flown, and which had worked so well for us, since 1981.

Boeing versus Airbus

The French were not happy, to say the least, and lobbied government, in particular (by now Major General) Sitiveni Rabuka in his capacity as the properly elected Prime Minister. In April 1997 they invited him to visit France on a state visit and invested him with a military medal for bravery, which was fair as he had saved some French soldiers when serving in Lebanon with the UN peacekeeping forces – strange though that they remembered to do this so many years later. We were later told they also made mention of a rather large aid cheque. Then, while they had him there, took him to Toulouse and filled his ear with all the wonders of the A320, and why the Boeing aircraft was wrong for Air Pacific. It seems he became convinced because a message was sent to Suva telling David Pickering as Minister for Transport and Civil Aviation, to direct Air Pacific to 'reconsider' the decision to buy the 737s. What is more, a copy of the message was given to the Fiji newspapers! We were front page for the wrong reasons – yet again.

Now, as it happened, David Pickering and I were in Beijing at the time. I was Chairing the annual PATA Conference as the PATA Chairman, and he was leading the Fiji tourism delegation. We both received faxed copies of the newspapers on the morning I was to Chair the grand opening ceremony in the Great Hall of the People in Tiananmen square. David and I nodded briefly to each other as I was being escorted in the official party to the dais. I knew we had kept him fully briefed during the selection process, and that he would be prepared to discuss the situation; but things were serious, and speed was of the essence.

Sketches of Fiji

I delivered my welcome address to the more than 1200 delegates in the Great Hall of the People, then sat at the head table while all the other dignitaries made their speeches, including the Premier of China. People probably thought I was making notes of what was being said – actually, I was writing a press release to respond to the Prime Minister's dictate. It was to say that we respected the PM's message and would respond to the Airbus sales pitch (and I used that expression) as a matter of urgency.

At the coffee break I showed it to David, and he agreed. I then gave it to Ernie Dutta and asked him to get it to Gerald as quickly as possible. If Gerald agreed with the wording then it was to be immediately released, which happened – more front- page stuff. There were long phone calls that evening, and we dispatched our Chief Pilot Captain Tuisue and Chief Engineer Barry Geddes to Toulouse.

The Conference ended the next evening and I left to return to Fiji even before the formal dinner was over. Tui and Barry reported that they were facing a wall of Airbus designers, engineers and pilots and that there was no purpose continuing the debate with them. Rabuka had left Toulouse by now and David got him to agree to put everything on hold until we all returned to Fiji.

While we waited for him to return, I briefed my Board and they remained in full support of our decision. When Rabuka got back we provided him, David Pickering and several other cabinet Ministers with a full brief, even though they had already seen a great deal of this

Boeing versus Airbus

during the selection process. They were somewhat mollified when we pointed out that the B737 actually had a high French content; in particular the avionics and the CFM engines which were built in France. The upshot was that government became convinced that we were right (again), and we went ahead with the Boeing order. Handling the public relations of this so as to not embarrass the Prime Minister was a bit nerve wracking, but we got through it well enough.

There was a sequel to this. Not long after the dust had settled, I was at the French Ambassador's residence to celebrate Bastille day. The 'champers' was flowing freely and by 10pm or so, after the speeches were over and the singing had started, one of my close friends, a well-known journalist, came over to me to say that the Ambassador had told him that Drysdale had taken a bribe from Boeing, and that USD 360,000 had been paid into an account in Vanuatu. I took it to be the booze talking and thought nothing more of it.

But a few days later David Pickering called me into his office with the Permanent Secretary. He said he had been told of this claim and asked directly whether there was any truth in it. Naturally enough I said 'no' and offered to give him an open letter addressed to any financial institution granting the Government of Fiji complete access to any account that I, or any of my family may hold. His permanent Secretary took that down as a note and David said, 'Thank you Andrew, that won't be necessary'. It may be just a coincidence, but the Ambassador left Fiji not long after. Oh! And I was never invited to Bastille Day celebrations again.

Sketches of Fiji

As an aside, it was at the end of that memorable 1997 Conference that PATA presented me with their highest honour of Life Member. I had been elected to the Board of Directors some eight years earlier and had headed PATA's aviation subcommittee for most of that time. I had also formed the view that the then heavily USA-focused organisation needed to re-focus to Asia where the future of tourism and aviation lay; and told them so. This did not go down well with my US colleagues.

The upshot was that the PATA Board asked me to write a report on the future of the organisation. I did so and, amongst other things, recommended that we move the headquarters from San Francisco, where it had been for nearly 40 years, to a city in Asia. This strategy paper was accepted by the Board and became known as the 'Drysdale Report'. It also caused the then CEO of PATA who lived in San Francisco to resign – which in my opinion was a good thing. PATA eventually moved to Bangkok. The organisation has changed enormously since then and has become far more relevant to the global travel, tourism and aviation industry.

Conquistadors del Cielo

One of the more interesting things that happened during those risky, mad Air Pacific years was that I was invited, twice, to attend the annual, 'secret', meeting of the Conquistadores del Cielo (Conquerors of the Sky). 'The what?' you say, and rightly so.

The CdC is a supposedly secret club whose members are some of the aviation and aerospace industry's top executives. It is in fact a not-for-profit American organisation founded in 1938 and limited to just 91 members. They meet twice a year. Once at the A bar A 'Dude' ranch high in the Wyoming mountains. That meeting is very exclusive, just members plus 10 'invitados'. The second is at a golf course somewhere in the USA and open to a wider audience; but again, only by invitation.

Because of antitrust laws, the group is watched very carefully by the American Securities and Exchange Commission but were given exemption many years ago and that continues. They have a strict rule 'leave your sword at the door' i.e. absolutely no discussion on business – or they throw you out with immediate effect.

I was invited to attend two of the four-day-long Dude ranch meetings (1991 and '93) by Jim Worsham who lead the General Electric team that give the world the GE high by- pass jet engine. He was a genuine Kentucky Colonel who had served in US Army artillery units during WW II and hated guns. The members of CdC are *the* names of Aerospace and Aviation, albeit with a heavy USA bias. For those of you who know your aviation history, Crandall, Rowe, Shrontz, Douglas

Sketches of Fiji

(yes, that one) and Mc Donald (yes that one), Kelleher, and British Airway's Sir Colin Marshall have all been members. There were also members of the NASA space program – Neil Armstrong (no introduction needed), Alan Shepherd (the USA's first man in space) and Jim McDivit (Commander of Gemini 4). It's an amazing list and I enjoyed spending time with them. Armstrong is (was) an absolute gentleman and quite shy. Jim McDivit taught me how to throw knives – he was an expert. I still have the knives.

They spend their time riding horses, shooting all sorts of guns, including a genuine 1860s buffalo rifle, throwing knives, archery, fly fishing, gambling at poker (for extraordinary winnings), tennis, golf, and in fact almost any sport where you can be competitive in your late 40s or older. Great camaraderie; and at the end is the 'Ceremony'. They dress up as Spanish Conquistadores, complete with armour, genuine swords and helmets and, carrying blazing torches, ride horses across a ridge and down into a valley to a huge campfire. There they farewell members who have died and initiate new members in a ceremony which includes dubbing with a sword.

One of the activities is gun slinging – as in wild west cowboys. They have a genuine Colt 45 revolver and holster. You strap this gear on and stand facing an open space with the back of your knuckles pressing on a pressure switch. The gun is loaded with blanks. On command you draw and fire by fanning the trigger hammer – pulling the trigger is far too slow. You will have seen the action in cowboy movies. The clock starts when your knuckles leave the pressure switch and stops with the percussion sound of the bullet firing – clever engineering stuff. At 70 years of age Jim Worsham beat them all; his time was 1.1 seconds.

It was an amazing experience, and one I will long remember. After the second attendance, and after I had been discreetly observed and checked out by the inner circle of 'kingmakers', Jim told me my name had been placed on the list of possible future members once a vacancy was created. This only happened when a member died, stopped attending, or was kicked out for breaking the 'leave your sword at the door' rule. It was an exceptional honour; but I left Air Pacific before that happened.

Dreketi

As the relocation to Nadi rolled out in 1992/3 I had moved into a house in the 'CAAF Compound' at Namaka, Nadi that had been built for the Pan American manager when they operated to Fiji. For reasons that I never understood, I could not warm to that house. James, who was working at the Sheraton by now, joined me. Liz and Jackie travelled from Suva whenever they could, and I was in Suva regularly. Richard was still at boarding school, and David had gained a BA at the University of the South Pacific and was working in Suva.

We had rented our house in Tamavua and began looking around for somewhere to build in the Nadi/Lautoka area. We, at least I, gave very little thought to what would happen after the second term of five years with Air Pacific was completed. For months we drove all over the Nadi/Lautoka/Momi countryside looking for a site to build a special home. Eventually we found a six-acre cane farm on a ridge above Saweni and Vuda bays with spectacular views over almost 360 degrees. The mountains of the Nadi highlands to the East, Mamanuca islands to the West, Nadi to the South, the Yawawa chain of my Blue Lagoon days and Lautoka to the North. We couldn't quite see the city, but no problem with that.

We bought it from a cane farmer – all his Christmases had come at once - and had it rezoned residential. That's easy to say; it took months to get past the bureaucracy because it was a working cane farm at the time. In the end I told the boss of the Lands Department

Dreketi

that we were planning to grow flowers commercially, which was true. Friends of ours, Tippi and Ian Simpson, who owned the helicopter company, bought the parallel ridge and we both went to see our architect friend Stu Huggett to ask him to design our homes for us.

Stu's firm had been the architects for two extensions to our Suva house and a major extension had been completed just before we de-camped to Lautoka in the Blue Lagoon days. His firm had also been involved in the design of the Blue Lagoon ships. We knew Stu and his wife Gilly very well, both socially and in business. His initial idea was to dig out the sandstone the property lay on and use it to build the house. Grand plan, but no one could tell us if the stone was of construction grade, so we moved to plan 'B'. This was a large 'Queenslander' style home opening out on all sides with multiple French doors. The design was to use all Fijian hardwood. And that's what we built.

All the fittings were imported, and I paid many a visit to Home Depot in Honolulu and Los Angeles, returning on one trip with more than 200 four-inch, brass hinges in my suitcase. There were 68 doors – each of the multiple external French doors was double and had both a glass inner pair of doors and a heavy louvered outer pair that acted as hurricane shutters.

There are many stories to be told of that building and of the parties, even during construction. We celebrated my 50th. birthday there whilst it was still just a shell (with toilets).

Sketches of Fiji

New Year's Eve after we moved in was a massive party and I had to turn the water off under the house as that was the only way to stop the revelers from hosing everyone - throwing water at New Year is a Fijian custom.

Colin Dunlop, our naval architect from the Blue Lagoon days, got out his bagpipes and played, marching up and down outside the house in his full highland regalia. What our Indian cane farmer neighbours thought of that heaven knows. My mother Nell had a great time though, singing along, and bobbing up and down as one does.

At midnight, the hills rang out to Auld Lang Syne complete with kilted Scottish piper, our hands clasped to each other, and tears streaming down the faces.

Then, as the celebrations settled down to more drinks and storytelling, Colin walked out to the edge of the ridge in front of the house, and there, silhouetted by the moon, under the tropical stars he played 'Amazing Grace'. Grown men suddenly needed to look at their feet. I'm sure the spirit ancestors of the early Fijians would have approved of that happening at their legendary Vuda 'First Landing' just below us at the bottom of the ridge.

A Hotel? Madness!

Airlines should not get involved owning or running hotels. Repeat that after me!

So, what did we do – we got involved in building a new hotel.

It goes like this. The soft underbelly of our grand plan was that, if we were to add all that capacity to our fleet, and fly to those new destinations, and carry over 50 per cent of Fiji's tourists, then we needed the hotel room-nights to accommodate them. Seems simple, but by the early '90s Fiji was, seasonally at least, completely full in tourist hotels of any reasonable standard. I make that distinction because the Fiji Hotel Association would cry nonsense whenever I said that we didn't have enough hotel rooms. There were two reasons for this; first they had to represent all their members including the very basic motels in the backblocks of Nadi, and second, they were existing hoteliers, many were owners of their own hotels, and they weren't keen to see more competition.

Compounding the problem was that Fiji at the time was positioning itself as a quality destination with high yield per tourist, not something a very basic motel would do. The major growth market was Japan and they demanded high quality accommodation. An equally compounding problem was the political insecurity arising from the coups that meant few investors were prepared to put their money into Fiji at the time, certainly not into very expensive tourism bricks and mortar.

Sketches of Fiji

This became increasingly concerning as delivery dates for the new aircraft approached and I had many a public and private dispute with the hotel fraternity – albeit we always remained friends outside of the ring. I also spoke to several of the big international hotel chains. They were interested, but only in managing the property, not in owning the real estate.

The day came in 1995 when I said to my Board that if no one else was going to do it, then we would have to. Let's get that into perspective; there had been no new hotels built since 1987, no new hotels were mooted, and no foreign investor had shown the slightest interest in doing so. Nevertheless, my ever-supportive board said, 'Okay, give us a plan'.

Strange things sometimes come out of the woodwork. In 1992 the Japanese market was booming, and demanding high-quality hotels, and along came a fellow called Dr. Bungo Takahashi and a company called Electronics Industry Enterprises (EIE). In tow he had a fellow called Steven Norrie, a New Zealander allied to a large, and later controversial, New Zealand investment firm, Faye Richwhite. It's a long story, but their plan was to buy the then Regent Hotel at Denarau and to develop a tourism marina plus more hotels, villas and homes on the island. There were three problems – they needed increased flights to Japan and to the US (we were planning that anyway), they needed a commitment of at least one large hotel being built, and they needed land swaps from native land to freehold at Denarau island.

A Hotel? Madness!

Based on government assurance the land swap would happen, and our assurance that we would provide the flights, they began the process. They also bought a small parcel of Air Pacific shares and were given a position on the Board. This went to their Fiji manager, Andrew Thompson (son of Sir Ian, and a friend). The bit that was missing in the formula was the hotel.

Bungo and Co. were throwing money around freely, and Norrie's interest was in a commission on the deals. There was a little problem though; EIE was reportedly illegally using Japanese retiree's pension funds. Ultimately EIE went broke along with several Australian companies they were linked to, including a number of Christopher Skase's developments. As I heard it Bungo's Chairman went to jail – Bungo got off. Still, the momentum had begun, and the project continued, driven by Norrie, under a development company called Tabua Investments. Today it is 'Denarau', Fiji's tourism hub.

The land swap duly took place and, through an off-the- shelf company called Richmond Ltd. (ex our solicitor Barry Sweetman's firm) Air Pacific acquired a block of land to build a hotel next to the then Regent (now Westin) hotel.

We also negotiated a deal with the Hyatt chain for them to manage our hotel as a Grand Hyatt based on the Grand Hyatt in Bali. In fact, the plans were a clone of that hotel. This entailed lots more heavy-duty negotiations in Los Angles – as it happened, right next door to the ILFC offices. And lots more fast learning for this aircraft engineer.

Sketches of Fiji

We recruited an Australian, Adrian Black, to be the project manager and a local engineer Dallas Foon as his deputy.

Plans were completed, contracts let, and site work began. But by then my time with Air Pacific was coming to an end. I left for Australia in late 1997, in 2000 George Speight conducted his 'mutiny' and Hyatt withdrew. Sometime later, however, the Accor group took up the mantle, and today the hotel is the Sofitel at Denarau. It is profitable and paying dividends to Fiji Airways. I still say airlines should not get involved in hotels – so there!

Towards the end in Fiji

As we rolled into mid 1997 it was time to start thinking about my contract that was coming to an end early in 1998. Gerald and I had briefly touched on this and he indicated that the Board would like me to stay on for a third term subject to the position being advertised. That was good for the ego and I kind of got used to that idea.

But then I began to ask myself what new things I would do in a third five-year stint after the drama of the move to Nadi, beating the unions at their game, introducing the new fleet, starting the hotel and building a profitable national airline. I found myself looking at more of the same and knew that that was not going to be good enough. I had become too comfortable with the success we had achieved. Try as I might, everything I came up with was just incremental change to what we already had, and I'm not good at that - so I began to wonder.

There was another factor that was more subtle. Over the years there had been a gradual shift in attitudes such that we local Europeans were being seen by some, and I emphasise some, as not being part of the true local community. It was difficult to pin down, but it was there.

My position also meant that it was increasingly difficult for me to just be one of the 'local gang'. I tried very hard to retain the old lifestyle as much as possible, but when you are out most evenings hobnobbing with the foreign embassies, government Ministers and business leaders, it is not easy to then share a roti parcel with the cleaners.

Sketches of Fiji

This gradual drift was not helped by my insistence on wearing a tie at all business events and in the office. This was a deliberate policy of mine to build a culture of professionalism in the company. Casual shirts in the office does not do this. In similar vein I introduced a new crew uniform that went away from the 'aloha' look to a smart suit. But the effect of this formality was to distance me from many of my old mates even further.

I was in the news almost every week, and often on the front page of the newspapers. As much as I wanted, with great sincerity, to retain the links to the simple, down to earth, past and upbringing, it just wasn't possible. The society I lived in was not going to allow that to happen. I like to think that I hadn't become a snob, and I'm not bemoaning my lot; it was more that the society of my youth had simply faded away in the years post-independence and post the coups; and there was nothing to replace it that I felt belonged to me.

I was still locked into my daily stresses and loving what I was doing - but even I began to come to the realisation that, as they say in Fiji, 'time's up'.

And then we left Fiji

At the same Beijing PATA conference in June1997 that I spoke of earlier, I was standing in the buffet line for dinner with a friend, Captain Trevor Howarth who founded and owned Australia's Captain Cook Cruises. We got talking about things. I mentioned that my contract with Air Pacific was coming up for renewal, and he said he was planning to take his company to a public float and to retire. To do that he needed someone to prepare the company by introducing the necessary corporate governance processes and modern management practices. He readily accepted that his rule had been law in the cruise company, and that this needed to change if it was to become publicly listed. We looked at each other and went to a quiet corner. The upshot was that he offered me the position of Managing Director of the company and he would become Chairman. I accepted.

Because I was a Fiji citizen, I had to obtain a residency permit to live and work in Australia – yes, even though I had been born there. I went through the bureaucratic mill, including a full medical with X-rays. The irony was that when the permit finally came through, I could enter the hallowed halls of Australia because my wife was a New Zealand citizen courtesy of her father having been a Kiwi. Indeed, my passport carried the command that I was 'not to enter Australia to reside before Elizabeth Madeline Drysdale'. Weird; all our family except me were born in Fiji, they could all live and work in Australia - I was not, and I was born there!

We left Fiji on FJ911 on 27 September 1997. I went to the galley on the flight to Sydney to say farewell to the crew. They had all signed a card; there were tears.

A thought on Air Pacific

We did all those things; and at times we placed the company at extreme risk. If we had got the numbers wrong, if we had failed in the implementation of the strategic and fleet plan, or if the global market turned, or if there was another coup, or if any number of things had happened, it was entirely possible that, burdened with that fleet, burdened with the cost of the new hangar, and still settling down from the move to Nadi, the company could have collapsed. But it didn't.

We got it right, the dice fell our way, and the profits grew.

There was one other rather unique factor in our favour – Rabuka's coups. Strange to say I know, but had Fiji been bowling along with nominally quiet politics and had there been an elected Parliament at the time of the decision to move to Nadi, exit domestic flying, get rid of the ATRs and build the jet fleet - it simply would not have happened. Politics, egos, emotion and vested interest would have stymied the plan. As it was, the military-appointed interim government, and the ordinary citizens of Fiji, were looking for (I can even say, were desperate for) positive stories. We gave them that.

The first coup in May of '87 came as such a shock that people were still trying to come to grips with what had happened when the second coup in September knocked them flat. The rumour machine was extraordinary, and rarely a day would go by without some new story being circulated – always intrigue, drama and negativity.

A thought on Air Pacific

The Air Pacific story was different. Here was the little national airline, still burdened by heavy debt and 'negative shareholder worth', now setting out to become a major player in the Pacific's airline industry, and it was led by Fiji citizens. It was a good, positive, story - and a ray of hope. I was deeply conscious that we had made some very big promises, and we had to perform. Did I feel the pressure? Yes, at times. It would come from a casual remark, or a moment of reflection sitting on an aircraft, or after dinner, or suddenly from nowhere; but mostly it was just 'get on with the job', deal with the issues, and do what must be done.

I inherited a company that had the biggest 'negative shareholder worth' in the history of Fiji. The company's operations were propped by loans from Westpac, who in turn relied on Government guarantees. These were, to say the least, shaky, post Rabuka's coups. We changed that. We were profitable in every year of my ten years as CEO and the company remained profitable for many years after I left. By 1990 shareholder value had become positive again and continued to grow over the years.

We retired the debt in three years and began paying tax and dividends to the shareholders. As per our plan, by year three we were carrying more than 50 per cent of the visitors to Fiji and over 60 per cent of the freight. We moved the company from Suva to Nadi, built the hangar and headquarters, and created a safe, profitable, international airline for our country. By the time I left we were employing over 900 Fiji citizens and every one of the senior executives was local.

Sketches of Fiji

At my farewell in September 1997 more than 500 staff and their families gathered in the grounds (*Rara*) of the Mocambo hotel. It was a tremendously moving evening.

There was a yagona ceremony, speeches and the ladies of Air Pacific presented mats and tapa. Even more moving, they had composed a special *meke* and song to say farewell. There are many highlights of that night, but one that is deeply embedded in my memory was when I walked over to my old friends from the Nausori engineering days who were gathered quietly at one end of the ground. Saying farewell to these men who had shared hard biscuit and bully beef with me in the early hours of the mornings so long ago was a bit emotional.

In 2016 some of the old hands arranged a reunion. I wasn't able to attend because of my University lectures, but I did send a message to George Faktaufon who worked with me in those early years and which I repeat here:

George, I'm thinking of you all this week and am very sorry I can't be there; but it is a critical exam time for my students, and I need to be here for them. Please give my very best wishes to all the old (in inverted commas) friends and comrades. My message to you all is 'we did it'. Yes, we had expatriates from time to time– good, bad and indifferent – but at the end of the day it was us, the Kai Vitis, who made Air Pacific and Fiji Airways what it is today. We were the ones who stayed at our duty and made it happen. We did it, and we can all be very proud of what we did.

A thought on Air Pacific

We handed on a strong, profitable, company to those youngsters (again in inverted commas) to take the company to the next level. We created a safe airline, a sound commercial base, a strong corporate culture and a vision for the future. Full marks to us. My very best regards Andrew.

If only I could list all their names here - but they know who they are, and my heartfelt thanks goes to them all for their friendship over the years and their unfailing support, advice and damned hard work, often in very trying circumstances.

Vinaka vaka levu to all of you.

So, why these notes?

Everyone has a story – everyone. This, in part, is mine

I believe an understanding of where we come from shapes us, and impacts those around us, more than we normally give credit to. These are the things that provide our lives form and perspective, especially in the early years. Yes, they fade a little as we carve out our own lives and deal with what life delivers to us, but they never go away. Over the years I've been acutely conscious of the importance of this as our kids have, from time to time, sought these stories from me.

I wanted, as far as my poor writing skills would allow, to try to capture at least some of the stories from my life. In particular to try to tell what it was like as a local European growing up in Fiji at the end of the Colonial era, the pioneering Fiji Airways days, political independence, then the coups; and importantly, how we locals built a strong national airline for our country in the aftermath of those coups. In many ways I'm writing these notes for those wonderful people who worked with me in those exciting, scary, Air Pacific days. It's the least I can do.

I opened these notes with a quote from Gerald Gould's poem 'Wander thirst'. I'll close with a quote spoken by the wonderful English actress Maggie Smith at the end of the film *2nd. Best Marigold Hotel*. She said, 'There's no such thing as an ending; that's just the place where you leave the story'.

Lolomas Andrew

Sketches of Fiji

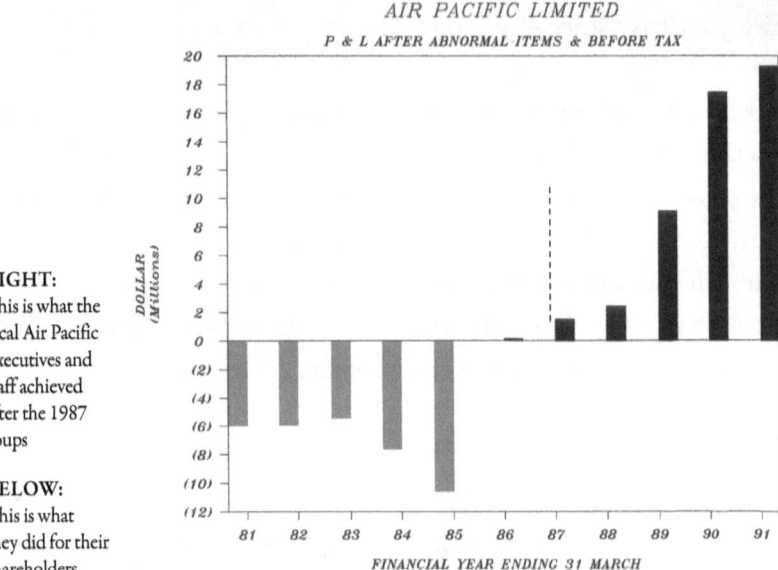

RIGHT:
This is what the local Air Pacific Executives and staff achieved after the 1987 coups

BELOW:
This is what they did for their shareholders

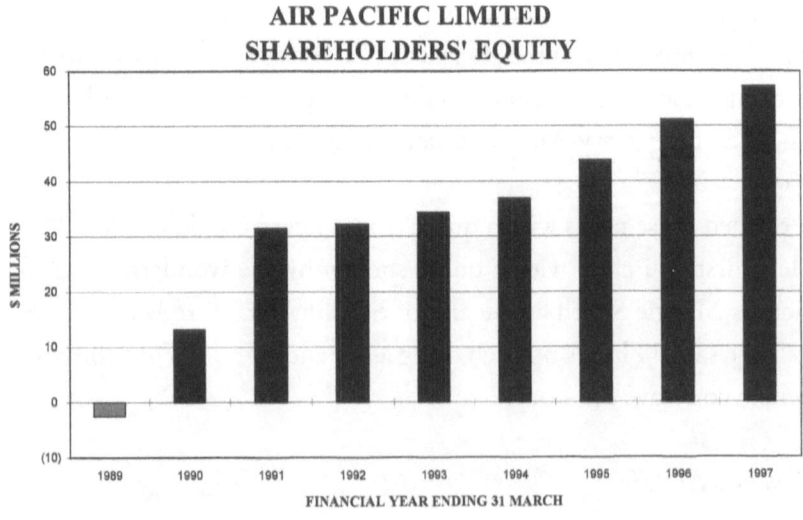

Sketches of Fiji

LEFT:
My mentors Marriott and Wilson

BELOW:
Air Pacific Executives 1997. Standing from left Capt. Tuisue, Mua Taukave, Ernie Dutta, Tony Wong, Manoa Kamikamica. Seated from left, Josephine Yee Joy, self, Ramendra Narayan

Sketches of Fiji

RIGHT:
Nadi Hangar spaceframe structure

BELOW RIGHT:
Qantas CEO John Ward and self signing for QF to codeshare on our flights

BELOW:
Inaugural Tokyo/ Nadi Flight they couldn't find a pair of silk gloves big enough for Ratu Mara

Sketches of Fiji

LEFT:
Last bolt for the Hangar roof self and Jone Sowata

BELOW LEFT:
Self and Chairman Gerald Barrack relaxing in Honolulu

BELOW:
Jo Kamikamica, Deputy PM and Minister for Finance and Economic Planning

CREDIT: BOEING

Sketches of Fiji

RIGHT:
B767 signing -
Self, Pleuger,
Chairman, Hazey

BELOW:
June 1997 PATA
Annual Conference
Great hall of the
people self and
Chinese Premier
Li Peng.

Sketches of Fiji

ABOVE:
Our Home at Dreketi

BELOW LEFT:
Dreketi veranda looking East

www.ingramcontent.com/pod-product-compliance
Lightning Source LLC
Chambersburg PA
CBHW031404290426
44110CB00011B/248